WHAT'S NEXT?

Unconventional Wisdom
on the Future of the World Economy

Edited by David Hale and
Lyric Hughes Hale

Yale UNIVERSITY PRESS

New Haven and London

Chapter 21, "The Future of Corporate Compliance" is reprinted from *Corporate Compliance Practice Guide: The Next Generation of Compliance* with permission. Copyright 2009 Matthew Bender & Company, Inc., a member of the Lexis-Nexis Group. All rights reserved.

Yale University Press books may be purchased in quantity for educational, business, or promotional use. For information, please e-mail sales.press@yale .edu (U.S. office) or sales@yaleup.co.uk (U.K. office).

Set in Galliard Old Style type by Westchester Book Services
Printed in the United States of America.

Library of Congress Cataloging-in-Publication Data

What's next? : unconventional wisdom on the future of the world economy / edited by David Hale and Lyric Hughes Hale.
        p. cm.
   Includes bibliographical references and index.
   ISBN 978-0-300-17031-3 (pbk. : alk. paper)
   1. Economic history—21st century.   2. Economic forecasting.   I. Hale, David.   II. Hale, Lyric Hughes.
   HC59.3.W47 2011
   330.9—dc22

                                                         2010053413

A catalogue record for this book is available from the British Library.

This paper meets the requirements of ANSI/NISO Z39.48-1992 (Permanence of Paper).

10 9 8 7 6 5 4 3 2 1

WHAT'S NEXT?

For our children, who have allowed us to travel the world : Aria, Erin, Devin, Harmony, Jennie, and granddaughter Cadence.

CONTENTS

PREFACE

The current global financial crisis has exposed the limits of economic forecasting. Or has it? Was it simply that the best voices were not heard over the media cacophony? Perhaps the data itself were misleading and inaccurate. Perhaps as economic actors, bureaucrats, and politicians, we are too focused on immediate events to take the future into account, even though we know that we should. Regulators might have underestimated the greed and cunning of Wall Street operators. Or we, as human beings, just might not be wired to understand and predict the future.

Throughout this period of economic turbulence, my husband, economist David Hale, and I have been exposed to other voices that have helped us to make sense of the enormous changes that have taken place on a global basis since 2008. We have been informed by commentators whom we believe to be some of the best thinkers in the world. Most of them are independent intellectuals, with no loyalty or responsibility to financial institutions, who are not well known outside of their area of expertise. Our realization that not everyone has had access to these authors was the impetus for this book.

We began the grand task of asking these authors, many of them friends, to write about their vision for the future, based upon their respective fields of knowledge. We hope this kaleidoscope of information and opinion will create a triangulated perspective that will allow our readers to formulate their own version of "What's Next?"

As the global financial crisis became a juggernaut, the public appropriately raised the question, why didn't anyone, economists in particular, see this coming? What is the value of economic research? Two new closely allied fields, behavioral economics and neuroeconomics, have attempted to bring the human factor to bear on neoclassical theories. Nobel Prize winner Paul Krugman has also blamed a reliance on what he calls mathematical elegance in economics. Doubts about statistics, once largely confined to third world countries, and in particular China, have surfaced in first world countries.

The herd mentality, the weakness of financial regulatory bodies, and institutional deficiencies are now commonly discussed. Seemingly benign technological advances are also seen as having a detrimental effect, due to the speed and interconnectedness of markets. And globalization has created efficiencies and contagion effects simultaneously. The small town in Norway, which lost its savings to international bankers selling "sure" investment instruments, would be an example of financial asymmetry.

As Berkeley economist Barry Eichengreen has said, "We now know that the gulf between assumption and reality was too wide to be bridged. These models were worse than unrealistic. They were weapons of mass economic destruction."

My own opinion is that what we are witnessing are the growing pains of the internationalization of markets. Lessons learned, we will create greater long-term stability. A gradual economic rebalancing will take place. Inexorable trends, such as outsourcing of US manufacturing to China, will reverse themselves over time. In fact, that has already begun to happen. Concerns over logistics costs, rising wages in China, and productivity issues such as just-in-time delivery have now given US companies an edge. US manufacturing has made a gradual recovery, which in turn will create more jobs. The unanswerable question is when.

Many of our contributors have bravely tried to answer this question. They have ably presented their knowledge and experience and have offered their assumptions for debate with the reader. Our goal is not only to help you answer the question "What's Next?" but also to spur you to explore "What If?"

We would like to thank our many contributors for their efforts. In this quickly moving world, faced with the realities of publishing, they have been asked to update and prognosticate into the distant future. No matter how things turn out, this book will give you a frame of reference, and a perspective, that goes beyond the current received wisdom.

We would like to express our gratitude to the members of the staff of David Hale Global Economics. Sandy Abraham provided creative inspiration and enthusiasm, and is responsible for editing the graphic presentations throughout the book. Sandy worked with the firm's clients in the investment world to gain valuable feedback. Economist Mark Zoff worked tirelessly for many months, coordinating, updating, copyediting, and rigorously fact-checking the work of the contributors in a fast-changing environment for forecasters. These efforts have combined to create a book that is at once visionary and scholarly, useful to both professionals and the reader who simply wants to know more about what is going on in the financial world than what is reported in the media, and at a more profound level. Kenneth Dam, our friend of many years, who critiqued the manuscript and provided a wealth of valuable suggestions that allowed us to improve the text throughout. Given the scope of this book, very few reviewers would have had the breadth to accomplish this difficult task. We cannot thank him enough.

Finally, we would like to thank our editor at Yale Press, Michael O'Malley. Without his encouragement and optimism, this book would not have made the rough passage between concept and conclusion.

Lyric Hughes Hale

INTRODUCTION

David Hale

After more than two years of turmoil in the financial markets and a severe recession during the early months of 2009, there are clear signs that the world economy is poised for a sustained recovery. China's highly stimulative monetary and fiscal policies helped to sustain the economy while exports recovered. The US consumer has begun to spend again. German manufacturing orders have bottomed, and exports benefitted from the Greek crisis in the monetary union. British house prices are increasing. And rising commodity prices are buoying confidence in Latin America and Africa.

This book will examine the outlook for 2011 and beyond from a variety of regional perspectives. It will also examine new developments in tax policy, corporate governance, climate change, and communications. The goal of this compendium is to provide original insights from a diverse mixture of independent analysts and forecasters. The contributors include the founder of the Hong Kong currency board, the former prime minister of Peru, the former research director of the central bank of Botswana, the founder of a Mexican fund management group, economic analysts in Hong Kong, a former director of the Davos World Economic Forum, and many other distinguished authors.

There are certain issues that loom large in the intermediate-term outlook. Will the recovery in US final demand be sustained? Can Chinese microeconomic policy support high growth for another year? How will European countries such as Britain cope with dramatic fiscal tightening?

Will the upturn now occurring in commodity prices boost the growth outlook for Latin America and Africa? Will central banks remonetize gold after a long period of selling it? Can the US dollar continue to be the world's dominant reserve currency when the country is confronting massive fiscal deficits and the Federal Reserve has slashed interest rates to zero?

The chapters of this book are organized into eight parts. The first four focus on economic trends in major regions of the world: the Western Hemisphere, Europe, Asia, and the Southern Hemisphere. The next section focuses on the outlook for the dollar as a reserve currency and the future of gold. The sixth part examines the energy market, Iranian politics, and the challenges posed by the issue of climate change. The seventh part focuses on a variety of policy issues, including financial regulation, taxation, corporate compliance, and the prospects of a Tobin tax to finance global public goods. The final section focuses on investment decision-making and the diminishing returns from information technology.

In the first chapter I argue that the United States has embarked on a sustained recovery as a result of significant monetary and fiscal stimulus from 2009 to 2010. I also focus special attention on the resilience of the corporate sector. The corporate sector slashed employment by eight million jobs from 2009 to 2010, which pushed the unemployment rate up to 10.1 percent. The job losses had a devastating impact on personal consumption, but they set the stage for large gains in productivity. Productivity increased by over 4 percent in 2009, and it grew at an 8 percent annual rate during the third quarter of the year. No other country has been able to restructure as aggressively as the United States. In Germany and Japan, output fell at a rate of 6–8 percent, but job losses were only 2–3 percent. As a result, productivity fell sharply in both countries. The United States therefore entered 2010 10–12 percent more competitive vis-à-vis Europe and Japan than it was at the beginning of 2009. The gains in competitiveness, coupled with the cheap dollar, should trigger an export boom. The US corporate sector is also running a free cash flow surplus exceeding $755 billion. This number is unprecedented in the modern era, and explains why firms are boosting investment on productivity-enhancing technology. The great uncertainties in the US outlook center on public policy. As the unemployment rate remained at 9.6 percent during the fourth quarter of 2010, the Federal Reserve embarked upon a program of quantitative easing. The Fed pledged to purchase $600 billion of government securities in the eight months through June. Federal Reserve Chairman Ben Bernanke said that the policy would help to reduce long-term bond yields and bolster the equity market. Finance ministers in Brazil, China, and other developing countries said that the policy was designed to devalue the dollar. Several Republican economists warned that the policy could be inflationary. The Fed will continue the policy for as long as it perceives the economy to be weak. If employment growth rebounds to 200,000 per month by the second quarter of 2011, it will suspend the policy. If employment growth remains lackluster at only 100,000 jobs per month, it could commit to purchasing another $500 billion of securities during the second half of 2011. The Republican victory in the midterm elections also set the stage for a compromise on tax policy with the Obama administration which will generate $797 billion of fiscal stimulus in 2011 and 2012. As a result of this policy action, most US economists have increased their growth forecasts to the 3.5–4.0 percent range. The tax cuts will increase the federal deficit during 2011 and 2012, and it is unclear at this stage how the nation's leadership will address the issue of deficit reduction. The chairmen of the president's commission on deficit reduction proposed a multiyear program of both tax increases and spending cuts to reduce the deficit by $3.8 trillion by 2020, but it was criticized by both liberal Democrats who are protective of transfer payments and conservative Republicans who are opposed to all tax increases. The deep partisan divides in Washington over fiscal policy could make it impossible to achieve any meaningful deficit reduction until interest rates rise sharply after the Fed abandons its policy of quantitative easing. There is little pressure on Congress to act when the Fed is monetizing the deficit. Congress will not be able to tell the voters that there is a clear economic trade-off for deficit reduction until there is a real danger of bond yields rising sharply. Such a time is coming, but it may not be until late 2012 or 2013.

Joshua Mendelsohn believes that Canada's economy is showing clear signs of recovery that will continue. Canada has benefitted from having a stronger banking system than the United States and has avoided reckless property lending. The Canadian household sector is less leveraged than US households. Home sales rose sharply in early 2010 because of record low interest rates. Canada is also in a far better fiscal position than the

United States. After several years of the government running fiscal surpluses, the public debt share of GDP fell to 21.7 percent in 2008, which is
the lowest of any OECD (Organization for Economic Cooperation and
Development) country. Canada introduced a stimulative fiscal policy in
early 2009, and it will have run a deficit of 3.7 percent of GDP in 2009 and
2.8 percent in 2010. There is no risk of the deficit climbing to the high
levels that are now prevailing in Britain or the United States. Canada has
reduced the corporate tax rate from 26 percent in 2002 to 19 percent currently, and is planning to reduce it to 15 percent in 2012. The fact that
Canada will be cutting taxes as the Obama administration is planning tax
increases will enhance Canada's competitive position. Canada needs more
corporate investment because its productivity performance has lagged
during recent years. Canada is better positioned than the United States to
cope with the climate change challenge because it obtains only 15 percent
of its electric power from coal compared to 50 percent in the United States.
Canada's concerns center on its rapidly growing tar sands industry in Alberta. Some members of the US Congress want to restrict imports of oil
from Alberta on the grounds that it is dirty. Therefore, Canada intends to
closely coordinate its environmental policies with the new policies that are
emerging from the Obama administration. Canada's problem in the short
term is that the Obama administration cannot get support in the US Senate
for its own cap-and-trade policy.

Tim Heyman reviews Mexico's *annus horribilis* in 2009. Real GDP fell
by 7 percent—the sharpest decline since 1932. Mexico was very vulnerable
to the sharp downturn in its important US export market, especially for
automobiles and other durable goods. It also is suffering a long-term decline in oil output because of inadequate domestic investment and political barriers to foreign investment. The year 2010 in Mexico will have been
iconic because it was the two hundredth anniversary of independence and
the one hundredth anniversary of the revolution that brought down Por-
firio Díaz. Mexico will have a cyclical recovery in 2011 as the United States
returns to a real GDP growth rate in the range of 3 percent, but Heyman
believes that Mexico's long-term performance will depend on how it man-
ages four critical issues. First, it has to find a way to exploit its deep offshore oil potential. The United States drills one hundred wells per annum
in the deep waters of the Gulf of Mexico while Mexico drilled only four

wells in four years. The government has to find some way to reconcile the need for foreign investment with Mexico's legacy of nationalizing foreign oil companies in 1938. The second reform Mexico needs is a stronger tax system. The current system collects only about 10 percent of GDP, far less than any mature economy. Pemex, the state oil monopoly, helps to compensate for the low tax receipts, but Pemex is becoming a less reliable source of revenue. Mexico must therefore find a way to obtain more revenue from consumption or income taxes. The third area for potential reform is security. Mexico has to improve the recruitment and training of its police force in order to fight the war on drugs, kidnapping, and extortion. The federal police will also have to work more effectively with local police. The final area for reform is politics. The end of the Institutional Revolutionary Party's (PRI) political dominance has led to new conflicts between the president and Congress. The president is far weaker than he was in the era of PRI control. And members of Congress are very beholden to their parties because they cannot seek reelection. Heyman suggests that the election rules should be changed to allow for reelection, and that the presidential election should be resolved by a run-off that would produce a clear majority for the winner. He believes that the next president will have to pursue far-reaching reforms in order to be popular. He concludes that the next stage of Mexico's march toward modernity will be motivated by necessity, not choice.

Pedro Pablo Kuczynski explains how Latin America coped with the global financial crisis of 2008–2009. It had two major advantages compared to past crises: lower public debt ratios and greatly improved banking supervision. Latin America had also enjoyed current account surpluses in 2007 and early 2008 because of the global commodity boom. As a result of these advantages, it did not have to turn to the IMF for help, and Brazil and Mexico only had to obtain credit swap lines from the Federal Reserve that they did not even have to use. Kuczynski is optimistic about Latin American growth in 2010 and beyond, but he feels that Mexico and Brazil, the two major countries in the region, are not achieving their full potential because of structural problems with cartels and government regulation. Mexico has declining oil output because the government cannot open up the sector to foreign investment. Brazil has a high tax share of GDP with low government productivity. He fears that the region could suffer from "reform fatigue." Latin America's great advantage today is demographics. There is steady growth occurring in the labor force because of high birthrates in recent decades and increasing female participation in the labor force. Latin America is also much younger than the old industrial countries. Only 8–9 percent of the population is over sixty years old, compared to 16 percent in the United States, 22 percent in Europe, and 25 percent in Japan. The challenge for Latin America will be to capitalize on the next commodity boom by pursuing more aggressive reforms of education, taxation, and infrastructure.

Anatole Kaletsky has written a commentary on how Europe resolved the crises of its monetary union in May and November 2010 with rescue packages for Greece, Ireland, and the Iberian Peninsula. Germany, France, and other countries made a clear statement that they would not allow debt-ridden nations such as Greece to default, and that they intend to protect the monetary union. They used the stress test of Europe's leading banks to guarantee that they would protect the solvency of the banking system as well. Kaletsky believes that Europe enjoyed stronger growth than the United States during the middle quarters of 2010 because it had a more severe recession, but he does not think that European output will regain its former peak until 2012. He is concerned that European fiscal policy could constrain growth and that it will not be fully offset by monetary accommodation. He therefore believes that Europe will need a major currency depreciation in order to compensate for its fiscal policies.

Louis-Vincent Gave notes that Asian stock markets are now discounting high growth expectations, and thus are trading at premiums to traditional OECD markets. Gave reviews the four key factors that have driven economic performance in the West over the past decade, and suggests that some of the factors are still driving Asian growth. These factors are the emergence of three billion new producers, creation of a global economy, and the great moderation of steady low-inflation economic growth, and financial innovation. The financial revolution that drove markets in New York and London is still evolving in East Asia. East Asia is also free of two problems that now loom over the old industrial countries—a legacy of private debt that financed asset inflation and large fiscal deficits. Gave's new concern is that China could soon confront labor shortages. He is also concerned that China has excess savings, but understands how the excess has resulted from robust profits, not just deferred consumption. Gave finishes by offering a few conclusions about investment alternatives that track broad stock indices such as exchange-traded funds (ETFs). He favors utilities and stable growth stocks linked to the consumer. He does not think that the infrastructure and commodity stocks that led the market from 2000 onward will outperform again.

Robert Madsen reviews the structural factors that have depressed Japanese growth since the 1990s. The country has a bias toward over savings, which it has dealt with through export-led growth. As a result, it suffered a severe downturn during the global financial crisis of 2008–2009. Japan will also be vulnerable if the global economy loses momentum again during late 2010 and 2011. The Bank of Japan (BOJ) has added to the economy's problems by failing to stop deflation. The BOJ's refusal to pursue a more aggressive policy has limited Japan's ability to counteract the large increases in the yen exchange rate as well. There is little potential for Japan to pursue a more stimulative fiscal policy because the public debt is now approaching 200 percent of GDP. Japan has had no problem funding its deficit because the buyers are almost entirely local, but the Ministry of Finance does not want to expand the debt any more than necessary. Japan will therefore be heading for an extended period of growth in the 1.0–1.3 percent range, with deflation holding nominal growth close to zero or less. It is impossible to predict when Japan's debt could produce a financial crisis, but it does loom as a possibility at some point.

Richard Katz reviews the great volatility in Japanese politics during 2009 and 2010. The Democratic Party of Japan (DPJ) won a major victory in the 2009 elections and formed a government in place of the long dominant Liberal Democratic Party (LDP). Their popularity then fell sharply, and they suffered a major defeat in the election for the upper house of the Diet in July 2010. They also changed prime ministers in May 2010, but the new leader, Naoto Kan, frittered away an early lead by discussing the possibility of hiking the consumption tax after the Democrats promised to leave the tax unchanged through 2013. The LDP made a comeback in the mid-term elections, but only in rural seats that they had lost in previous elections. They could not challenge the Democrats in urban areas. The voters also supported a new party, the "Your Party," which is committed to carrying out reforms that began in the Koizumi era. The elections have produced a remarkably confusing situation, and it is not clear if the Democrats will be able to recover. What is certain is that the era of one-party dominance in Japanese politics is over. There could be a further splintering of the political system, and Japan may be unable to produce a strong government for several years. Such an impasse could leave many important policy questions unresolved and jeopardize Japan's ability to play a global leadership role.

Keith Jefferis discusses the economic outlook for Sub-Saharan Africa. The global financial crisis reduced Africa's growth rates from 5–6 percent to 1–2 percent. The crisis weakened commodity prices, reduced income flows from diasporas, depressed foreign direct investment, and adversely affected tourism. The upturn in commodity prices since March 2009 has revived optimism about African growth in 2010 and beyond. Jefferis expects robust growth in East Africa. Kenya is still suffering from political divisions, but Uganda has had large oil discoveries. The Democratic Republic of the Congo (DRC) has immense potential to increase its mining output, but the country still suffers from insurgencies in its eastern provinces. West Africa should benefit from the rebound in oil prices, but Nigeria has had a banking crisis because of high levels of margin lending for stock market speculation. Ghana will became an oil producer in 2010, and oil revenues could reach $4 billion per annum. South Africa had a successful FIFA World Cup in mid-2010, which should boost future tourism, but the event put an immense strain on public services. Southern Africa could experience new power supply problems as the regional economy recovers. The climate change issue is also a problem because South Africa depends heavily upon coal, and it will have to build new coal-burning stations in order to improve power supplies. Zimbabwe has begun to recover because the government withdrew the local currency in early 2009 after a bout of massive hyperinflation, but the political situation remains tense because President Robert Mugabe is still reluctant to share true power with the Movement for Democratic Change (MDC). It will be difficult for Zimbabwe to attract foreign investment until the political logjam is broken.

Iraj Abedian reviews the impact of the global recession on South Africa's economy and political process. Abedian notes that South Africa's macroeconomic performance has compared favorably with many emerging market economies since 2000. The African National Congress (ANC) government pursued responsible fiscal policies, and monetary policy was allowed to combat inflation. Abedian notes that South Africa must now confront some significant structural challenges such as the inadequacy of the national education system and the skills shortage it is creating. He also says that the government has failed to create an effective industrial policy or address critical supply-side issues such as power supply. There were power shortages during early 2008 because of the South African public utility's (Eskom) failure to invest in new capacity, and productivity in the public sector has declined. These factors are depressing South Africa's competitive position. Abedian notes that the new government under President Zuma offers both hope and anxiety because there are sharp divergences on many issues among the ministers. The recession will also swell the public sector deficit from 3–4 percent of GDP to 11–12 percent in 2010 and 2011. These large deficits will pose a challenge because welfare spending is on a trajectory to rise to a level above education spending, and there will be great reluctance to curtail public expenditures significantly.

Saul Eslake reviews how Australia was able to avoid a recession in 2009 and the potential risks that lie ahead. Australia emerged from the recession unscathed because its banks had not invested in toxic assets, and the government agreed to guarantee their liabilities after the Lehman bankruptcy. As Australian banks have high loan-to-deposit ratios, they depend on global wholesale funding that might have been at risk without a guarantee. The government also announced timely fiscal stimulus packages through targeted tax cuts and increased infrastructure spending. Meanwhile, the Reserve Bank slashed interest rates to 3.00 percent from 7.25 percent and gave a significant boost to the incomes of mortgage borrowers. Australia also benefitted from the resilience of the Chinese economy, and the share of its exports going to China rose to nearly 25 percent from 12 percent two years ago. Eslake says that the fortunes of China's economy will now loom as a major risk factor for Australia. If China has a sudden slump, Australia will be caught in the backwash. Australia was better prepared than many other countries to cope with the crisis because its government had run fiscal surpluses for several years. The fact that there was no public debt in 2008 allowed the Rudd government to run stimulative fiscal policies without having to worry about a large run-up in the ratio of government debt to GDP. Most other G-20 governments are deeply envious of Australia's fiscal situation. Eslake concludes by noting that Australia's benign economic performance during the global financial crisis did not protect its government. The Labor Party dismissed Prime Minister Kevin Rudd in June 2010 over disappointment about his environmental policies, and then went on to lose a parliamentary election in late August. Most of the G-20's political leaders were envious of Kevin Rudd's economic record, but he went down in history as the first political leader to lose office over the issue of climate change.

John Greenwood offers an optimistic view of the dollar's prospects of continuing as a global reserve currency. He reviews the process by which the dollar displaced the British pound as the dominant global currency during the early decades of the twentieth century. He then analyzes the prerequisites to be a reserve currency in the modern era. They are that the currency be widely available outside its home economy, that it be fully convertible, that it be supported by a large economy, and that it have a developed financial system. When these factors converge, they generate network effects in which the greater the number of people that are using the currency, the more beneficial it becomes for the users, and the more dominant it becomes. He thinks that the euro is not fully competitive with the dollar because there is no market for European government debt. Instead, investors have to choose between the debts of individual nation-states, of which the largest debtor is Italy. The yen suffers from the low interest rates in Japan and growing investor concern about the credit quality of Japanese government debt. The public debt will soon exceed 200 percent of GDP, and massive fiscal deficits will loom in the future. Greenwood does not regard the Special Drawing Rights (SDR) as a serious alternative to the dollar because there is no market for SDR securities. It is instead an accounting unit of the IMF, and all SDRs are deposited at the IMF. China has some preconditions for establishing a reserve currency, such as a large economy, but its capital markets are underdeveloped and the currency itself is not fully convertible, although there were some significant developments in the RMB's liberalization process in the second half of 2010. Therefore, Greenwood expects the dollar to remain dominant almost by default.

I also review the recent rally in the gold price and suggest that the outlook is still positive. Investor demand for gold has been buoyed by the creation of exchange-traded funds. They now hold over 2,000 tonnes, and could easily expand to levels matching Bundesbank holdings (3,400 tonnes). The production of gold has failed to rally with the price. South African output has slumped while China, Australia, and other African countries have been producing more, but total output has been static. There are three factors that will determine the intermediate-term outlook for the gold price. The first will be how long central banks restrain interest rates to promote economic recovery. Low interest rates have traditionally been positive for gold. The second factor will be investor confidence in the dollar. Investors will be very concerned about how the United States resolves the problem of its fiscal deficits and how the Fed conducts monetary policy. The third factor will be Chinese demand for gold. Chinese private demand for gold has been steadily increasing, and the central bank could make purchases to diversify its large foreign exchange reserves. During the early years of the twentieth century, the United States signaled its rise as a great economic power by accumulating larger gold reserves than Europe. China could now do the same.

Albert Bressand believes that 2009 was the year in which the "peak oil" theory of finite reserves proved to be untrue. Oil reserves expanded after a long period of decline, and there was a sharp increase in estimates of natural gas reserves because of new developments in utilizing shale gas. Bressand suggests that Brazil could be producing 5.7 million barrels per day in 2020, and there are major new oil discoveries occurring in West Africa and Central Africa. Ghana became an oil producer in 2010. Uganda will soon follow. Bressand also believes that Iraq could triple or quadruple its oil production. The oil-producing countries are very concerned about efforts to reduce climate change, but they took comfort from the fact that the Copenhagen summit failed to produce any clear agreements. The International Energy Agency (IEA) estimates that even if the world can agree to hold the CO_2 levels in the atmosphere below 450 parts per million of CO_2-equivalent, hydrocarbons will retain a 68 percent share of global energy consumption, and the oil price in 2030 will be $90 per barrel. Bressand notes that the world will have to spend $26 trillion on energy investment over the next twenty years to increase oil output. In 2009, investment fell to $442 billion from $524 billion in 2008. Bressand expects that investment will continue to occur over the next twenty years because there are no practical alternatives to our current heavy dependence on hydrocarbons. He expects the 2010 Gulf of Mexico oil spill to produce demands for more environmental protection in Europe and North America, but he does not believe that developing countries will be as restrictive. Libya, for example, will continue to drill in the Mediterranean Sea. There will also be more demand to restrict shale gas development in the northeastern United States because of concerns about groundwater pollution. The United States has been able to significantly expand its gas reserves since 2006 because of shale gas development, so it would be unfortunate if the new restrictions go too far.

Narimon Safavi reviews the open-ended political situation in Iran. He believes that Iran is creating a civil society that will ultimately have the potential to change the country's direction. He notes that Iran has had three major revolutions over the past one hundred years, the third of which led to the establishment of the Islamic Republic in 1979. The 2009 election was another opportunity to promote change, but it was held in check by authorities. Safavi believes that Iran is now controlled by an industrial-militia complex that is led by the Revolutionary Guard. This group rigged the 2009 election to consolidate its hold on power, but it is now vulnerable to divisions among the elite. Safavi examines recent conflicts over control of Azad University and the inability of either faction in the conflict to achieve its goal. Safavi believes that the pro-reform forces will ultimately prevail because only they can deliver an effective, competent government, but it will be a long struggle.

Brian Fisher and Anna Matysek review the climate change issue and its implications for public policy. They note that 183 countries and the European Union have ratified the Kyoto Protocol for regulating carbon emissions. The European Union is now going beyond the Kyoto Protocol by proposing to reduce carbon emissions by 30 percent (rather than 20 percent) from 1990 levels by 2020. The United Kingdom has also announced a 26–32 percent reduction from 1990 levels by 2020 and a 60 percent reduction by 2050. The United States did not sign the Kyoto Protocol, and while the Obama administration sought to implement a cap-and-trade system for carbon emissions and the House approved such a plan, the Senate avoided ratifying it because of concern among coal-burning states about the economic consequences. China has offered to promote more energy-efficient technologies, but it has been reluctant to accept a target for carbon emissions reductions on the grounds that it is still a developing country. Fisher and Matysek are pessimistic that the current negotiations will be effective in curtailing carbon emissions. They believe that the global average temperature could rise by three degrees Celsius over the next one hundred years, and that the world will have to adapt to a significant amount of climate change.

Tim Congdon focuses on bank regulation. He does not believe that inadequate US bank capital played a role in causing the recent financial crisis. He notes that leading US banks entered the crisis with the highest capital ratios in several years. He fears that attempts to impose higher capital ratios will depress credit and money growth. He also warns that financial activity could shift from areas with excessive regulation to areas that are more lightly regulated. As China has an immense pool of excess savings, he believes that Shanghai is a strong contender to emerge as a global financial center. Congdon wants the major central banks to take stronger actions to promote money growth and a recovery of asset prices in order to strengthen bank capital. He does not want the banks to improve their capital ratios by shrinking their balance sheets. He believes that such actions will only impede the recovery of the global economy and set the stage for more capital erosion through loan losses.

Andrew Sheng offers the case for a Tobin tax to finance global public goods. He reviews the origin of the idea in the 1970s and the recent proposal of it by Lord Adair Turner of the Financial Services Authority in London. Sheng says that the world is caught in a collective action trap that encourages a race to the bottom for financial regulation and taxation. He believes that a Tobin tax offers many advantages, including money to finance global public goods, increased data availability on financial transactions, and a tax on bank profits to reduce the bonuses that encourage speculative activity. Sheng estimates that the global value of foreign exchange turnover is $800 trillion and that the value of stock market trading is $101 trillion. If we were to apply a 0.005 percent tax on financial transactions, the tax would produce $45 billion of revenue. The essential prerequisite for such a tax is that all G-20 countries agree to apply the same tax, so as to discourage countries from pursuing financial services business by avoiding the tax.

Jack Mintz reviews the outlook for future tax policy in the wake of the global recession and large increases in the fiscal deficits of many countries. He notes that the IMF is forecasting that public debt will expand to 85 percent of global GDP from 62 percent before the financial crisis. The old industrial countries are experiencing the largest deficits. The emerging market countries, by contrast, are expected to record a modest decline in their debt burdens over the next five years. Aging populations in the developed countries will only exacerbate these problems. He thinks that competitive factors will force countries to rely more heavily on consumption-related taxes. The most popular consumption tax in the world today is the value-added tax, which the United States is unique in not having. He also thinks that some countries will rely on excise taxes or higher user fees for public services.

Michael Lewis analyzes the impact of the Dodd-Frank Wall Street Reform and Consumer Protection Act on the economy. He believes that the new law will have a modestly contractionary effect by depressing bank profits and imposing more regulatory barriers on consumer lending. He also notes that the legislation failed to address the true cause of the financial crisis—the role of Fannie Mae and Freddie Mac in providing large amounts of subprime mortgage credit to homebuyers. Congress plans to address the future of these agencies in 2011. The Federal Reserve has received more power from the legislation, but there was tremendous controversy in Congress about the Fed's role in propping up troubled banks. Lewis notes that there was also great controversy over the issue of "too big to fail" because of Republican allegations that the new law would not curtail bank size, but he says that the regulatory authorities now have more power to "unwind" the positions of large entities that could pose a systemic risk. He does not believe that the new law will prevent future financial crises, but it will prevent a repetition of many of the factors that led to the recent one. Banks will have to retain 5 percent of the assets they securitize. It will be easier to sue the rating agencies. There will be greater transparency of derivatives trading as more volume moves onto centralized exchanges. The law can modify behavior, but it cannot prevent future excesses in some asset markets.

Carole Basri examines how the recent financial crisis will affect the future of corporate compliance. She notes that the crisis has led institutions to reduce their headcounts in compliance and ethics departments. She views this as a negative development because the crisis itself resulted from a breakdown of compliance and ethics at leading banks and brokerage houses. She believes that governments will have a critical role to play in promoting improved corporate governance. She also believes that the public can play an important role by creating more ethics and compliance programs in business schools, law schools, and other institutions. The US government itself has been less effective at prosecuting the financial criminals in the recent crisis than it was in the past. The US government will have to strengthen the law enforcement process in order to promote more respect for the law among senior bankers.

Thierry Malleret examines the process of investment decision-making. He suggests that many people did not foresee the recent financial crisis because they did not want to see it. He believes that human beings find it difficult to make rational choices and are instead influenced by emotions, beliefs, and feelings. He also believes that the big winner from the crisis will be neuroeconomics. Malleret reviews studies that suggest that we suffer from "bounded rationality" and that we have clear limits on our capacity to digest large amounts of information. Our language also makes it difficult to describe complex, nonlinear systems. Instead, we try to over-simplify and are subject to herd behavior. Malleret states that investment firms do not employ neuroeconomists because they do not help people make good decisions. They instead help people to avoid bad decisions. Most investors are confident that they do not need the advice offered by neuroeconomists, but Malleret thinks that one of the legacies of the recent crisis could be a greater willingness to listen to them.

Mark Roeder analyzes the role of information in the modern economy. Roeder notes that the spread of the Internet has changed how people absorb and use information. He quotes Nicholas Carr, who asserts that the Internet is impeding people's ability to concentrate and contemplate. He believes that technology is encouraging us to be shallow and never dwell on one subject for long. The Internet can also cause us to become excessively narrow because we can choose to see only the information we want to see, whereas an ordinary newspaper could expose us to many topics. Roeder also notes that brain imaging technology has indicated that the Internet activates reward pathways that have been linked to addiction. He believes that we have entered a period of diminishing returns in which we have greatly increasing access to information but inadequate understanding of how to use it.

These chapters reflect a diverse set of views on both important macroeconomic and microeconomic questions. They have a generally positive bias toward the global economic outlook at the end of 2010, with caveats about monetary policy. They cover a diverse mixture of microeconomic questions ranging from the future of oil supply to the challenges posed by climate change. The goal is to provide the reader with concise views about challenges that people will confront in the financial service sector over the next few years. There is no way to predict precisely what will come next, but the issues reviewed in this compendium will play a major role in shaping the future.

PART

WESTERN HEMISPHERE ECONOMIES

1

THE US RECOVERY
David Hale

The Business Cycle Dating Committee of the National Bureau of Economic Research has said that the great recession of 2008–2009 ended in July 2009. The US economy had a growth rate of 1.6 percent during the third quarter of 2009 followed by 5.0 percent during the fourth quarter and 3.7 percent during the first quarter of 2010. Growth then slowed to 1.7 percent during the second quarter of 2010 and 2.0 percent during the third quarter. The recovery has taken many by surprise because of the severity of the crisis in the financial markets in late 2008. The stock market fell sharply. The commercial paper market froze. Bond spreads rose to unprecedented levels. Bankers cut credit lines. Consumers reacted to these shocks by slashing their spending, especially in up-market retailers. Corporations sharply curtailed capital spending. As the credit crunch hit the global economy, exports fell sharply as well.

How Government Intervention Ended the Financial Crisis

Government intervention rescued the economy. The Federal Reserve slashed interest rates to zero and expanded its balance sheet from $900 billion to $2.2 trillion by injecting large amounts of liquidity into the financial system. After the Lehman Brothers bankruptcy, the Treasury Department persuaded Congress to approve the $700 billion TARP rescue package. As catastrophic as the Lehman bankruptcy proved to be for the markets, it is doubtful that Congress would have supported a bank rescue package without the Lehman shock. The US banking system needed a rescue because it had written off $1.2 trillion of bad debt as of the first quarter of 2010, and had only $1.3 trillion of equity capital in 2009. The Obama administration then persuaded Congress to enact a $787 billion stimulus program in February 2009. The program had provided $568 billion of stimulus as of November 2010.

There are several reasons to believe that the recovery will continue through 2011. The yield curve is positively sloped. Consumers have demonstrated that they are once again willing to spend. There has been an upturn in home sales, which is finally boosting residential construction after a severe three-year recession. The nonresidential construction share of GDP fell from 6.2 percent in 2006 to 2.2 percent in the third quarter of 2010, a record low. The corporate sector is running an unprecedented cash flow surplus in excess of $225 billion. This surplus will boost capital spending on high-technology capital goods in order to boost productivity. The United States enjoyed over 6 percent productivity growth between 2009 and 2010 because of the loss of over eight million jobs. Private sector employment during the recession fell by 7.4 percent in the United States, compared to only 2–3 percent in Germany and Japan. As their corporate sectors could not aggressively shed jobs, their productivity fell by 5–6 percent from 2009 to 2010. The US corporate sector therefore entered 2010 10–15 percent more competitive than it was in 2009 compared to Europe and Japan. These productivity gains, coupled with the cheap dollar, should trigger an export boom.

The momentum these factors created in the economy should have produced a growth rate in the 2.5–3.0 percent range in 2010. Such a recovery is not robust when compared to the growth rates that followed the severe recessions of 1974–1975 and 1981–1982, but it is respectable for an economy that is in the midst of significant deleveraging and rising household savings rates. The household sector repaid $900 billion of debt from 2009 to 2010. Bank lending to the business and household sector has been declining since early 2009. The great risks in the US outlook center on public policy and the economy's potential growth rate after 2010.

An Unbridgeable Ideological Chasm Has Emerged between the Major Political Parties

The Obama administration ended 2010 reconsidering the policies it had promoted during its first two years in office. It was on the verge of accepting Republican proposals to allow the Bush tax cuts that were enacted during 2003 to continue for everyone rather than hiking marginal income tax rates on Americans earning over $250,000 per annum. It abandoned proposals to introduce a cap-and-trade program for carbon credits. It will instead attempt to regulate carbon emissions through actions by the Environmental Protection Agency. The Republican victory could allow progress on one type of policy initiative. It will increase the odds of Congress enacting the free trade agreements (FTAs) negotiated by the Bush administration with South Korea, Colombia, and Panama. The Obama administration initially had no stated trade policy, but it decided to endorse the FTAs in 2010 in order to promote export growth. Its problem was that House Democrats were reluctant to enact new FTAs because of opposition to them from trade unions. The Republican Congress will now allow the administration to pursue export growth through new trade agreements.

The White House is projecting that the deficit could decline to 4.2 percent of GDP by 2020, but it is assuming an average nominal growth rate of 4.9 percent during the next ten years. If growth is more subdued, the deficit could easily escalate to 5–6 percent of GDP. The White House is also projecting that the ratio of government debt held by the public to GDP will rise from 53 percent to 66 percent over the next ten years, but many private analysts believe that it will rise to 77 percent because the economy will experience weaker growth than the administration is forecasting. Presidents Ronald Reagan and George W. Bush ended their terms at 45 percent and 53 percent, respectively. The administration assumes that gradual deficit reduction will take place as the economy's growth rate accelerates to an average rate of 5.9 percent between 2012 and 2014. If the US economy only grows at an average annual rate of 2.5 percent between 2010 and 2015, federal spending will rise to 26.5 percent of GDP in 2015. Medicare and Medicaid expenditures combined would climb from 4.73 percent of GDP to 5.78 percent. Social Security's share of GDP would rise from

4.93 percent to 5.44 percent. The defense share of GDP would decline from 4.92 percent to 4.14 percent. Interest payments would jump from 1.28 percent of GDP to 3.45 percent. As two-thirds of the federal debt has less than a two-year maturity, it is possible that this estimate could be too low. The rising government share of GDP suggests that the structural deficit will be at least 5–7 percent of GDP. Most economists believe that such deficits will be unsustainable and think that the administration should aim for a target of 3.0 percent of GDP.

The core problem is that the Democrats and Republicans have radically different visions for the future. The Democrats want to create a European-style welfare state in the United States that will permanently increase the federal government share of GDP to 25 percent. The Republicans want to restrain the tax share of GDP to its traditional level of 17–18 percent. There is no simple way to bridge this gap. As a result, the deficit is likely to remain large until there is a strike by bond buyers that will trigger large increases in bond yields. There is no way to predict when such a strike may occur, but it is likely to happen when private credit growth revives and investors become concerned about the risk of crowding out. Many Democrats privately support the idea of a national value-added tax (VAT). If the United States imposed a 10 percent VAT, it could raise sums equal to 5 percent of GDP. But the president has ruled out tax hikes on people earning less than $250,000 per annum. This leaves the option of hiking the top marginal income tax rates back to 45–50 percent, where they were before Ronald Reagan's presidency. Such a tax increase will generate massive protests from small businesses and high-income earners. It would also undermine the support that President Obama enjoyed from highly educated people during the 2008 election. Obama supported raising income tax rates to pay for health care reform in 2009, but he has not yet commented on how he will solve the budget deficit problem. There can be little doubt that fiscal policy ranks as one of the great uncertainties hanging over the US economy through 2015. The risk of new tax increases is high, but no one can predict what form they will take. The lack of visibility on fiscal policy is one of the factors that is restraining new hiring and investment by business.

Why the Turn in Monetary Policy Will Be Different This Time

As unemployment remained at 9.6 percent as of November 2010 while the core inflation rate had declined to 0.6 percent, the Federal Reserve decided in early November 2010 to pursue a policy of quantitative easing. It will purchase $600 billion of government securities between November 2010 and June 2011. The Fed will also recycle another $350–$400 billion of funds from maturing mortgage-backed securities in its portfolio into yet more government securities. The Fed will thus effectively monetize all of the federal government's borrowing needs through June 2011.

Fed Chairman Ben Bernanke began talking about such a policy at his speech at the 2010 Economic Policy Symposium in Jackson Hole, Wyoming, in late August, so the market had time to prepare for the change. It had a major impact on investor psychology. The US equity market rallied 14 percent during the three months following his speech, and the trade-weighted value of the dollar fell 5 percent. The price of gold and other metals rallied. After announcing the policy change, Mr. Bernanke wrote an op-ed column in the *Washington Post* explaining that he hoped the policy would bolster consumption by encouraging asset inflation in the equity market.

The Fed move was controversial. Finance ministers and central bankers in many other countries regarded it as a policy action designed to promote US dollar devaluation. German Finance Minister Wolfgang Schäuble was among the most outspoken and called the policy "clueless." Chinese officials expressed concern that the Fed was promoting dollar devaluation. Brazilian Finance Minister Guido Mantega warned that the world was confronting the risk of a "currency war."

Central bankers in developing countries were concerned that the Fed action would both promote dollar devaluation and encourage a surge of capital flows to emerging market countries that might create asset bubbles. Several countries therefore took action to regulate capital flows. Brazil imposed a 6 percent tax on capital flows to its bond market. Thailand imposed a 15 percent tax on foreign purchases of bonds. Taiwan restricted foreign investment in its bond market. Indonesia introduced longer maturity bank deposits for foreign investors. Peru and Chile liberalized restrictions on the international investment policies of their pension funds in order to encourage capital outflows and lessen upward pressure on their currencies.

The Fed's new policy is open ended. It will last as long as the Fed feels is necessary to reduce unemployment. If the economy's growth rate accelerates to 3–4 percent and job growth rises to an average of 200,000 per month by the second quarter of 2011, the policy will cease. If growth is more lackluster and average monthly employment gains remain at 100,000, the Fed could do another $500 billion of quantitative easing during the second half of 2011. The Fed will also have to be sensitive to the inflation rate. Its policy change has encouraged a rally that was already underway in the price of oil, base metals, and agricultural commodities. These price gains could boost the inflation rate by 0.3–0.5 percent and depress consumer real incomes.

In mid-December, the US economy received a further boost when the Obama administration and Congressional Republicans agreed on a $797 billion tax cut package for 2011 and 2012. They agreed to extend the Bush tax cuts, reduce Social Security taxes by 2 percent, and offer business 100 percent first-year depreciation allowances. The action had a dramatic impact on expectations of the US outlook. Most economists promptly upgraded their forecasts for 2011 growth to the 3.5–4.0 percent range. The new confidence also coincided with a strong finish to retail sales during the Christmas season. The economy enjoyed its most robust sales growth since 2006. Retail sales began to improve during the autumn, but the magnitude of the rebound during the fourth quarter took most observers by surprise. They had perceived that the household was still deleveraging and would thus be unable to spend. In fact, the household sector has reduced its leverage by nearly one trillion dollars since 2009 while the financial obligation ratio (interest, payments, property tax payments, etc.) declined from just under 19 percent in 2007 to below the thirty-year moving average of 17.2 percent by the second quarter of 2010. The household sector's savings rate of 5 percent is allowing it to accumulate financial assets or repay debt at an annual rate of $600 billion.

The dramatic rebound in corporate profits since 2009 has already triggered a healthy rebound in capital spending with growth rates exceeding 20 percent during the first half of 2010. The corporate sector should be able to sustain a growth rate of investment in the 10 percent plus range during 2011. Spending on high-technology capital goods has already exceeded its previous peak. Transportation and industrial equipment are still catching up.

The housing sector has traditionally played a supportive role during business recoveries, but during 2010 it has been missing in action. There is an excess supply of 2.5 million foreclosed homes on top of a vacancy rate of 2.5 percent for the housing stock near the end of 2010. Home sales rallied because of a government tax credit during 2009 and early 2010, but then fell sharply. They were starting to rebound in the second half of 2010 because of low mortgage rates and depressed home prices. The United States should have a core housing demand of 1.6 million units because of 1.2 million new households being formed each year and 400,000 homes burning down. Household formation declined during 2008 and 2009 because of job losses and is now rebounding. As the annualized rate of housing starts was around 600,000 during the second half of 2010, it will probably take a year to clear inventory and set the stage for an upturn in construction. Fannie Mae is forecasting that housing starts will rise from 580,000 in 2010 to over 700,000 in 2011 and 1.1 million in 2012. As the economy lost 2.1 million construction jobs during the recession, such an upturn could add several hundred thousand jobs.

As a result of increasing consumption, robust business investment, and a delayed housing recovery, the odds are high that the economy's growth rate will rebound to the 3.0–4.0 percent range by the first half of 2011. In such a scenario, quantitative easing will probably end in June 2011.

The Fed's policy will also force other countries to pursue expansionary monetary policies in order to prevent their own currencies from appreciating excessively. Japan has engaged in currency market intervention and announced its own quantitative easing program to stem the appreciation of the yen. Developing countries in both East Asia and Latin America are engaging in currency intervention that could nurture more domestic monetary growth. The European currency has suffered from investor concerns about the debt servicing problems of peripheral countries such as Greece, Ireland, and Portugal. The European Union intervened to rescue Greece in May 2010 and created a special fund to help other countries, which helped Ireland in November. Germany then undermined market confidence in the peripheral countries by suggesting that it would encourage them to pursue debt restructuring that might penalize bond holders. Investor concern about the periphery of Europe has hurt confidence in the European currency and caused it to slump despite the Fed's quantitative easing program.

There is one country that has been engaging in massive intervention to restrain its currency for several years, but will now allow it to appreciate against the dollar. That country is China. As China has a current account surplus exceeding 5 percent of GDP and over $2.5 trillion of foreign exchange reserves, there is a general consensus that its currency is undervalued. China allowed it to appreciate by 20 percent between mid-2005 and mid-2008, but then re-pegged it during the global financial crisis. In the second half of 2010, it allowed the renminbi to appreciate by 3 percent, and will probably allow another 3–4 percent appreciation during the first half of 2011. There could be further gains of 6–7 percent during 2012 and 2013. China has been proceeding cautiously because of concerns that there could be a double dip in the global economy, but its own economy has been enjoying a growth rate in the 9–10 percent range because of highly stimulative monetary and fiscal policies. The inflation rate also rose to 4.4 percent in October 2010, and could climb higher during the next few quarters. China tightened monetary policy through administrative guidance over bank lending and a 25 basis point interest rate hike in October 2010. It is likely to raise interest rates further in 2011. As China needs a tighter monetary policy to restrain inflation, it has good domestic reasons to encourage currency appreciation, not just a need to defuse protectionist threats from the US Congress.

How Deficits Could Define the Obama Presidency

The United States is currently confronting unprecedented policy uncertainties. The current fiscal deficits have no precedent in peacetime. They have been easy to finance so far because private credit demand collapsed in late 2008 and 2009, but at some point it will recover. When the Fed finally tightens monetary policy, government bond yields could rise sharply, pushing up mortgage rates and jeopardizing the housing recovery. Companies will also be alarmed by a rising cost of capital. The Obama administration has not yet offered any clear strategy for deficit reduction because it has not been necessary. But as the economy gains momentum, concerns about fiscal policy will become a dominant issue in the financial markets. The deficit could become the issue that ultimately defines the Obama presidency.

The president appointed a commission for deficit reduction. The two co-chairs of the committee, Alan Simpson and Erskine Bowles, released their proposals in November 2010, which consisted of a program with $4 trillion of deficit reduction through 2020. They called for $1.464 trillion of cuts in discretionary spending and $733 billion of cuts in mandatory spending. They also asked for $733 billion in revenue enhancement through reductions in tax expenditures such as allowances for health care spending, mortgage interest rate deductions, etc., and other tax reforms. Their proposals drew immediate fire from House Minority Leader Nancy Pelosi (D-CA) and conservative Republicans for threatening entitlement programs and popular tax allowances, but they at least offered a set of ideas that attempted to hold the tax share of GDP below 21 percent while reducing federal spending to 22 percent of GDP. In 2010, the recession had reduced the tax share of GDP to only 14.8 percent while the Obama stimulus program had boosted the spending share of GDP to 25.4 percent.

The resolution of fiscal policy uncertainties will play a major role in shaping the business cycle post-2010. If the government were to introduce a 10 percent VAT in 2012 or 2013, it would depress consumer spending. The Fed might have to offset the fiscal drag by easing interest rates. If there is no change in fiscal policy, bond yields could rise to 7–8 percent and jeopardize the upturn in the housing market. Large interest rate hikes would also raise the cost of capital and depress investment. There is no way to predict exactly how these policy uncertainties will play out. Congress will be reluctant to raise taxes or slash spending without a crisis in the markets. The administration will also be apprehensive about proposing unpopular tax hikes. Only one thing is certain at this point. The United States is on a fiscal trajectory that will ultimately be unsustainable. The path by which Washington discovers that it is unsustainable will be a decisive factor in shaping the business environment before and after the next presidential election.

2

THE CANADIAN ECONOMY: PROSPECTS AND CHALLENGES

Joshua Mendelsohn

Global Overview

Spurred by massive government stimulus measures and unprecedented monetary easing, the global economy is recovering. Most countries are showing positive growth again, with the strongest performance in the emerging Asian economies, notably China. However, the recovery process will be uneven and there is the risk of reversal in some regions. In particular, the pace of recovery in the United States and Europe is likely to be sluggish and fitful. Apart from the obvious need to repair the financial system and recover from the damage caused by the combination of the financial crisis and the housing market collapse, efforts by governments and central banks to reign in budget deficits and unwind monetary stimulus put in place to combat the recession will lead to more sluggish economic performance than otherwise would be the case in the latter part of 2010 and in 2011. The sovereign debt crisis in Europe, triggered by Greece in the spring of 2010 and amplified by developments in Ireland in the fall, has only intensified this risk, as many European countries have felt the need to act sooner than they otherwise might have in working to consolidate their fiscal positions. This has not only been true of countries that consider themselves to be in the direct line of fire, such as Portugal, Spain, and Ireland, but even the United Kingdom has introduced one of the most stringent budgets in many years. Other countries, notably Germany, have refused to consider additional stimulus measures to further promote global growth as has been called for by the United States. In the United States, there is a debate between those calling for a start to fiscal consolidation and those arguing for delaying the process and, more recently, in the face of the weak employment situation and signs that the recovery has lost momentum, additional stimulus measures. As part of an agreement reached in December 2010 to extend the Bush tax cuts for two years to all taxpayers, the Obama administration also obtained additional temporary stimulus measures (including a 2 percent reduction in payroll taxes for 2011 and an extension of expanded unemployment benefits for the year), which will bolster growth in 2011. However, with the mid-term congressional elections resulting in the Republican Party displacing the Democratic Party as the majority party in the House of Representatives, as well as making gains in the Senate, further fiscal stimulus is highly unlikely, and calls for fiscal consolidation will intensify. While the unwinding of fiscal stimulus is not expected to result in a reversion to negative growth, it will certainly take some momentum out of the global recovery. Given the integrated nature of the global economy, the effects will be felt at least to some degree in all regions.

From both a short- and long-term perspective, there are also grounds for concern about possible adverse effects from policy measures that are under consideration or have been put in place, however well intentioned, that could inhibit growth by creating uncertainty and adversely affecting business and consumer confidence and the allocation of resources. Examples of such measures include those aimed at preventing a recurrence of the financial crisis and those dealing with global warming, US health care reform, and tax policy, to mention a few.

While the above clearly pose risks to the recovery process, the global economy is still seen to be moving forward. After showing negative growth of 2.0 percent in 2009, the global economy is expected to have grown by about 3.7 percent in 2010 and slow to about 3.3 percent in 2011. The global recovery should reinforce the prospects for the Canadian economy. The fact that growth will be led by emerging economies, particularly in Asia, with their strong demand for energy and industrial materials, bodes well for Canada's resource sectors. Prime Minister Stephen Harper has made the point that Canada needs to increase its ties with Asia, as its more traditional markets in the United States and Europe will tend to be slower growing. True as this is, the fact remains that the United States is likely to continue to be Canada's main trading partner by far for many years to come, and its performance will remain the main external force affecting the Canadian economy. After registering a negative 2.6 percent growth rate in 2009, the US economy is forecast to have grown in the order of 2.8 percent in 2010 and to grow about 2.9 percent in 2011. Canada is expected to have outperformed the United States in 2010, with growth in the order of 3.0 percent, but will lag the US performance in 2011, with growth in the order of 2.7 percent.

The Canadian Economy

The second half of 2009 saw Canada emerge from recession. After three consecutive quarters of sharp declines in real GDP (averaging −4.3 percent seasonally adjusted annual rate), the economy grew at annualized rates of 0.9 percent and 4.9 percent (respectively) in the final two quarters of 2009. GDP growth accelerated to 5.6 percent in the first quarter of 2010, but then slowed sharply to only 2.3 percent in the second quarter and an even slower 1 percent in the third quarter. The rebound in economic growth largely reflects the relatively strong performance on the domestic front, with the external sector acting as the key constraint. From the third quarter of 2009 through the first quarter of 2010, growth in final domestic demand averaged 5.1 percent at seasonally adjusted annualized rates (SAAR), with the second and third quarters of 2010 slowing to a still very respectable average growth of 3.7 percent. For the five quarters through the third quarter of 2010, the 4.5 percent growth in average final domestic demand was a sharp reversal from the 4.2 percent decline experienced during the recessionary quarters. Growth in consumer spending was up a healthy 3.9 percent (SAAR) through the first quarter of 2010, before slowing to 2.3 percent in the second quarter as government incentives for home renovations ended, but accelerating to 3.5 percent in the third quarter. Following five quarters of sharp declines through mid-2009, business investment in machinery and equipment has been gathering momentum, averaging growth of 17.7 percent over the five quarters ending September 2010. Inventory building was also a more significant contributor to growth in the first three quarters of 2010. The key negative for the economy has been the external sector. Although export growth has turned positive in recent quarters, it has been offset by a much stronger growth in imports, thereby detracting from GDP growth. The strong investment in machinery and equipment noted above, much of which is imported, in part explains the rise in Canadian imports and the deterioration in the trade account. However, this investment should be viewed as a positive as it should contribute to enhancing productivity. At the same time, the growth in exports has been held back by the relative weakness in the US and global economies, improved but still soft energy (especially natural gas) and other commodity prices, longer-term structural challenges (such as the much downsized US auto industry), and the challenges posed to Canadian competitiveness from the strong Canadian dollar.

The 5.6 percent first quarter 2010 GDP growth rate likely represented the high-water mark for this recovery, with growth in more recent quarters already showing sharp deceleration. The much slower pace of growth is expected to continue in the second half of 2010 and in 2011. After growing by a forecasted 3.0 percent in 2010, growth in 2011 is forecast to slow to about 2.7 percent. As noted above, however, at the time of this writing the situation is still quite fragile and downside risks remain until the global, and especially the US, recovery is on more solid footing.

The downturn in Canada was relatively shallower than in other G-7 countries and the recovery more consistent than in all other G-7 countries. This reflects the fact that Canada's economic fundamentals are in many respects sounder than those of the United States and indeed most developed countries, and, barring sharp adverse external developments, should help the recovery process continue.

The Canadian banking system has been and continues to be one of the strongest, if not the strongest, banking system in the world. Despite all the turmoil, no Canadian bank has been at risk of failure. Key factors contributing to the strong performance of Canadian banks include a nationwide banking system with a strong retail deposit base and more emphasis on traditional, well-diversified lending as opposed to new exotic products. Even more important is a rigorous and focused supervisory regime overseen by the Office of the Superintendent of Financial Institutions (OSFI), with clearly defined objectives and a principles-based approach to regulation as opposed to a rules-based approach (as in the United States). This, in turn, has contributed to a more conservative risk appetite by banks. As part of this process, Canadian bank capital requirements were, at the time of the onset of the financial crisis, and continue to be well in excess of Basel II standards and that of many of their global bank counterparts. Minimum Canadian banks' Tier 1 and Tier 2 capital ratios were already at 7 and 10 percent, respectively, when Basel II requirements were at 4 and 8 percent. Moreover, Tier 1 capital was required to be at least 75 percent common equity. Since then, Canadian banks have significantly increased their capital ratios and, at well into double-digit territory for both Tier I and total capital, are well ahead of the new 7 percent Basel III capital guidelines agreed to at the November 2010 G-20 meeting in Seoul. Along with the constraints noted above, Canadian banks also face a regulatory limit on total leverage of twenty time's total capital, which has been more conservative than in most other jurisdictions. (Depending on individual institution performance, OSFI can allow a somewhat higher ratio or demand a lower ratio.) Separately, regulations affecting home buying and the mortgage market also helped Canada and its banks avoid the housing meltdown that occurred in the United States and other countries. Given the performance of the Canadian banking system, Prime Minister Stephen Harper successfully argued against calls from the United States and others for the general imposition of a special tax on major banks, although individual countries can still apply such a tax, at the June 2010 G-8 and G-20 meetings hosted by Canada. Additionally, there is no pressure to overhaul legislation governing the financial system in Canada for risk-management purposes, although banks would like access to such markets as auto leasing. The one change the federal government is trying to make involves the creation of a national securities regulator to replace the current provincial system, which is seen as inefficient and out of date.

Canada also has not suffered from the real estate debacles that have occurred in the United States and parts of Europe. Markets did overheat in some regions, notably Alberta, but this was because of the influx of people into the province due to the strength in the energy sector in recent years. A combination of institutional and regulatory factors prevented the development in Canada of a mortgage market akin to that which proved so disastrous in the United States. Virtually all mortgages in Canada are "full recourse" loans, whereby the borrower remains obligated to repay the full value of the mortgage even if the borrower's home is foreclosed upon. Thus, unlike in many jurisdictions in the United States, where the borrower can simply "mail the key to the bank and walk away," if, for example, the value of the property falls below the mortgage principal, Canadian borrowers can have other assets and even future earnings attached by the lender. Home mortgage interest is not tax deductable in Canada either (but capital gains on a home are also not subject to tax). Full recourse mortgages and no mortgage interest tax deductibility significantly reduce the incentive to take out excessively large mortgages. Indeed, there is an incentive to accelerate mortgage repayment. Unsurprisingly, a large proportion of mortgages in Canada are insured. Any mortgage with less than a 20 percent down payment must be fully insured for the life of the mortgage. The majority of mortgages are insured through Canada Mortgage and Housing Corporation (CMHC), a federal Crown corporation. Canadian banks tend to originate and hold most of their mortgages as well, encouraging a much more prudent approach to lending. Subprime mortgages and their variations accounted for, at most, 5 percent of mortgage origination in Canada, and mortgage securitization has been far more limited than in the United States.

Canadian households were also never quite in the same dire straits as their American counterparts. As one measure, Canada's household net worth-to-disposable-income ratio did not deteriorate nearly as sharply as in the United States, in good part reflecting the more stable housing market noted above. As can be seen in Figure 2.1, the recovery in the stock market and a much more buoyant housing market have resulted in the further strengthening of this ratio as Canada moved through the early part of 2010, and the gap between Canada and the United States has remained quite wide.

Canada's employment picture has also been far brighter than most countries and certainly the United States'. Over the period from August 2009 through November 2010, Canada created 437,000 jobs, offsetting nearly all of the employment loss experienced during the downturn. After peaking at 8.7 percent in August 2009, the unemployment rate was down to 7.6 percent in November 2010. This rate is still well above the 6.1 percent level that prevailed before the onset of the recession, but this is due to the influx of people into the labor force over this period (not the exit of workers,

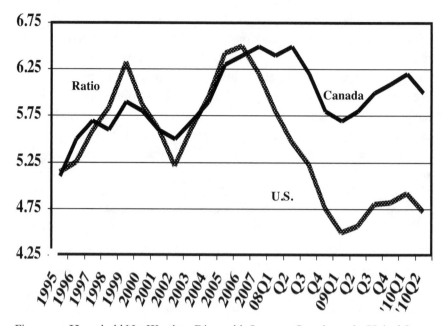

Figure 2.1 Household Net Worth to Disposable Income, Canada vs. the United States
Source: Statistics Canada, FRB

as has occurred in the United States). Moreover, most of the increase in employment has been in full-time positions, with the bulk also being in the private sector. The pace of employment growth going forward will likely slow. Still, the recovery in the labor market to date—as well as further, albeit slower, improvement going forward—augurs well for consumer confidence and spending.

That being said, growth in consumer spending will likely proceed at a slower pace compared to early 2010, as pent-up demand is satiated, government stimulus to promote home renovation has ended, and the buildup of debt in recent years causes consumers to take a break. With respect to the last point, in good part owing to the strong housing market and mortgage demand, the ratio of household debt to personal disposable income stood at 149 percent at the end of the first quarter of 2010 (compared to an already high 142 percent in early 2009). Even the Bank of Canada has raised concerns over the growing consumer debt load. (See Figure 2.2.) The fear is that with interest rates having nowhere to go but up, increasing debt loads make households more vulnerable.

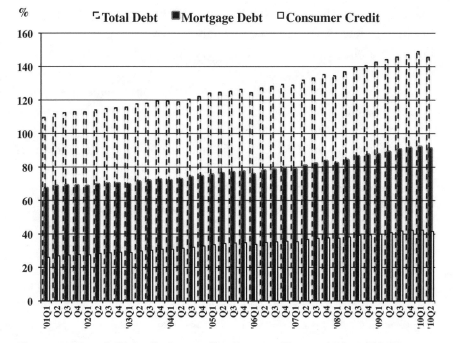

%   ⌐Total Debt   ∎Mortgage Debt   ⌐Consumer Credit

Figure 2.2 Household Credit Outstanding, Percent of Personal Disposable Income
Source: Bank of Canada, Statistics Canada

As of the time of this writing, there are indications that the pace of credit growth was slowing, and it will slow further as the housing market softens.[1]

Rock-bottom interest rates, pent-up demand, and prospective government measures that prompted home purchasers to advance their buying plans resulted in ballooning home sales in the latter half of 2009 and early 2010, with average sales of existing homes exceeding 500,000 (SAAR) in the final quarter of 2009 and the first quarter of 2010(compared to sales in the mid-300,000 level during the depth of the recession). Sales have since fallen off, and trended in the low 400,000 unit range in the second half of 2010 through November. Home prices, which were rising nearly 20 percent year over year in late 2009 and early 2010 have also decelerated, and have recently been flat on a year-over-year basis based on data from the Canadian Real Estate Association (CREA). The slowdown in the housing market was not surprising as the market was being pumped up by special factors earlier in the year. The pressure from pent-up demand and low interest rates was reinforced through the early spring by the impending imposition of more stringent mortgage eligibility and down-payment requirements introduced by the government in its efforts to preclude the risk of a US-style housing bubble. The harmonization into a single tax (HST) of the federal Goods and Services Tax (GST) and the provincial retail sales tax in Ontario and British Columbia as of July 1, 2010, also contributed to housing demand. Prior to harmonization, the provincial retail sales tax was not applied to housing. Under the new system, the tax will apply to the price of newly constructed homes above a certain price threshold ($400,000 in Ontario and $525,000 in British Columbia), causing prospective buyers to accelerate their plans. There was a certain amount of confusion about the applicability of the new tax on housing. Some prospective buyers may well have thought the tax applied to resale homes as well as newly constructed homes, thereby prompting added resale demand. The desire to avoid the added sales taxes that would now be applied to home sale and purchase-related services, such as real estate commissions and legal fees, likely also prompted some sales. Once these measures came into effect, the housing market cooled off quickly. Housing starts have also started to ease back. For the balance of 2010 and into 2011, the housing market is expected to remain much softer than what prevailed over the latter part of 2009 and into early 2010, with prices generally flat and possibly even falling in some areas. However, a still-buoyant labor situation and relatively low mortgage rates should limit the degree of weakening, and a major decline in prices is not expected. Nevertheless, a flattening in home price increases, and even more so a downward correction in prices, would adversely affect the growth of household net worth, one of the strengths noted above.

In contrast to the household sector, Canada's corporate sector has seen its financial position improve, with debt-to-equity ratios declining while corporate profits have been on the rise. This puts firms in a good position to invest in coming quarters. The stronger Canadian dollar and the introduction of the HST in Ontario and British Columbia, which allows for the recapture of sales taxes paid by business on inputs, reinforces the case for investment. In fact, in contrast to households, which accelerated their purchases in certain areas, the impending introduction of the HST may well have caused firms to delay investment spending until the harmonized tax was in place.

The Fiscal Situation

Canada's fiscal position is also much healthier than nearly all of its developed country counterparts. This reflects the fact that between fiscal 1997–1998 and 2007–2008, Canada consistently ran budget surpluses, resulting in a progressive reduction in the federal debt. On the eve of the financial turmoil, not only did Canada start off with a small budget surplus, but the federal debt-to-GDP ratio was down to 29 percent. The aggregate of provincial governments also ran surpluses from fiscal 2004–2005 on, further reducing Canada's debt load. Based on OECD measures, by 2008, the country's general government net financial liabilities as a percent of GDP were down to 22.4 percent, which was well below any other G-7 country.[2]

Reflecting the impact of the global recession on Canada and efforts to mitigate it, in its October 2010 Update of Economic and Fiscal Projections, the Department of Finance projected deficits in the order of $55.6 billion and $45.4 billion in fiscal 2009–2010 and 2010–2011, respectively (equal to 3.6 and 2.8 percent of forecast GDP, respectively), and diminishing through 2014–2015, at which time the deficit is forecasted to be $1.7 billion, or 0.1 percent of GDP. Despite these deficits, the federal government's debt-to-GDP ratio is forecasted by Finance Canada to peak at a relatively low 35.3 percent in 2010–2011. Whether the government will be able to meet its deficit reduction goals remains to be seen.[3]

Many of Canada's fiscal projections rely on consistently good economic performance, with nominal growth projected to average 5.0 percent over the 2010–2014 period, and the government's ability to contain the growth of program spending at a time when demographic pressures will be building. With the 2010 nominal GDP growth rate now looking to exceed the economic growth assumption in the budget (about 5.8 percent compared to 4.9 percent) and the unemployment rate turning out to be below the budget assumption (8.0 percent compared to 8.5 percent), the government will get a head start toward meeting its budget deficit targets and should have no trouble meeting the G-20 target of cutting the budget deficit in

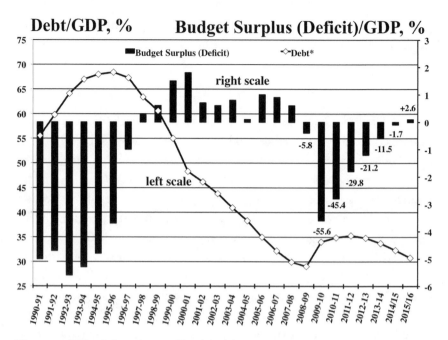

Figure 2.3 Federal Government Fiscal Position
Source: Finance Canada—Update of Economic and Fiscal Projections (September 2009) and Budget 2010

half by 2013. (See Figure 2.3.) Still, if it is to achieve its ultimate goal of eliminating the deficit and stabilizing its debt at a low level, it would appear that Canada has run out of room to cut taxes, and spending will need to be restrained over the coming years.

Monetary Policy, Interest Rates, and the Dollar

In the face of worsening global economic and financial conditions, the Bank of Canada reduced its overnight rate from 4.50 percent in the fall of 2007 to a low of 0.25 percent in April 2009, and committed to hold this rate until mid-2010, barring any buildup of inflationary pressures. Strong growth in the last quarter of 2009 and the first quarter of 2010, coupled with positive indicators for the second quarter and the Bank's measure of inflation running not far below its 2.0 percent target, led the Bank to raise its overnight rate by twenty-five basis points in June 2010 and a further twenty-five basis points in July to 0.75 percent. Despite signs of a softening economy, the Bank raised the overnight rate again in September to 1.0 percent. Given increased global uncertainties and with the pace of economic growth in Canada slowing, the Bank has since shifted to a holding position and the overnight rate is expected to remain at 1.0 percent into early 2011. Given the lowered expectations for economic performance in 2011, although continuing to move back to more normal interest rates, the Bank will do so in a measured way, with the overnight rate gradually approaching 2.0 percent by the latter part of 2011.

Undoing other measures taken during the period of extreme economic and financial stress is less of a challenge for the Bank of Canada than for many of its counterparts. Unlike the Fed, the Bank of Canada did not need to acquire poorly performing assets from commercial banks and avoided quantitative easing. Instead, the Bank injected liquidity into the financial system by purchasing short-term liquid assets, making the unwinding process much easier.

Although still strongly influenced by commodity prices, the Canadian dollar now appears to be reflecting other forces as well. The soundness of the Canadian financial system, Canada's strong fiscal position and economic prospects compared to the United States and Europe, prospects for rising interest rates, and a generally more negative sentiment toward the US dollar played a part in the sharp appreciation of the Canadian dollar in the latter part of 2009 and in 2010. The currency is generally expected to trade at about its current level ($1.01 Cdn/US) for the balance of 2010. Going forward, with global uncertainties dissipating and US and global growth and commodity prices providing a more positive picture, and with the Bank of Canada resuming a gradual tightening policy in 2011, the Canadian dollar should also gain strength and will likely test parity with the US dollar again. However, a sharp and rapid appreciation of the Canadian dollar above parity would be of some concern to the Bank of Canada and would likely cause it to slow the pace of any monetary tightening.

Risks

The positive, albeit moderate, prospects for the Canadian economy could be thrown off course by any number of external factors, some of which are noted below.

- Of greatest concern is the possibility of the US economy suffering another downturn. This would clearly have a significant direct adverse impact on Canada's external sector and overall economic growth. To the extent that a sharp reversal in the United States would also contribute to weaker performance globally, Canada would be affected by weaker non-US markets and commodity prices.
- As noted earlier, Canada benefits from strong growth in emerging countries due to their demand for energy and other industrial commodities, China being the most notable case. In part due to its unwillingness to allow its currency to appreciate more sharply inflationary pressures are building in China as is a real estate bubble. Should efforts to contain these pressures result in a sharp slowdown in China's growth, commodity exporting countries such as Canada would clearly suffer.
- Given that many countries, especially the United States, are already experiencing significant budget deficits, additional efforts to offset renewed economic weakness with fiscal stimulus would only worsen the situation. Moreover, the impact on the economy may be even less than measures to date, as markets and taxpayers increasingly worry about the fallout from further fiscal deterioration. The likely absence of further fiscal stimulus puts the burden of trying to revive the economy on the back of monetary policy. Indeed, in the United States, with the Fed funds target rate set at 0.00–0.25 percent, the Fed has already introduced a new round of "unconventional" measures, the so-called quantitative easing (QEII), which will result in a further expansion of an already bloated Fed balance sheet. This expansion raises the risk of future inflation and generating asset bubbles, but under present circumstances it is not being taken as a serious concern.
- Another key risk is the introduction of protectionist measures in a slow growth and high unemployment environment. As the global financial crisis took hold, the G-20 members committed to avoid imposing protectionist measures. To a reasonable degree they have stuck to their agreement. That is not to say that no measures have been introduced. Indeed, many more trade impediments were put in place if one includes the host of "beggar thy neighbor" policies that were introduced. These include the "buy America" provisions of the US stimulus package and

various export tax rebates implemented by China, to name but two clear examples. More recently, the implementation of QEII in the United States, although argued on grounds of reviving domestic demand, clearly has implications for the US dollar, leading to depreciation and, through capital flows, having undesirable effects on other countries. Efforts by one country to promote its trade position raise the risk of other countries following suit.

- We also cannot dismiss the possibility of new financial crises erupting or of older ones bubbling up again. Indeed, the debt and banking crises that hit Ireland in November 2010 have intensified concerns about the financial health of Portugal and Spain, with the latter being of particular concern given the size of its economy.

As sound as Canada's fundamentals are, it is unlikely that the country could avoid the economic and financial fallout from such developments.

Some Longer-Term Issues and Challenges

Although Canada has many positive attributes, the country is not without its challenges. While Canada's fiscal situation is relatively healthy compared to many other developed countries, it faces the demographic challenge of an aging population, which will put added pressure on government spending. The year 2011 will see the oldest of the baby boom generation reach sixty-five, and the pace of retirements will quicken thereafter. While losses suffered due to the financial crisis may cause some prospective retirees to delay exiting the labor force, this will not change the longer-term reality. In addition, the recession has thrown off the government's efforts to "pre-fund" future expenditures by further reducing its debt ratio. Hence, getting the fiscal situation back on track as quickly as possible is critical.

The aging population also means that labor force growth will be slower, implying lower potential growth and all that entails in terms of income growth and government revenues. Higher participation rates and increased immigration could offset some of these issues. With respect to the latter, Canada is introducing policies that will help expedite the accreditation of immigrants to Canada with foreign professional and trades credentials. Well-trained foreign doctors driving taxis in Toronto do not ease the shortage of family physicians.

The real key to providing for the future, however, is improving Canada's productivity performance, which has been lagging badly since the turn of the twenty-first century. There are many reasons given for this lag, including the mix of Canada's industries, the slower diffusion of new technologies, lack of sufficient competition in some areas, and less capital available per worker. In an effort to promote investment and enhance productivity and competitiveness, the federal and provincial governments have worked to reduce the tax burden on business in recent years. The federal general and manufacturing and processing corporate tax rates have been reduced from 26 percent and 22 percent, respectively, in 2002 to 18 percent in 2010, and will drop to 16.5 and 15 percent, respectively, in 2011 and 2012. Capital taxes on nonfinancial corporations have been eliminated at the federal level as well as in some provinces, and other provinces have lowered their rates. Also, as noted above, on July 1, 2010, Ontario and British Columbia harmonized their sales taxes with the federal GST, allowing companies to recapture provincial sales taxes as well as the GST paid on all inputs. All of this should improve the position of firms, making them more competitive and helping to promote investment.

Another recent move of note is the federal government's decision to allow Globalive to provide mobile phone services in Canada despite the fact that it is largely financed through a foreign-owned firm (Orascom Telecom). Canada has often been criticized for limiting foreign ownership in various sectors, including telecoms, thereby limiting competition and its benefits. It remains to be seen if this is just a one-off decision or a crack in the door. In this context, the federal government's rejection of Australian mining giant BHP Billiton's effort to acquire Potash Corporation of Saskatchewan has raised questions over Canada's openness to foreign investment. It should be kept in mind, however, that this is only the second time the government has rejected a transaction out of the more than 1,600 proposals that have been reviewed and approved since the Investment Canada Act came into being in the mid-1980s.[4] (The Investment Act only applies to transactions where the value of the target company's assets is Canadian $300 million or higher.) The government has said that it will be reviewing the act, and this will hopefully result in greater transparency. From a broader perspective, Canada needs to adapt to the changing global economic structure. This means that sectors that have previously been given special consideration at the expense of others may no longer merit such special treatment. Indeed, the reallocation of resources may go a long way toward improving Canada's overall economic performance.

No analysis of Canada would be complete without raising the environmental challenges. For Canada, with its energy-producing sector and many important industries that give off greenhouse gases (GHG), global efforts to contain GHG emissions pose both risks and opportunities. The risks stem from the prospect that stringent guidelines agreed to by Canada's trading partners, especially the United States and/or globally, will adversely affect Canadian industry, both domestically and from a trade perspective, by significantly raising costs or imposing other constraints. Of particular concern to Canada was the passage in the US House of Representatives of the American Clean Energy and Security Act of 2009 (the Waxman-Markey bill). Given the outcome of the November 2010 Congressional elections, however, it is very unlikely that a major environmental bill will pass Congress before the next presidential election in 2012. Having said this, both the overall targets of any environmental legislation, and, perhaps even more important, the mechanisms by which these targets are expected to be achieved are critical. It is for this reason that the Canadian government has been holding off on its own proposals, as it wants to get a better perspective of what US legislation and/or regulatory changes (as imposed by the Environmental Protection Agency) will look like; it will then try to harmonize, as best it can, Canada's climate change policies with those of the United States. If Canada's policies are seen as less stringent or not in sync with those of the United States, Canadian firms may find themselves shut out of US markets or having to purchase border permits for their products to compensate for laxer emissions standards. Under some elements of proposed legislation, Canadian hydropower exported to the United States might not qualify as a renewable energy source. State-sponsored measures in the United States are also of significance, as in the case of California's low-carbon fuel standard, with its significant adverse implications for Alberta's oil sands. Climate legislation can also be used as a back door for protectionism, and this must be guarded against. Having said this, climate legislation can also open up opportunities. Alternative sources of cleaner energy often come to mind, but technologies developed by emitting industries or others to reduce emissions can generate new products and new industries in their own right.

Notes

1. For scenario analysis, see Bank of Canada, *Financial System Review*, December 2009, 21–25. Additional refinement can be found in *Financial System Review*, June 2010, 24–25 and 57–62.

2. Canada Department of Finance, *Fiscal Reference Tables*, October 2010, Table 55.

3. The provinces will also run deficits, the most significant being that of Ontario.

4. Industry Canada, Investment Canada Act, Quarterly Statistics, October 7, 2010, Table A.

MEXICO'S INTERMINABLE TRANSITION—2011 AND BEYOND

Timothy Heyman

2010—A Year of Recovery

For Mexico, 2010 was a year of recovery from the *annus horribilis* of 2009. The fall in 2009 GDP of 6.5 percent had been the worst among OECD and major emerging countries except Russia (Table 3.1), and Mexico's worst since 1932. (See Figure 3.1.)

This dismal 2009 performance had been caused not only by Mexico's dependence on the United States but also by internal factors. A hitherto unknown strain of flu (A/H1N1) was discovered in Mexico in April and paralyzed the country for a week, with measurable direct economic effects and incalculable indirect effects on morale and image. Oil production fell to 2.6 million barrels per day, compared to its peak level of 3.4 million in 2004. Formal unemployment rose as high as 6.4 percent, its worst level since October 1995. Drug violence continued, as did a wave of kidnappings and extortion, particularly in cities outside the capital. The main opposition party, the Institutional Revolutionary Party (PRI), along with its allies, won a congressional majority in mid-term elections in July, but this led to even more legislative gridlock. A fiscal package designed to counteract the oil income shortfall was almost entirely emasculated, with the three main parties (National Action Party [PAN] [right], PRI [center], Party of the Democratic Revolution [PRD] [left]) incapable of reaching a sensible agreement. Mexico's debt (rated BBB+, two notches above an investment grade of BBB−) was downgraded to BBB, its first downgrade since

Table 3.1 GDP 2009

Country	GDP 2009 (percent)
Brazil	−0.2
Canada	−2.6
China	8.7
Euro area	−4.1
India	5.7
Japan	−5.2
Mexico	−6.5
Russia	−7.9
United Kingdom	−4.9
United States	−2.4

Source: IMF (2010)

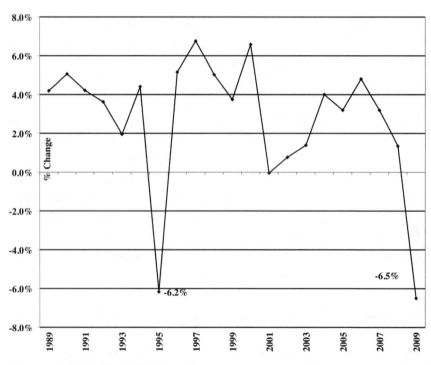

Figure 3.1 Mexico: Real GDP Growth
Source: United Nations Statistics Division (2009) and IMF (2010)

1995. Meanwhile, other countries that were previously considered Mexico's peers in the emerging markets universe were hardly affected by the financial crisis.

Recovery in 2010 was predictable, due mainly to the absence of the extraordinary combination of factors that caused the collapse of 2009. With the United States growing by an estimated 3 percent, it was probable that Mexico would grow by more than 4 percent (Table 3.2), with an increase in exports to the United States, particularly automotive, providing a major contribution. Oil production stabilized (Figure 3.2), and the overall trade balance was helped by higher average oil prices than in 2009. Countercyclical government stimulus, particularly in construction and infrastructure, also contributed to the recovery. Formal unemployment fell to 5.1 percent in June, and inflation was even lower than forecast.

Gubernatorial elections in July 2010 in twelve states were broadly positive for the PRI, which won nine out of twelve races. Indeed, it won three states from the opposition: Aguascalientes and Tlaxcala (PAN) and Zacatecas (PRD). However, its losses in three states (Oaxaca, Puebla, and Sinaloa) to coalition PAN-PRD candidates represented a far greater loss in voter population than its gains (8.1 million vs. 2.6 million) and a reduction in the voter population of PRI-governed states to just 50 percent of the total voter population for the first time since the PRI's founding in 1929. It also showed that there might be a way for the PAN and PRD to slow down the PRI juggernaut in the run-up to the all-important congressional and presidential elections in 2012 (Table 3.3).

Table 3.2 Mexico: Economic Forecast for 2010 and 2011

Indicator	2010	2011
GDP growth (percent)	4.4	3.7
Inflation (percent)	4.7	3.9
28-day interest rate (percent)	4.7	5.8
Exchange rate ($/US$)	12.5	12.8
Fiscal deficit (percent of GDP)	2.4	2.2
Commercial deficit (US$ bn.)	6.9	12.6
Current account deficit (US$ bn.)	8.4	13.8
Foreign direct investment (US$ bn.)	16.9	19.7

Source: Analysts' consensus compiled by Bank of Mexico (July 1, 2010)

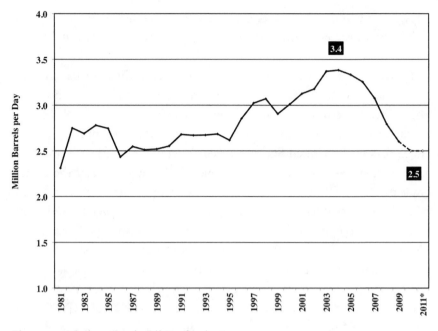

Figure 3.2 Mexican Crude Oil Production*
*Forecast
Source: Energy Information Administration (2010) and SHCP (2010)

Table 3.3 Gubernatorial Elections: Results 2010

State	Party of incumbent	Winner in 2010 elections
Aguascalientes	PAN	PRI
Chihuahua	PRI	PRI
Durango	PRI	PRI
Hidalgo	PRI	PRI
Oaxaca	PRI	PAN-PRD
Puebla	PRI	PAN-PRD
Quintana Roo	PRI	PRI
Sinaloa	PRI	PAN-PRD
Tamaulipas	PRI	PRI
Tlaxcala	PAN	PRI
Veracruz	PRI	PRI
Zacatecas	PRD	PRI

Source: Instituto Federal Electoral (IFE) y El Universal (2010)

Increased drug violence in the northern states cast a cloud on the social, economic, and investment climate and led to President Calderón's appointment in July 2010 of his fourth interior minister in four years. He replaced Fernando Gómez Mont with Francisco Blake Mora, who is a hard-line security expert from the border state of Baja California.

The year 2010 is iconic because Mexico is celebrating two hundred years since declaring independence from Spain in September 1810, and also, uniquely among Latin American nations, one hundred years since its Revolution in November 1910. As is typical for such events, some questions were raised about the organization of the celebrations (the coordinator having been changed five times) and the transparency of the budget, but the many events and exhibitions related to the bicentenary went off without a hitch, and, possibly, contributed to a greater consciousness of Mexico's identity, achievements, and challenges, which may eventually be reflected in the ballot box.

For 2011, the economic outlook is again highly dependent on the US economy and world commodity prices. Broadly, more of the same is expected, with growth coming in at 3–4 percent, inflation staying around 4 percent, and the trade balance deteriorating slightly as the recovery gathers pace.

As in 2009 and 2010, other emerging markets are expected to continue to forge ahead. Following sixteen years of constructive presidencies (Cardoso and Lula), Brazil is looking forward to a smooth political handover to Dilma Rousseff, the winner of the October 2010 presidential election, that will consolidate its position as Latin America's leading country. Chile, a paradigm of economic and political stability, managed an orderly presidential changeover in March 2010 from left-of-center Michelle Bachelet to right-wing Sebastián Piñera. Having survived a devastating earthquake at the beginning of Piñera's presidency, and with the unexpected fillip of the extraordinary miners' rescue in October 2010, Chile will continue to benefit from the voracious import appetite of its Pacific trading partners. Colombians elected Alvaro Uribe's former defense minister, Juan Manuel Santos, to the presidency in recognition of Uribe's success in reducing violence and stabilizing the economy, and Santos is likely to maintain his predecessor's economic and social policies.

But the concern for Mexicans is not 2011. It is the medium and long term: whether Mexico can and will make the structural and institutional reforms to complete its transition to modernity.

1988—The Salinas Revolution

Mexico has been in this situation before. In 1988, the last year of President Miguel de la Madrid's *sexenio* (the Mexican president's six-year term in office), and six years after the country's virtual bankruptcy in 1982, GDP growth was at 1.3 percent, inflation was at 52 percent, and the government deficit was at 11.7 percent of GDP. The foreign debt contracted prior to 1982 was still unpayable, and the banking system, nationalized in 1982, was still in the hands of the government. In presidential elections that year, the official PRI candidate, Carlos Salinas, was opposed by a left-wing coalition headed by Cuauhtémoc Cárdenas, son of Lázaro Cárdenas, who was president between 1934 and 1940 and a historic figure for having expropriated the Mexican oil industry in 1938. Salinas won amidst widespread allegations of fraud. It seemed as if the country was economically unviable and politically ungovernable.

Salinas, who took office in December 1988, was surprisingly able to transform expectations and reality in the first two years of his sexenio. In 1989, he consolidated his power by successively jailing Joaquín Hernández Galicia ("La Quina"), the leader of the oil workers' union, and Eduardo Legorreta, one of the most prominent brokers in Mexico. In January 1990, following the collapse of the Berlin Wall in November 1989, Salinas realized at the World Economic Forum's annual Davos meeting that he would have to compete with the newly liberated countries of Eastern Europe. Salinas ordered the beginning of negotiations toward a North American Free Trade Agreement (NAFTA) and the reprivatization of the banking system. The banks were privatized between June 1991 and June 1992, and NAFTA was negotiated at a breakneck pace and approved by the US Congress in November 1993, with implementation of the agreement beginning on January 1, 1994.

By the end of 1993, Mexico was one of the top three emerging markets by market capitalization, and Carlos Salinas was feted as one of the key leaders of the emerging markets universe. Mexico became a member of the OECD and was held up as an example of successful sequencing of economic and political reforms (in contrast to Russia), with perestroika (economic restructuring) coming before glasnost (political opening). As if to reaffirm Mexico's international prominence, for the first time, a Mexican man, Octavio Paz, won the Nobel Prize for Literature (1990) and a Mexican woman, Lupita Jones, became Miss Universe (1991).

The prestige of the Salinas presidency evaporated with the Zapatista uprising in January 1994, two major political assassinations, the "Tequila Crisis" of December 1994, the first month of Ernesto Zedillo's sexenio (1994–2000), and the incarceration of Salinas's brother Raúl in 1995. But Mexico recovered rapidly with the help of a massive US-assisted bailout and continued to consolidate economically and politically under Zedillo. NAFTA led to an immediate increase in average foreign direct investment from US$5 billion to US$13 billion per year, and an average GDP growth (following the crisis year of 1995) of 5.5 percent for the rest of the sexenio.

2000—The Fox Revolution

Sooner than anyone anticipated, perestroika led to glasnost. The PRI lost the congressional majority it had held since 1929 in mid-term elections in 1997, and then, most importantly, it lost the presidency in 2000. Vicente Fox, an outsider, took over the right-wing PAN party and won against a lackluster PRI machine candidate, Francisco Labastida.

Twelve years of relative prosperity (Figure 3.3) meant that intensely nationalistic Mexicans were prepared to entrust their future to a man with a foreign name who had been the head of Coca-Cola in Mexico, and to remove the PRI, the party that had provided them with political stability for seventy-one years, from Los Pinos (the presidential mansion). It seemed as if Mexico's transition to modernity was close to completion.

Once in office, Fox turned out to be more a Walesa—historically important for having overturned a regime, but unable to consolidate a new one—than a Mandela, who was able to do both. To his supporters' dismay, he wasted little time in showing that campaigning and governing skills are not necessarily the same.

Shortly after assuming the presidency in December 2000, he frittered away his political capital with an untimely attempt to "solve" the Zapatista

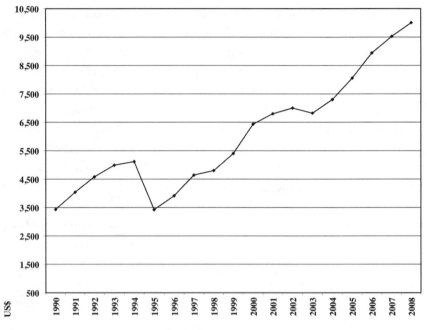

Figure 3.3 Mexico: GDP per Capita in Current US$
Source: CEPAL (2010)

problem, even though it was no longer a problem. His attempts to introduce ambitious reforms foundered as he mismanaged relations with an
ever more combative Congress. His relationship with George W. Bush,
who was elected in the same year, began splendidly as they flaunted their
shared interest in horses, ranches, and cowboy hats. But it was dented by
his tepid response to 9/11 and irrevocably damaged by his failure to support the United States in the UN Security Council on the Iraqi war.

As Fox's sexenio progressed, his marriage to his press secretary, Martha
Sahagún, turned the presidency into a soap opera. Meanwhile, as the PRI
fell further into disrepute and disarray following its catastrophic defeat in
2000, the opposition vacuum was filled by Andrés Manuel López Obra-
dor (AMLO), a firebrand demagogue who used his platform as Mexico
City's mayor (the second most important elected post in the country) to
wrest leadership of the leftist PRD party from Cuauhtémoc Cárdenas.

AMLO's cause was only helped by Fox's ham-fisted attempt to block
him from standing for the 2006 presidential election through a dubious

legal procedure. With Fox failing to transform himself from party out-sider to insider and to consolidate his hold on the PAN, Santiago Creel, his candidate for the 2006 presidential elections, was rejected by the party in favor of Felipe Calderón, an experienced congressional politician and scion of the PAN's founding elite.

2006—Calderón's First Four Years

Calderón's victory was a close-run thing. AMLO was buoyed not only by his own populist rhetoric, but by disappointment with Fox and the PAN. He lost, by the narrowest of margins, because he was un-able to move to the center in the latter stages of the campaign, and Calde-rón was able to present him as a clear threat to the hard-won gains earned by Mexico's newly emerging middle class after eighteen years of economic growth. AMLO's reaction to his electoral loss, which was to cry fraud and block Reforma (Mexico City's main thoroughfare) with a tent city for several months, seemed only to confirm the PAN's portrayal of him. Meanwhile, Calderón's supporters assumed that he was much more quali-fied than Fox to pilot needed reforms through Congress given his experi-ence with the legislature and PAN party politics.

But Calderón has also disappointed. At the beginning of his sexenio, he surprisingly declared war on drug gangs, extradited various capos to the United States, and made visible use of the army in what many considered to be police work, with the rationale that the police were part of the prob-lem. At the time, such action seemed necessary, courageous, and admirable. But two-thirds of the way through his sexenio, it is estimated that more than 28,000 have died as a result of the drug war since 2006. Despite a record level of highly publicized detentions of people, weapons, and drugs (Figure 3.4), Mexicans are concerned about whether the war is being "won," or whether it should even have been taken on in such a public way, as victory is likely to be distant, if not indefinable.

In implicit contrast to Fox, Calderón also openly proclaimed that he would seek "possible" rather than "desirable" reforms; that is, anything was better than nothing. But debilitating negotiations with Congress led to electoral, energy, and fiscal reforms that some regard as worse than noth-ing. Meanwhile, on Calderón's watch, Mexico suffered its *annus horribilis*

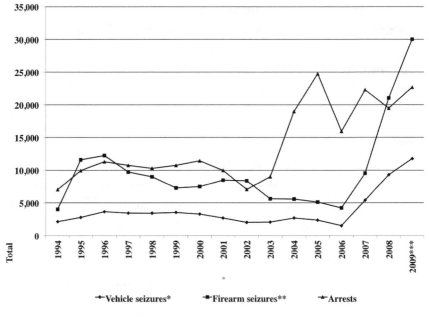

Figure 3.4 The War on Drugs
*Includes terrestrial vehicles, marine vehicles, and aircraft
**Includes long and short
***Data from January 2009 to June 2009, annualized
Source: PGR (2009)

in 2009, and although his government handled the flu crisis with more skill than most, he could not escape the blame.

In addition, encouraged by the PRD's post-electoral self-destructiveness, the PRI, third in the polls in 2006, regrouped impressively. After winning a series of off-year gubernatorial and local elections, the PRI and its allies sealed their comeback by taking a majority in Congress in 2009 and by winning nine out of twelve gubernatorial elections in 2010. In these elections, Calderón's new electoral strategy of forming coalitions with the PRD around candidates considered to be strong at a local level worked in the key states of Oaxaca, Puebla, and Sinaloa (although it was not obvious how the elected governors would actually govern). This could be the strategy for local elections up to the end of Calderón's sexenio, and even for the presidential election in 2012. But the PRI remains the front-runner to win the presidential election in 2012.

The Decalogue

Calderón himself realized that his sexenio had stalled in September 2009 when, in an unusual speech, he set out the agenda for his second three years, with indications that he would seek the "desirable," not the "possible," listing a Decalogue of desirable reforms (Table 3.4).

Given Calderón's record in the first half of his sexenio, skepticism about his ability to implement his Decalogue remained widespread and, thus far, seems justified. His decision a month after the announcement of the Decalogue to liquidate Luz y Fuerza del Centro, Mexico City's state-owned power company (which had become a byword for union cronyism, corruption, and inefficiency), led some to believe that Calderón meant business. However, almost one year after the Decalogue was announced, no other significant reform initiative had been presented. The ten items in the Decalogue reflect the structural reforms Mexico needs to complete its transition to modernity, which have been pending since 2000. All of the items are important, but four are critical: energy (included under economic reforms), public finance, security, and politics.

In the realm of energy, the decline in Mexico's oil production became particularly evident in 2009 (Figure 3.2). The key is the Cantarell field, discovered by a fisherman of that name in the Bay of Campeche in the 1970s, which at its peak in 2004 produced more than 2.1 million barrels per day—63 percent of Mexico's total production—but had fallen to an annualized 500,000 barrels per day in 2010. With offsets from some new

Table 3.4 Calderón's Decalogue

1	Fight against poverty
2	Universal health care
3	Quality education
4	Strengthening of public finances
5	Economic reforms
6	Reforms to the telecommunications sector
7	Labor reform
8	Regulatory reform
9	Public security
10	Political reform

Source: Presidencia de la República

production, Mexico's total production is expected to decline from 3.4 million barrels per day in 2004 to under 2.6 million in 2010.

Pemex, the state oil monopoly, estimates that production will remain at an average of 2.5 million barrels per day from 2010 to 2014. In recent years, Pemex's estimates have been routinely overoptimistic, sometimes by very wide margins. However, even if they were correct this time, Mexico's growing population and GDP imply an increasing domestic need for energy, with less remaining for exports, which has serious implications for Mexico's current account. It implies that Mexico requires a two-prong thrust: first, acceleration in its development of alternative energy resources and conservation techniques, and second, increased investment in exploration and production. With the first alternative requiring a long-term change in culture, attitudes, and processes, the quickest fix could come from the second.

Mexico has been slow to recognize its declining reserves (Figure 3.5) and has shown a worrisome inability to replenish them. The most promising

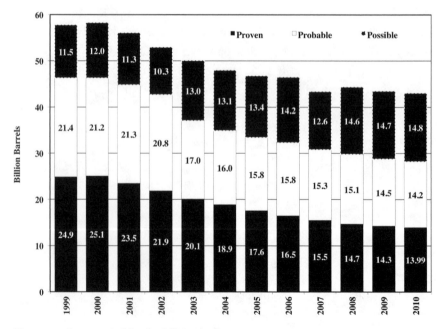

Figure 3.5 Reserves of Crude Oil Equivalent
Source: Pemex (2010)

area (even taking into account the catastrophic BP oil spill in 2010) is the deep waters of the Gulf, which are estimated to hold a potential 30 billion barrels in reserves, but this area can only be explored and exploited with technology and financial resources that Pemex does not currently possess. Participation with Pemex in this process is unattractive to foreign oil companies because the Mexican Constitution forbids them from owning any oil and gas that they find. Therefore, risk contracts and production-sharing agreements—routine elsewhere in the industry—are off-limits, and there can be no adequate compensation for the huge risks involved. The result is that while more than one hundred deep-water wells have been drilled annually on the US side of the Gulf, Mexico has drilled just four in the last four years at relatively shallow depths and with meager results. However, three semisubmersible rigs have been acquired by Pemex at huge cost (some $900 million) to drill in relatively deep waters during 2011. At least for now, Pemex intends to go ahead with the plan, regardless of what Washington says about restrictions for its side of the Gulf in the wake of the BP spill.

The energy reform of November 2008, which attempted to make drilling participation more attractive to foreigners, was heavily watered down by the opposition. The reform included provisions for more flexible contracts that would also provide incentives for improved results. But, two years later, despite talks with companies that were potentially interested, there was still no indication of how the contracts could provide the necessary incentives. Calderón's Decalogue proclaims an intention to deepen existing reforms, but the opposition claims that any private-sector involvement with Pemex amounts to "privatization." The oil nationalization of 1938 is considered an integral part of Mexico's national identity, and as some of the key privatizations that occurred during the Salinas sexenio (privatization of banks, for instance) are considered to have been botched, privatization has become a dirty word, fully exploited by the opposition.

A solution to this problem, given the political will, would be the introduction of the model that was adopted by Petrobras in Brazil. Petrobras is owned by the Brazilian government, but the government sold a portion of its equity to domestic and foreign outside investors on the stock market in 2000, which led to the strengthening of private-sector disciplines and transparency. Petrobras partners on a satisfactory basis with oil majors and recently discovered some of the deepest and largest oil reserves in the world. Its effect on Brazil's economic and stock market performance has been electrifying. However, even if all political barriers could be overcome, a transition to the Brazilian model would not be easy for Pemex given its inward-looking corporate culture and the power of its union.

The second critical reform for Mexico is strengthening public finance. Taxes collected in Mexico only represent approximately 11 percent of GDP. This has been augmented by the government's income from oil and other sources, which raises its total income as a percentage of GDP to 21 percent, but that figure is very low by international standards (Table 3.5).

The short-term challenge is to cover the immediate budget shortfall left by declining oil revenues. This was achieved by the compromise reached in 2010, but it did not prevent the downgrade in Mexico's debt rating to BBB.

Table 3.5 Total Tax Revenue as a Percentage of GDP in 2006

Country	Tax revenue as a percent of GDP
Sweden	49.1
France	44.2
Italy	42.1
Hungary	37.1
United Kingdom	37.1
Spain	36.6
OECD average	35.9
Portugal	35.7
Germany	35.6
Canada	33.3
Ireland	31.9
Greece	31.3
Australia	30.6
United States	28.0
Japan	27.9
Korea	26.8
Turkey	24.5
Mexico	20.6

Source: OECD (2008)

The long-term challenge is to set Mexico's government finances on a firm footing by raising the tax take and improving the efficiency of government spending. The current system has two structural problems. The first is that even law-abiding Mexicans are averse to paying taxes to a government that they do not think provides value for money. The second is that an estimated 30 percent of the Mexican economy is informal and therefore escapes the tax radar.

A broadly suggested solution to these twin problems is an extension of value-added tax (*impuesto sobre el valor agregado*, or IVA), currently at 16 percent, to include food and medicine, a measure opposed by both the PRI and PRD. It has been calculated that simplification of the current dual income tax system (with its many exemptions) and an 18 percent IVA on all goods and services, including food and medicine, would go a long way toward solving Mexico's fiscal problem.

The third area in urgent need of reform is security. Violence increased in 2010, particularly in the border states. Crimes involving narcotics gangs and politicians (including the murder of the PRI gubernatorial candidate in Tamaulipas and the kidnapping of Diego Fernández de Cevallos, PAN presidential candidate in 1994) received maximum publicity both in Mexico and abroad. The Decalogue mentions improvement of the police force as a way to fight the war on drugs, kidnapping, and extortion, implying a changeover of responsibility from the army to the Federal Police (Policía Federal). This process has two dimensions. The first is recruitment and training, which is a long and difficult process. The second is improving the relationship between federal and state governments, where governors have not always been happy to cooperate with what they perceive as federal meddling in their own affairs. This process has been exacerbated by the fact that a PAN executive has had to deal with a majority of PRI governors. In August 2010, as a possible alternative, public debate about the decriminalization of certain drugs (for example, marijuana) was encouraged, but the prospect seems like a long shot, especially as it would probably require coordination with the United States.

Finally, political reform is necessary. Mexican political life was transformed by the elimination between 1997 and 2000 of the PRI's monopoly on power. However, its institutions have not been modified to reflect the new political reality. The president, omnipotent when the PRI dominated all branches of government, is now structurally weak. Because of the no-reelection rule that has been in force since the 1910 Revolution, parties are beholden to their leaders, not their constituents, so they must vote en bloc rather than according to the ideas of their individual senators or congressmen. A solution that has been widely suggested is to introduce reelection, at least for senators, congressmen, and mayors. Another idea to promote stronger government has been to institute a second round of voting in presidential elections, which would leave just two candidates in the final round and a clear majority for one or the other. This could facilitate a situation where, once elected, a party would be able to carry out its electoral program and be judged accordingly at the next election.

The PRI, the PRD, and the 2012 Elections

The problem with three out of four of the structural reforms (energy, public finance, and politics) is that they depend on changes in either the constitution or the law and require a vote in Congress, which is dominated by the PRI and its allies. Calderón's political calculation in introducing the Decalogue was that if he is unable to pass further key reforms in the run-up to the 2012 elections, it is the PRI, now dominant in Congress, and to a lesser extent the PRD that will be to blame.

The PRI could have two broad reactions to structural reform. The first would be to continue to obstruct any specific proposal, as the PRI cannot afford the possibility of a success that would improve the PAN's electoral chances in 2012. The second would be to help the PAN pass critical reforms, however unpopular, before 2012 (when the PRI hopes to win the elections), so that they can reap the benefits without having to pay the political cost.

The PRI is not monolithic. Between PRI Senate leader Manlio Fabio Beltrones, congressional leader Beatriz Paredes, and State of Mexico Governor Enrique Peña Nieto, there are at least three factions with varying views and agendas. The most likely scenario (as of November 2010) is that the line of least resistance would be to obstruct the PAN in the run-up to 2012: that is, political gridlock will continue, not least through internal divisions within the PRI, but that the PRI will unite (as they did not in 2006) behind whomever they choose as leader in order to regain power in

2012. Peña Nieto is currently the front-runner for 2012, but his chances of success depend in some measure on his ability to mobilize his party behind a successful PRI candidate for the governorship in his state's 2011 elections against the PAN and the PRD, or even a possible PAN-PRD coalition candidate who is supported by Calderón.

Under normal circumstances, the PRD and its smaller party allies, Convergencia and PT, would be even more likely than the PRI to oppose any PAN reform initiative. However, since AMLO's 2006 defeat and subsequent intransigence, the PRD has divided into a moderate wing (which favored the coalitions that were successful in 2010), led by party leader Jesús Ortega, and the extreme faction led by AMLO, which was opposed to the coalitions; some kind of legislative coalition between the PAN and the moderate wing of the PRD cannot, therefore, be ruled out. Some attempt could also be made to reach out to Marcelo Ebrard, who as Mexico City's mayor is the most important PRDista in public office. But Ebrard is attempting to remain on good terms with both wings of the left in order to bolster his own chances for the 2012 presidential elections, and the July 2010 announcement by AMLO that he will again be a presidential candidate in 2012 makes this balancing act increasingly difficult.

It seems likely that, barring some major surprise (which is always a possibility in Mexico), divisions in both the PRI and PRD will impede major structural or institutional reform in the next two years. It may be significant that at this stage of the sexenio, none of a long list of possible PAN presidential candidates (which includes Ernesto Cordero [treasury secretary], Javier Lozano [secretary of labor], Alonso Lujambio [secretary of education], Juan Molinar [secretary of transport and communications], César Nava [president of the PAN] from the current administration, and Santiago Creel and Josefina Vázquez Mota from the Fox administration) has the national recognition and prominence of the most likely PRI or PRD candidates. This could further prejudice the possibility of a third successive presidential victory for the PAN in 2012.

Mexico as Emerging Market

There are many ways to define "emerging market." One useful definition is "a country where the process of basic institution building is not complete." You can find institutional deficiencies in any emerging market, as we have in Mexico. But despite the absence of institutional reform, Mexico has not stood still over the last ten years, and it will not over the next two. Its stock market, a relevant indicator, has performed better than the emerging markets' average since the end of 2000, when the PAN came to power (Table 3.6).

This performance reflects Mexico's basic strengths: its size, economic stability, and growing financial system. In population, land area, and US$ GDP, Mexico ranks between tenth and fifteenth in the world. The economic stability achieved by Salinas and Zedillo has been maintained by the PAN with strong finance ministers and stability at the Bank of Mexico. Owing to NAFTA and its geographic location, the Mexican manufacturing base has become even more closely integrated with the United States, especially in the automotive and electronics industry. Workers' remittances and tourism (first and third, respectively, among Mexican exports) are recovering with the US economy and have helped to compensate for the decline in oil exports (now in second place).

With an independent central bank that was established under Salinas, the financial system is dominated by global banks, including BBVA, Citi, HSBC, Santander, and Scotia, and was practically unaffected by the crisis. Over the last ten years the financial system has been greatly expanded by an obligatory pension system run by specialized fund managers, who at the end of June 2010 managed US$99 billion for 41 million accounts, with traditional mutual funds having grown to US$87 billion. This has led to a

Table 3.6 Mexican and BRICs Stock Market Returns: June 2001–June 2010 (annualized, in US$)

Country	Annualized return
Brazil	20.3%
Russia	19.3%
India	17.9%
Mexico	16.1%
China	13.5%
Emerging Markets Average	14.0%

Source: MSCI

boom in mortgages and housing, with more than five million mortgages placed since 2000. The combination of economic stability and financial market deepening has led to a growth of the middle class, now estimated to include 60 million of Mexico's 110 million inhabitants.

Mexico's impressive stock market returns also reflect the performance of world-class listed companies, which have continued to grow inside and outside of Mexico. América Móvil is one of the world's largest cellular companies, and it operates in both Mexico and Latin America. Mexican mining groups include Peñoles, the largest silver company in the world, and Grupo Mexico, the largest copper company by reserves and the fifth-largest producer. Televisa is the world's largest Spanish-language broadcaster, Cemex is the third-largest cement and concrete company, and Coca-Cola Femsa is the second-largest Coca-Cola bottler. Wal-Mart de México, listed on the Mexican Stock Exchange, is one of Wal-Mart's most successful subsidiaries.

The Curse of Comparison

But while Mexico has advanced, other countries have advanced further. In terms of stock market returns alone, three of four BRICs (Brazil, Russia, and India) have overtaken Mexico since 2000 (Table 3.6); China's stock market bears little relation to its buoyant economy. Given the expectations raised by the PAN in 2000, Mexicans are understandably frustrated by the decade's institutional stagnation. If 2011 and 2012 bring no further progress, as seems likely, Mexico could reach a point where whoever is elected president has no alternative but to push through the necessary structural reforms because he (or she) views it as the best way to keep his party in power. Carlos Salinas, having spent several years in self-imposed exile following his disgraced presidency, now visits Mexico frequently from his home in Europe and is widely believed to be actively attempting to return the PRI to Los Pinos, as well as to rehabilitate his own reputation. It would be ironic, but not surprising, if the next stage of Mexico's march toward modernity were motivated by necessity, not choice, and nostalgia for the past rather than hope for the future.

4

IS LATIN AMERICA CHANGING?

Pedro Pablo Kuczynski

Latin American countries arguably did better than most in facing the 2008–2009 world crisis. This positive outcome was a welcome change from the past, when high public debt ratios, fiscal deficits, and dependency on foreign credit gave pneumonia to most Latin American countries when the world sneezed.

Is Latin America a Single Entity?

The first issue in discussing "Latin America" is whether it exists as some kind of a single unit. There is huge diversity in the region, as there is in Europe and Asia. Demographically, there is a big difference between the more mature and aging populations of Argentina, Chile, and Uruguay and those that are farther north. There is an enormous contrast between the two industrial powerhouses of Brazil (nearly 40 percent of the regional economy) and Mexico (about 25 percent) and the others, which are primarily commodity exporters. In terms of income distribution, Latin America is one of the most backward areas of the world, with Gini coefficients in the 0.50 to 0.60 range (including progressive Chile), although there are some exceptions, notably Uruguay and Costa Rica. Politically, there are signs of increasing maturity and democratic stability, mostly in Brazil and Chile, and also perhaps in Colombia, Peru, Panama, Costa Rica, and Mexico. Argentina and Venezuela lead a pack of autocratic and somewhat unpredictable countries, including most of the Central American and

Caribbean countries. Incidentally, this last group, financed with oil subsidies from Venezuela, controls the Washington-based Organization of American States, even though the United States pays most of its bills.

Despite covering a huge area (it takes eleven hours by jet to get from Monterrey, Mexico, to Buenos Aires, Argentina), Latin America is viewed as one entity by financial markets. Perhaps this is the result of a shared Iberian colonial history, similar languages, and a common religion in Catholicism with its attendant economic accompaniments. Many parts of the region display similar traits, including modest savings, a general tendency to postpone politically difficult economic decisions, and low economic growth in comparison with resource potential. So we conclude that it is legitimate to talk about "Latin America" even if there are individual exceptions to every assertion, most notably Cuba.

Reforms Finally Benefitted Latin America in the 2000s

Led by the earlier example of Chile, many Latin American countries in the 1990s started programs of opening up their economies, balancing budgets, reducing inflation, and privatizing various sectors. Yet the 1990s were disappointing for most countries because the reforms did not go far enough. Mexico (1994–1995) and Brazil (1999) got themselves into major devaluations, and the Asian (1997) and Russian (1998) crises and subsequent US recession sealed the fate of Latin America's dismal performance in the 1990s and early 2000s. It was only after 2000 that reforms deepened and were effective. Activity first picked up in Peru in 2002 and then gradually got going in Brazil as the incoming Lula administration vastly exceeded skeptical market expectations. Chile kept up its 5–6 percent growth and Colombia sharply improved as well. After the 2002 devaluation, Argentina kept up its growth bounce-back despite notably investment-unfriendly policies, including high export taxes, huge consumer energy subsidies, and the state takeover of private pension funds. Only Mexico lagged among the major countries because it was hobbled by the inability to get basic reforms in energy policy and taxation through Congress.

Despite this uneven performance, all the major countries plus Uruguay and Panama had two positive things in common going into the 2008 crisis: lower public and private debt ratios, which were mostly the result (except for Venezuela) of improved public finances, and strong banking supervision. Most banks in the region are well capitalized, and there have been few financial failures as a result of the crisis despite some big losses from wrong-way hedges by a few large industrial companies in Brazil and Mexico. All of the countries benefitted from the tailwind of rapidly rising commodity prices beginning in 2005.

Fortunately, by the time the US crisis hit in mid-2008, governments had not yet succumbed to the temptation of spending this easy money, and they were able to face the crisis without significant balance of payments problems. Both Argentina and Venezuela experienced significant cash flow squeezes, but no major economy had to go to the International Monetary Fund. The United States organized large credit "swaps," or stand-by lines, for Brazil and Mexico, but they were not used.

The comparative performance of Latin America in 2009 is certainly creditable. If Mexico, which had a near 7 percent decline in GDP in 2009, is overlooked, Latin America's performance is comparable with Asia's, excluding China and India (Table 4.1). Of course, all of these statistics have to be taken with a grain of salt (some countries have questionable numbers, annual year-on-year numbers distort trough-to-peak trends, etc.), but the broad picture is clear. Latin America has done much better facing

Table 4.1

Real GDP Growth, Percent Year-on-Year	2007	2008	2009F	2010F
Latin America	5.4	4.4	−2	3.5
of which Mexico	3.2	1.8	−6.8	2.3
Lat. Am. excl. Mexico	6	5	−0.7	4.2
Asia (Non-Japan)	9.6	6.8	5.1	6.8
Asia excl. China and India	5.8	2.9	−1	4.7
China	11.9	9	8.3	8.3
India	9.4	7.3	6	6.5
Emerging Europe, M. East and Africa	6.8	4.3	−4.9	3.2
of which Russia	8.1	5.6	−6.4	2.3

Source: Deutsche Bank

the most recent crisis than it has been at facing problems in the past, and it is likely to perform well in the short and medium term.

What are the region's weaknesses? First, inflation. Chile and Peru are at one end of the spectrum, with negative or close to zero inflation in 2009. Argentina and Venezuela are at the other end, with consumer price indices gains in the 15 percent and 30 percent range (respectively) in recent years; these gains are likely to increase going forward. Venezuelan inflation is expected to have reached 50 percent in 2010. However, numbers from both countries have to be looked at warily. In the middle, the two big economies of Brazil and Mexico seem unable to surmount underlying inflation of about 4 percent, which is too high, especially given the worldwide recession. Although authorities in both countries will vehemently deny it, the basic cause is protectionism, both trade protectionism and protection of certain economic groups.

This leads us to the second weakness, which is below-potential long-term economic growth in the two leading countries that set the tone for the region with two-thirds of its GDP. Despite the decline in interest rates and inflation, the commodity boom from 2005 to 2008, and the more recent stock market hype, Brazil has been going along at a 5.0–5.5 percent growth rate since 2006 (obviously excluding 2009)—a creditable performance, but probably two points below its potential. Mexico, with long-term growth in the 3 percent range, has been performing far below its potential. These weak growth numbers endure despite demographic conditions that are the most favorable in the region's history for a great economic leap forward. Brazil, Colombia, Mexico, Peru, and Venezuela all have similar population profiles: rapidly growing labor forces that reflect past birthrates and the increasing participation of women in the workforce, sharply declining birthrates, and favorable dependency ratios—few old people, and not too many children. Only 8–9 percent of the population is over sixty years old, compared to 16 percent in the United States, 22 percent in Europe, and over 25 percent in Japan.

The favorable "window" for economic growth will last another twenty-five years. The only country that is currently taking advantage of it is Peru, where nominal GDP, with a fairly stable exchange rate, has grown from approximately $55 billion in 2001 to $127 billion in 2009 and approximately

$140 billion in 2010. The reasons for this strong growth include the metals boom (especially in gold mining), the rapid rise of consumer and mortgage credit that is leading to the emergence of a middle class, gradual fiscal reform (especially in public pensions), and a progressively more open economy (the average import tariff in 2010 was about 2 percent).

The big economies are going to have to push major reforms through if they want to realize their potential. Energy reform is long overdue in Mexico, even after the tough government decision in October 2009 to fire all 42,000 unionized staff members of Luz y Fuerza del Centro (the state utility for Mexico City that was well known for its inefficiency and theft of electricity). Given the decline in oil production, recent sales tax and income tax increases will only keep tax revenue stable at about 21 percent of GDP, including oil revenues. In Brazil, a high tax load that has not been matched by efficient government spending has arguably been a curb on economic growth.

Is a New Commodity Boom about to Benefit Latin America?

South American economies have taken advantage of the commodity boom, and they are likely to continue to do so, with expected growth in the 4–5 percent range in 2010 as of mid-2010 estimates. Central America, Colombia, and Mexico, whose economies are more oriented toward North America, will not have done as well as other countries in the region in 2010 as a result of a slow US recovery.

In the next five years, with continued fast growth in China, the steady emergence of India, and gradual recovery in North America and Europe, commodity producers in Latin America are almost bound to do well. China currently accounts for 37 percent of world steel production. The average Chinese citizen today is 20 percent larger than his or her parents and eats substantially more protein. By 2015 there will be almost three billion Chinese and Indian citizens, most of whom will be better fed, and all of whom will want a TV, a motorcycle, and/or a car. The implications for the global environment and pollution are daunting, but for commodity producers the possibilities are almost limitless. This potential growth outlook stands in contrast to the possible setbacks to strong economic growth that the "old" economies are facing, including high unemployment, huge central bank balance sheets that are difficult to exit without sparking (rightly or wrongly) market fears of inflation, the questionable US corn-based ethanol program (which is likely to further exacerbate food price pressures if the present lobbying effort to increase the ethanol mix in gasoline succeeds), and large structural fiscal deficits in the United States and most of Europe.

For the last ten years, a weakening US dollar has helped commodity producers. More likely than not, this trend is liable to continue. Latin American economies and governments, which viewed themselves as pariah commodity exporters, are likely to change their attitudes, and they will follow the earlier lead of successfully managed and diversified but commodity-based economies such as Canada and Australia.

The question is whether the free ride of a commodity boom will relax the pressures to reform education, taxation, and infrastructure, all three of which are liabilities in virtually all Latin American countries. Latin American countries appear to be entering another period of "reform fatigue." This seems to be a frequent historical occurrence. At present the lack of effort to achieve fundamental reforms may be the result of a combination of factors: hubris about how well most countries survived the crisis, elections in a number of countries (Chile, Colombia, Brazil at the end of 2010, and Peru in April 2011), and the fact that the big missing reforms,

Table 4.2 Major Latin American Economies' GDP Growth: 2007–2010 (Percent Year-on-Year Growth Real GDP)

Country/Region	2007	2008	2009	est. 2010	Population (millions)	GDP (millions)
Argentina	8.7	6.7	−3.3	1.5	43	326
Brazil	5.4	5.4	0.3	4.8	192	1,573
Chile	5.1	4.6	0.2	4.1	17	173
Colombia	6.8	3.5	0.2	1.5	47	212
Mexico	3.2	1.8	−6.8	2.3	108	1,040
Peru	8.4	9.3	2	5.5	29	127
Venezuela	8.4	4.5	−1	2.7	28	280
Total (Including Others)	5.4	4.4	2	3.5	535	4,100

Source: Deutsche Bank with author adjustments, 2008–2010

in particular labor market flexibility and some large remaining privatizations, are especially difficult to implement politically. The outlook for reform is good in Chile and Colombia, but uncertain in the others, especially Brazil. Reform is fundamental for future growth; with guarded prospects for reform, growth will stay below potential for several important economies, although it is likely to be better in some of the mid-sized economies such as Chile, Colombia, and probably Peru.

In the short run, meaning 2011 or 2012, the European crisis will put a damper on export growth rates for the countries that look toward the Atlantic and Europe, especially Argentina, Brazil, and Uruguay. But export growth will still be relatively strong because of China's seemingly insatiable appetite for food, minerals, and oil. Chinese imports of food and minerals are South America's meal ticket to financing a good part of its economic expansion in the coming years (Table 4.2).

5

THE WORLD BETS ON EUROPE, BUT THE UNITED STATES WILL PROBABLY WIN

Anatole Kaletsky

The near-death experience of the euro in 2010 transformed the prospects for the European economy and the European Union's political structure. The turning point was the summit of May 7–9, when European leaders agreed to the bailout of the Greek government, followed by the weekend of November 27–28, 2010, when the temporary mechanism created in May was abruptly converted into the permanent European Stability Mechanism (ESM) in order to stop a run on Irish banking system. Faced with the threat of a meltdown of the European financial markets, and acting under intense pressure from the US government to avoid a second Lehman-style debacle, Chancellor Merkel of Germany, who in May and November had adamantly opposed any collective fiscal responsibility for Europe's beleaguered sovereigns, eventually buckled. She agreed to ignore the "no-bailout" clause which had been her country's principal condition for agreeing to the creation of the euro, and offer all the other EU governments a package of financial guarantees worth nearly a trillion euros. As subsequently noted by Lord Kerr of Kinlochard, the British diplomat who drafted the Lisbon Treaty codifying the no-bailout clause in the EU Constitution, "it took only ten minutes to tear up a constitution that had taken ten years to negotiate."[1]

The result of May's "night of miracles," as one of Italy's European commissioners later described it, will now depend on the success of the much more comprehensive Irish bailout. If Germany accepts the transformation of national debts into collective obligations of the entire European Union, which is the logical implication of the European Stability Mechanism, then the risk of a break-up of the euro or of sovereign defaults within the eurozone will be effectively eliminated—at least until and unless the German public rises up in revolt against the potentially enormous new obligations they have been forced to bear.

The biggest question for Europe in 2011 therefore will be whether it is prepared to create a permanent federal mechanism for managing and sharing fiscal responsibilities, reinforcing the monetary union that was created in 1999. This question has both structural and macroeconomic aspects which will have to be addressed by policymakers and investors in 2011 and beyond.

The positive performance of the European economy and financial markets in the months following the May bailout suggested a newfound optimism about the structural sustainability of the euro and the political cohesion of the EU. It was still far from clear, however, whether macroeconomic policies in the eurozone and in Britain would be consistent with strong economic recovery, or whether they would condemn Europe to a long period of stagnation and relative decline comparable to the 1990s in Japan.

The sharp improvement in business and financial sentiment in Europe in 2010 was driven by three forces. First and foremost was the fact that all eurozone assets were massively oversold at the time of the May bailout, reflecting understandable but exaggerated fears about devaluations and sovereign defaults. Thus, there was nothing surprising about a powerful short-term rally when investors realized that Germany, the European Central Bank (ECB), and the IMF would use their combined financial firepower to prevent any European government from suddenly going bust.

Second, there was recognition that European governments were addressing the long-term contradictions in the construction of the eurozone. A monetary union without some degree of fiscal federalism and some willingness to accept automatic budgetary transfers had always seemed doomed to failure—and this was finally acknowledged by European leaders at the May 9 emergency summit. The challenge of creating a permanent mechanism for fiscal transfers from Germany and of fiscal restraints on the Mediterranean countries still lay ahead, but at least the issues were now understood, and there seemed to be a willingness to think about new political structures to replace the temporary mechanisms cobbled together at the summit.

Third, the election of an unprecedented Conservative-Liberal coalition on May 6, 2010, in Britain was deemed by the markets to represent an important milestone on the path back to fiscal solvency and financial stability for the whole of Europe. The new British government's extremely ambitious fiscal targets—a reduction in the general government deficit from 11 percent of GDP in 2010 to 7.5 percent in 2011, 5.5 percent in 2012, and just 3.5 percent in 2013—were greeted enthusiastically by the markets. This positive political and market reaction had a symbolic significance well beyond Britain. Of all the G-7 countries, Britain had the biggest deficits, the largest exposure to financial services and property, and the highest levels of household debt. Thus, if Britain could pull itself out of recession and financial crisis and simultaneously put its fiscal house in order, similar feats might be possible for every other European country—perhaps even Greece, Portugal, and Spain.

The Irish bailout and the parallel (and more important) announcement regarding the European Stability Mechanism (ESM) in November 2010 indicated that Germany had backed off its most dangerous demands. The most important facet of these events was the announcement that the ESM would become a permanent structure, which seemed to satisfy the six key requirements for a permanent solution to the euro crisis:

1. The temporary arrangements that were cobbled together for Greece in May 2010 were replaced with a permanent mechanism of collective responsibility for European sovereign and bank debts: In other words, the EU must take a decisive step towards fiscal federalism. This was always the main condition for a credible single currency.
2. No burden-sharing for any senior bank creditors, so as to avoid triggering Lehman-style bank runs across the eurozone: According to the news reports and briefings from Brussels and Dublin, these seemed to have been confirmed in the Irish bailout. But the language of the Irish program was rather ambiguous, and contained ominous warnings for owners of bank bonds.
3. No haircuts or burden-sharing on any sovereign debts currently outstanding: This seemed to have been promised by only applying the

proposed Collective Action Clauses (CACs) to new debts that are issued after mid-2013.

4. No arbitrary limits on the amount of funding potentially available to support EU sovereign borrowers: Unlike the European Financial Stability Fund, which was limited to €750bn (including IMF money), the ESM appears to be open-ended. The amount of financing on offer will be determined by negotiations between the country, the European Commission, the ECB, and the IMF.

5. An unequivocal commitment from Germany to contribute unlimited sums to the ESM, either through direct lending or sovereign guarantees: This was the most uncertain part of the package following the initial announcement, since Germany's signature on the ESM proposal did not mean that German politicians understood the country's limitless commitment to fiscal transfers the deal seemed to imply.

6. A promise from the ECB to continue offering unlimited liquidity support to all eurozone banks, regardless of their financial condition: This promise was repeated for the Irish banks by the Irish central bank governor.

If the six points above are eventually confirmed, which was an uncertain prospect at the time of writing, as investors and their lawyers look more closely at the terms of the ESM and the Irish rescue—and if German politicians stick to the consensual script that they apparently agreed to in Brussels—then the euro crisis is probably over.

But these remain big ifs—especially the second one.

Assuming that the protection of all pre-2013 bondholders is genuine, European finance ministers have accepted a potentially enormous fiscal burden on behalf of their electorates. Greece, for example, will need to have all its debts refinanced continuously by the ESM for many years ahead. The CACs to be applied to new debts after 2013 will effectively lock Greece out of the bond markets until its fiscal position has been transformed. Private bondholders will surely lend no new money to Greece on any reasonable terms once the CACs come into force, leaving the whole of the Greek national debt to be continually refinanced by the ESM—not just for a few years, but forever!

The biggest threat to this package must therefore be political credibility. Will investors really believe that the EU will redeem at 100 percent, and then continually refinance Greek debts worth more than 150 percent of GDP—and that they will continue to do this until the last Greek bonds outstanding have been faithfully repaid? Even if that is the honest intention of the EU leaders in 2010, will future German and French politicians maintain this generous formula so that they can honor the promises made years before.

If they do, the euro crisis is probably over. But if German politicians revert to demanding that existing investors must share the burden of losses, if Bundesbank President Axel Weber starts hinting that he will vote against extending liquidity support on the ECB council, or if German, Dutch, etc. voters go into open revolt against the potentially enormous and permanent fiscal obligations suddenly imposed on them by the November 2010 announcements, then this package will unravel.

If this proposal is taken at face value, the pre-2013 bonds issued by *all* European sovereigns (including Greece and Ireland) should quickly converge to the same yield as German debt. By contrast, post-2013 debt issues from the weak sovereigns will simply cease to exist. Once the CACs come into play Greece, Ireland, Spain, etc. will be unable to sell any bonds at all to private investors, and will have to be refinanced entirely by the ESM. In effect, therefore, the financing of the peripheral governments will become a federal obligation of the European Union—and that presumably will mean that the EU takes permanent control of Greek fiscal policies. This would mean a bigger move towards fiscal federalism in one weekend than the US has managed in 250 years, which is possible, but seems unlikely. In view of this, one may well conclude that the ESM proposal is simply not realistic, and therefore that the promises made to bondholders in November 2010 cannot be believed.

Unfortunately, the success or failure of the policies espoused by eurozone leaders at their May summit, by the new British government in its budget a few weeks later, and by the November announcements cannot be judged until 2011 and beyond. The improvement in economic statistics shortly after these momentous political events in the spring of 2010 encouraged politicians, investors, and business leaders, but it revealed nothing about the prospects for the European economy once the policies of fiscal austerity are fully implemented in the years ahead. To judge how much Europe's prospects have really improved after the 2008–2009 recession, whether in absolute terms, or in relation to the United States and Japan, it is therefore important to distinguish between financial and business sentiment, macroeconomic policy, and structural reform.

There have been several genuinely positive developments in Europe since the Lehman crisis, which investors and businesses only began to recognize once the survival of the euro was finally guaranteed by the German government: the seriousness of fiscal consolidation plans in Southern Europe; the competitiveness of many world-class European companies that had dramatically improved their management and productivity in the past decade; and the cooperative relationships between business and government that were helping to reposition many European industries toward future growth sectors such as alternative energy, advanced infrastructure, and high value-added services. Looking at the eurozone as a whole, the fiscal outlook also contrasted favorably with that of the United States, Britain, and Japan. Public spending control had been surprisingly effective in most of Europe during the recession, and indeed in the decade before, in contrast to the free-spending policies advocated in the United States by the Obama administration, and practiced covertly by the Bush administration and the Brown government in Britain in the years leading up to the credit crunch.

None of this means, however, that the eurozone is about to emerge in 2011 from its long period of economic underperformance in relation to the United States and Britain. Neither does the recent contrast between the bullish sentiment in Europe and the pervasive gloom in the United States and Britain imply that Anglo-Saxon macroeconomic policies of aggressive monetary and fiscal stimulus were counterproductive. Still less should the experience of Europe be presented, as it has been by the new government in Britain, as evidence that pre-Keynesian policies of fiscal tightening in recession will *strengthen* economic growth.

Starting with the good news for Europe—and the relatively bad news for the United States—there are two main trends likely to influence economic conditions in 2011.

The first is that almost all European governments are undertaking serious programs of long-term fiscal consolidation. These could, at least in theory, fix the budgetary blowouts created by the financial crisis. The new fiscal policies, if fully implemented, will start to tackle the long-term demographic challenges facing European governments by reducing their pension obligations and health costs. In the United States, by contrast, there is absolutely no political consensus on how to deal with budget problems. Democrats and Republicans are united only in their refusal to talk about reductions in Social Security and Medicare. And both parties are equally unwilling to contemplate any radical tax reforms, such as European-style consumption or energy taxes, that might allow entitlement programs to be properly funded without raising income tax rates to punitive levels. If American politicians refuse to discuss either serious spending cuts or major tax reforms, the whole country will eventually descend into the same fiscal chaos as California. In Europe, by contrast, the danger of California-style budgetary gridlock was always confined to a few relatively unimportant government entities, such as Greece and Portugal, and has now been effectively eliminated by German and federal European debt guarantees.

This leads to Europe's second item of genuinely good news. The decision to follow the sovereign bailouts in May 2010 with a series of stress tests on the European banks in the summer left the financial system reasonably secure. This was not because the stress tests were tough, transparent, or even truthful. On the contrary, the "worst-case scenario" envisaged by the regulators was only a mild recession, and no consideration at all was given to such obvious risks as default, restructuring, or any other permanent impairments of sovereign debts. But as in the case of the 2009 US stress tests, the real value of this exercise was not in the risks it identified, but in what it implied about government and central bank guarantees. Government regulators and the ECB made clear that all banks passing the stress tests could henceforth be regarded as "safe."

The implication was that, in the event of a financial disaster, such as a sovereign default, any bank that had passed the stress tests would be provided with unlimited support by the ECB. As a result, the counter-party risks and uncertainties created by the Lehman crisis have gradually disappeared in Europe, just as they did in the United States in 2009. This was good news for liquidity in all European financial markets. With solvency risks removed, the outlook for bank profits is even better in Europe than in the United States as a paradoxical consequence of the ECB's refusal to buy large quantities of eurozone government bonds. The ECB has, instead, supported the Greek, Irish, and Iberian governments indirectly by providing liquidity via repos to their banking systems, which would in turn use loans from the ECB to buy Greek, Irish, and Spanish bonds. This roundabout approach to sovereign debt monetization will guarantee large profits to European banks from playing the yield curve, and as a result the European banks could be recapitalized surprisingly quickly.

Four Major Headwinds Will Dampen European Recovery

As a result of the two factors mentioned above, fiscal and financial conditions in Europe should continue to improve in 2011, but the improvements will be counteracted by at least four major headwinds to economic recovery.

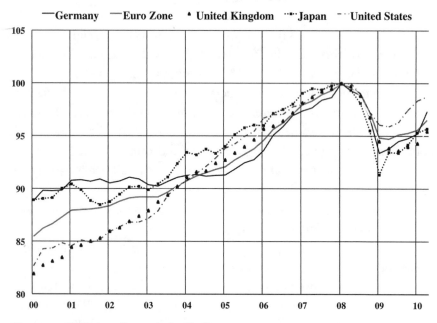

Figure 5.1 GDP since Pre-recession Peak
Source: Thomson Reuters

European Economic Activity Remains Very Weak

While the second half of 2010 was marked by upside surprises in economic statistics and repeated upgrades to European growth forecasts, these developments need to be put into perspective. Although Europe appeared to be enjoying a stronger recovery than the United States by mid-2010, this was largely a statistical artifact, reflecting the fact that Europe fell into a much deeper recession than the United States in 2008. As a result, Europe will still be much further from a full recovery than the United States, even by the end of 2011. This is illustrated by Figures 5.1 and 5.2, which show GDP and industrial production in comparison with pre-recession peaks.

GDP in the second quarter of 2010 was just 1.1 percent below its peak in the United States, while it was 2.7 percent below its peak in Germany, and 3.6 percent below in the eurozone as a whole. The US economy will almost certainly have recovered to its pre-recession level by early 2011, while the eurozone economy will probably not return to its pre-recession

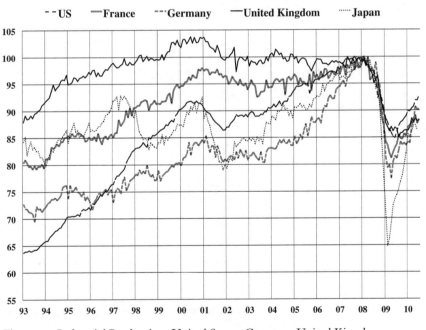

Figure 5.2 Industrial Production: United States, Germany, United Kingdom, France, Japan (2007–2008 peak = 100)
Source: Thomson Reuters

level until late 2012 or even 2013. Moreover, industrial production and GDP grew much more rapidly in the United States than in Europe during the twenty years before the crisis. As a result, US industrial production was 49 percent higher in mid-2010 than it was in 1990, whereas German production was only 23 percent higher and French production was only 3 percent higher than twenty years earlier. This suggests a perverse explanation of the surprisingly optimistic business and financial surveys in Europe. Such surveys typically ask industrialists and investors whether conditions are better or worse than normal. If normal conditions are perceived (as they have been in French industry, for example) as twenty years averaging a 0.1 percent annualized growth rate, then a further decade of such stagnation begins to be viewed as normality or even good news.

The very weak growth expectations in Europe were illustrated in Gave-Kal's third-quarter 2010 Quarterly Strategy Chart Book by comparing the long-term GDP trends in the United States and France (Figures 5.3 and 5.4).

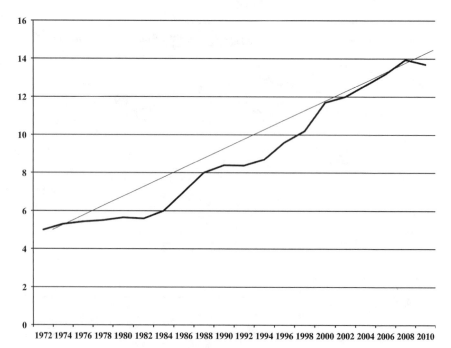

Figure 5.3 US Economy Usually Recovers to Trend after Recessions (US GDP with 1973–1980 Trend)
Source: Thomson Reuters

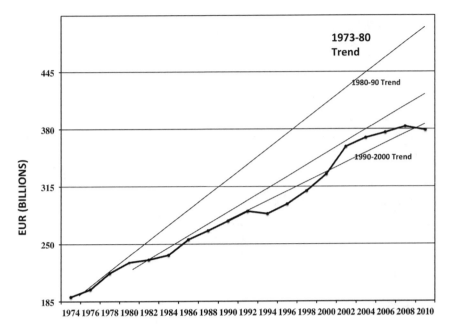

Figure 5.4 Growth Trends Deteriorated in France after Each Recession
Source: Thomson Reuters

The Euro Remains Very Expensive

The rise of the euro that followed the sovereign bailout in the
spring of 2010, although partially reversed during the Irish bank crisis,
creates another reason for caution regarding Europe's prospects in 2011.
Although European, and especially German, politicians and industrialists
frequently assert that their businesses are unaffected by exchange rates,
such claims are implausible in an environment where inflation is almost
zero in competitor economies. Additionally, European productivity has
been falling as a result of labor-hoarding during the recession. The currency risks for Europe can be seen from the euro's real trade-weighted
exchange rate. Figure 5.5 shows the trade-weighted exchange rate index,
calculated by the Bank for International Settlements, against the currencies of other major industrialized countries. It reveals that in the summer
of 2010 the euro was as expensive as at any time in history, apart from the
period immediately before and after the Lehman crisis. Relative to its long-
term average, the euro at $1.30 was roughly 15 percent more expensive than

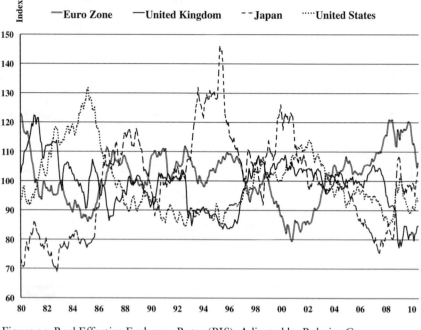

Figure 5.5 Real Effective Exchange Rates (BIS), Adjusted by Relative Consumer Prices (1980–2007 Average = 100)
Source: Thomson Reuters

the dollar, 25 percent dearer than the pound, and even more overvalued than the yen.

Figure 5.6 compares the euro's exchange rate against the major currencies with another "broader" exchange rate index that includes Central European emerging markets and smaller Asian countries, which are all important trading partners for Europe. On this basis, the euro looks less overvalued. But this is somewhat deceptive because similar indices for the dollar and the pound make these currencies look even cheaper. Given that European exporters sell goods and services that compete primarily against the output of other advanced OECD economies, rather than of emerging markets, the euro's exchange rate in the 2008–2010 period created a greater competitive handicap than at any other time in the past thirty years. The fact that Europe's current account moved only slightly into deficit merely illustrates the dislocation between global inventory cycles and the weakness of European domestic demand. If European domestic demand be-

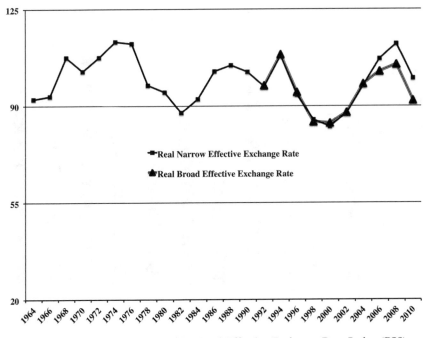

Figure 5.6 European Monetary Union Real Effective Exchange Rate Index (BIS), Adjusted by Relative Consumer Prices
Source: Thomson Reuters

gins to accelerate in 2010, net exports will subtract substantially from European economic activity and production.

This risk is further underlined by Figure 5.7, which shows relative hourly labor costs around the world, as surveyed annually by the US Bureau of Labor Statistics (updated using current exchange rates). This "absolute" measure of competitiveness or purchasing power parity does not depend on any expectation of mean reversion, but rather on the concept that an hour of manufacturing labor should cost about the same in advanced economies with access to similar technology and managerial know-how. On this basis, the euro appeared to be overvalued by 26 percent against the dollar and by 34 percent against the pound in the third quarter of 2010. Even if the euro weakened substantially from this level, which seemed a reasonable expectation, the lagged effects of currency overvaluation should continue to be seen in European industrial production statistics at least until the end of 2011.

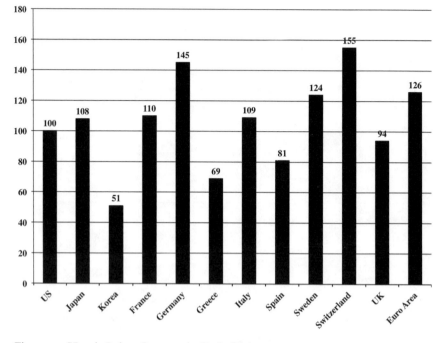

Figure 5.7   Hourly Labor Costs at the End of July 2010
Source: GaveKal Research

Europe's Post-Lehman Recovery Did Not Refute Keynesian Economics

Despite the anti-Keynesian rhetoric of the German government and other European authorities, fiscal policy in the key European economies after Lehman was only slightly less stimulative than in the United States. In Germany, according to OECD estimates, the general government deficit widened from zero in 2008 to 5.4 percent of GDP in 2010. The result was a somewhat bigger fiscal stimulus than the 4.2 percent of GDP experienced by the United States during those two years, or the 4.6 percent of GDP experienced by the eurozone as a whole. The real difference between the fiscal policies of Germany and the United States was not in their response to the Lehman crisis, but in their budgetary positions prior to the recession. While Germany started from a position of fiscal balance before the financial crisis, the Bush administration had already permitted the US budget deficit to explode from 2.8 percent of GDP in 2007 to 6.5 percent in 2008.

Thus, the theory of "Ricardian equivalence," which asserts that consumers and businesses will boost their spending in response to deficit reductions by their government (a theory, incidentally, which Ricardo himself mockingly dismissed) has not been vindicated by the experience of Europe and Germany—at least not yet. The fiscal stimulus in most of Europe is still going strong and will not be reversed until 2011. Only then will we know whether the fiscal tightening promised by European governments will prove beneficial, whether it will drag the eurozone into a 1930s-style debt depression, or whether governments will simply revise or abandon their ambitious fiscal plans.

In the past, anti-Keynesian economists and politicians have often predicted that "confidence" would be boosted by fiscal tightening, and that these confidence effects would outweigh the deflationary impact of budget cuts or higher taxes. In practice, however, such predictions have usually turned out to be wrong—disastrously so in Japan in 1997 and Germany in 2005.

History shows that fiscal tightening has usually proved deflationary, as Keynesian economics predicts, except in cases where fiscal tightening was counterbalanced by a much more stimulative monetary policy, as it was in the mid-1990s in the United States, Sweden, Canada, and Britain. Unfortunately for Europe—and even more so for Britain, where the government has promised a particularly aggressive fiscal tightening in 2011—the current monetary starting point is completely different from where it was in the early 1990s, when interest rates were above 10 percent in much of the world. The scope for monetary policy to be loosened much further is limited, and an easing comparable to the seven hundred basis-point reduction enjoyed by Britain from 1992 to 1997 is literally impossible.

Europe thus faces severe risks from Keynesian fiscal contraction in 2011. These risks are particularly acute in Britain, where the planned reduction in the fiscal deficit is of around 4 percent of GDP, and where financial confidence effects from fiscal consolidation are bound to be more limited than in the periphery of the eurozone since Britain never suffered from the financial panic that gripped Greece or Ireland, and since British long-term interest rates are already quite low.

To put this argument another way, any narrowing of public-sector deficits must be compensated, as a matter of arithmetic, by a narrowing of the private-sector surplus. But if public deficits are to be reduced, the corresponding narrowing of the private-sector surplus can be achieved in two very different ways. The healthy resolution is for the private-sector surplus to diminish as a result of rising investment. The unhealthy resolution is for the surplus to diminish because of falling profits, personal incomes, and private savings.

There is not much evidence that households and businesses will invest more or save less in response to the confidence effects of cuts in public spending. There are, however, good reasons to expect higher investment if extremely low interest rates come to be seen as a permanent fact of life and not just a temporary aberration, or if the exchange rate sharply depreciates. This is why fiscal tightening can usually be offset by a stimulative monetary policy. And this is why interest rates all over the Western world are likely to remain near zero for the indefinite future, as central bankers try to facilitate the tightening of fiscal policy they all want to see. There is, however, a limit to the amount of fiscal tightening that can be offset by monetary policy. And in Europe, that limit may well be exceeded in the coming years, both because of an overly aggressive fiscal tightening and because of an overcautious response by the ECB.

Monetary Policy in Europe Is Tighter and Less Pragmatic Than in the United States

While it is widely believed that monetary policy has "always" been traditionally tighter in Europe than in America, the figures do not bear this out. In the years before the crisis, the ECB was generally somewhat *more* expansive than the Fed, probably because Europe was experiencing a slower rate of financial innovation and remained more of a cash economy. Money supply grew more rapidly in Europe whether attention focused on the monetary base, which is directly controlled by central banks, or at broad money, which is the monetary gauge that has correlated best with long-term inflation and GDP growth (see Figure 5.8). After the crisis, however, this relationship abruptly reversed. While the Fed did its utmost to provide monetary stimulus for more than a year after Lehman, the ECB reversed course much more quickly—encouraging both the monetary base and broad money to contract from the middle of 2009.

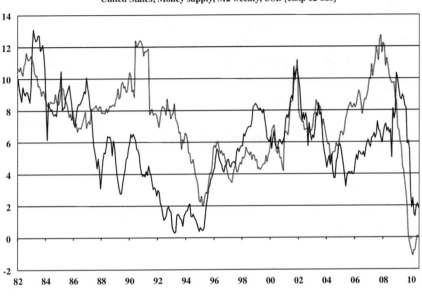

—Euro Zone, M3, Anount Outstanding, EUR [c.o.p 12 obs]

—United States, Money supply, M2 weekly, USD [c.o.p 12 obs]

Figure 5.8 Broad Money Growth (European Moneary Union M3 and US M2)
Source: Thomson Reuters

To be more specific, the ECB had expanded the monetary base more rapidly than the Fed in the years before the crisis—by 8.2 percent annually compared with 6.1 percent from 2000 to 2007. Its response to the crisis was, however, much weaker than the Fed's. The peak monetary base expansion in the eurozone was just 39 percent compared with 110 percent in the United States, and by December 2009 the ECB was shrinking the euro monetary base by 8 percent. As a result, broad money growth collapsed from 7 percent in January 2009 to a *negative* 1 percent a year later. Even Japan had never seen this kind of contraction in broad money. Not surprisingly, this premature monetary contraction was soon followed by the Greek crisis.

Without evidence of major philosophical changes at the ECB, there is no reason to expect a significant reform of monetary policy in 2011. This leaves only one possible mechanism to offset the fiscal tightening that lays ahead—a depreciation in the exchange rate. But to compensate for the sort of severe fiscal tightening planned in Europe for 2011 and 2012, the euro would have to fall substantially—at least another 15–20 percent against the dollar and the pound from the levels that prevailed in the summer of 2010.

Such a depreciation would make sense economically and would still leave the eurozone as the world's most expensive productive region (in terms of absolute labor costs). It is far less clear, however, whether such a large devaluation will be acceptable to the United States' and Europe's other trading partners—and whether it will happen quickly enough to prevent a major slowdown in the European economy in 2011.

Notes

1. Lord Kerr of Kinlochard, "Europe's Crisis, Britain's Challenge?" Panel discussion, European Council on Foreign Relations, London, UK, June 15, 2010.

PART

III

ASIA

6

ASIA'S PARADIGM SHIFT

Louis-Vincent Gave

From 2000 to 2010, having an overweight exposure to Asian equities in a global equity portfolio was, by and large, the easiest "major trade," if only because Asia was both a "return to the mean" trade (with very undervalued stocks in the wake of the Asian crisis and TMT bust) and a "momentum" trade (with faster growth). In 2000, having stock-picking skills did not matter much in Asia. What counted was having the courage, foresight, and cash to pick up dominant blue chips like Samsung Electronics or DBS Bank at attractive valuations.

Fast-forward to 2010 and things have undeniably changed. Asia has become the world's great hope for growth, and this perception is, unsurprisingly, amply reflected in equity market valuations. Most Asian equity markets are now trading at significant premiums to Western markets, which has never happened before, at least not for very long (Figure 6.1).

This valuation premium may of course be warranted given Asia's stronger growth outlook. But it also means that Asian equities need to deliver on investors' expectations or face a new de-rating. Or to put things differently, Asian equity markets are clearly no longer a positive "return to the mean" trade. They are now a full-blown "momentum" trade. And unfortunately, equity market momentum has not been too hot recently. But is the recent negative momentum a reflection of global trends? Or is it an Asia-specific problem? And if it is the latter, then what does it mean for investors who have telecast plans to overweight Asia in their portfolios?

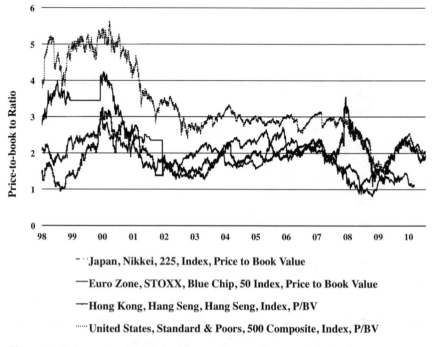

Figure 6.1 Price to Book of United States, Europe, Japan, and Hong Kong
Source: GaveKal Research

Putting Asia's Premium in Context

In his recently published book *Capitalism 4.0*, Anatole Kaletsky reviews the four key megatrends that have underpinned growth from 2000 to 2010. These are:

- The emergence of three billion new consumers, producers, and savers: The interaction between three historic events set off this dynamic megatrend—the breakup of the Soviet bloc, the opening up of China, and the end of proxy wars between communism and capitalism in the developing world. The result was that almost the entire world population found their lives guided for the first time by the invisible hand of market forces instead of being ruled by the iron fists of communism and feudalism or the clumsy robotic grip of central planning.

- Globalization: It transformed almost every economic activity in every country, as the principles of market competition, private enterprise, and free trade won universal acceptance after the breakdown of central planning and state ownership. In effect, the entire world economy started moving toward a NAFTA-style free trade area, if not quite a European-style single market. As this policy change interacted with the new technologies of zero-cost communications and cheap transport, the classical economic principles of specialization and comparative advantage began to operate with unprecedented effectiveness across the world. The result was an upsurge of productivity growth and wealth creation, especially in China and other previously backward Asian countries. The process of globalization transferred many manufacturing industries from the advanced economies to the developing world, vastly increasing the world's productive capacity. The transfer of industrial activity made the world economy more prosperous and more stable, which brings us to the third megatrend.

- The Great Moderation: A period of unprecedented stability in inflation, unemployment, and economic cycles that created twenty years of almost continuous growth throughout the world economy that lasted right up to the recession of 2008–2009. As the world began to recover from the recurrent crises of the 1970s and learned to live with pure fiat money, governments and central banks gained previously unimagined freedom to manage their economies and stabilize both inflation and unemployment. Policymakers gradually reverted to the active demand management that had been abandoned. Moreover, globalization stabilized the world economy by suppressing inflation and shifting many volatile manufacturing industries from America and Europe to China and other emerging economies. This transfer of industry not only made advanced economies less susceptible to inventory and capital investment cycles, but also helped to stabilize emerging economies, most notably in Asia, by reducing their dependence on subsistence agriculture, the most volatile industry of all.

- A Financial Revolution: This resulted from the adoption of a free-market philosophy, the buildup of savings in the rapidly growing Asian economies, and the stability created by globalization and successful demand management. With risks of bankruptcy and unemployment diminished in the stabilized economies of the 1990s, businesses and consumers felt that they could borrow more than ever before, and banks were more willing to lend. Meanwhile, the demystification of money meant that debt ceased to be a moral or theological issue and became just another consumer product. Financial innovation also meant that savings that were previously locked up in property and other illiquid assets could be used as collateral to support consumer and business borrowing. This attractive new feature of property, summed up in the saying "My home is an ATM machine," led to an increase in the value of homes relative to other more traditional investments such as stocks and bonds. The result of this revolution was that ordinary home-owners and small businesses gained opportunities to smooth their spending over their entire lifetimes and to manage their finances in ways that had been available only to large multinational companies and wealthy family trusts. This financial revolution was responsible for the boom-bust cycle that exploded in the 2007–2009 crisis, but the changes in traditional attitudes to debt, in property values, and in views about reasonable levels of borrowing may have changed structurally.

Looking at Asia, the first two of the four megatrends—the emergence of three billion new capitalists, both producers and consumers, in Asia and the unification of the world economy into a single market—are hopefully still on track and have not been derailed by the Great Financial Crisis. Meanwhile, the "Great Moderation," currently a discredited notion in the West, is still a visible reality in the East (if only because, as mentioned above, Asia is still weaning itself off a highly unpredictable agricultural cycle). Simultaneously, the "Financial Revolution" is still only now unfolding its many benefits on the Asian financial landscape. In short, Asia in 2010 looks nothing like most Western markets, which are confronting two very serious problems.

The Western World's Two Distinct Problems

The first problem the OECD faces is that from 2000 to 2010 the private sector created a lot of assets (real estate in the United States, Spain, the United Kingdom, Ireland, etc.) against which a considerable amount of debt has been collateralized by commercial banks. As the prices of these assets fall, a Fisher-like "debt deflation" looms.

The second problem is that, for structural reasons, a growing number of OECD countries are confronting a very challenging budgetary situation. The credit crunch, bank bailouts, and recession only account for 9 percent of the increase in long-term public debt burdens in major advanced economies. The remaining 91 percent of the long-term fiscal pressure is due to the growth of public spending on pensions, and health and long-term care. In other words, the credit crunch and recession did not create the present pressures on public borrowing and spending. They merely brought forward an age-related fiscal crisis that would have become inevitable once a majority of the baby boomers retired around 2020.

The solution to the first problem is simple monetary economics 101: Central banks have to buy assets in the hope of preventing a collapse in asset prices. These purchases need not be accompanied by a rise in the budget deficit. Instead, they trigger a sharp rise in the local monetary base, which is not inflationary as long as the prices of the underlying assets do not go up; if credit creation in the private sector remains muted, they are unlikely to do so. The rise in the monetary base compensates the decline in bank lending and the decline in the velocity of money. Over time, the hope is that these assets stabilize and gradually move off the central bank's balance sheet. In the near term, the central bank's action also usually leads to a weaker currency, which in turn allows for an "export-led" growth rebound.

The solution to the second problem is, however, far more painful, and there is little the central banks can concretely do to help. The onus is on governments to start cleaning up their balance sheets and income statements. This process may have started in the United Kingdom, and perhaps in Japan and certain European countries, though not without some backlash (witness the sudden stress that French President Nicolas Sarkozy found himself under when he tried tightening the government's belt). Meanwhile, in the United States, there have been few concrete measures to encourage the market that the right steps are being taken (the health care debacle was clearly a missed opportunity), and the rhetoric has grown increasingly antibusiness (bashing of banks, bashing of insurance companies, bashing of big oil, etc.).

Confronting the above dilemma, the natural reaction of central banks should be to follow Bagehot's advice to "lend freely and at a high price," otherwise the risk is that nothing will be done to address the "unfunded" problem. Worse yet, Western economies could fall into the trap of what Jacques Rueff called "subsidizing expenditures that give no returns with money that does not exist," a path which invariably leads to inflation. Even more disturbingly, such a path could conceivably lead to growing suspicion of the fiat monetary system, which, as Anatole Kaletsky indicates in *Capitalism 4.0*, has been the bedrock of the post–Bretton Woods economic miracle.

Obviously, Asia has neither of the above two problems, which helps explain why most investors are keener to increase their risk in the East while decreasing their risk in the West. But of course this does not mean that Asia does not offer investors challenges.

The First Challenge: Stepping into the Unknown

A cliché among professional investors is that the four most expensive words in the English language are "This time it's different." But while it is dangerous to ignore the cyclical nature of financial markets, and of human behavior more generally, it is undeniable that the driving forces of economic and business activity—technologies, social structures, and political institutions—can and do change. Thus, the four most expensive and foolish words in the English language are not "This time it's different" but "Everything's always the same." At least, this much is obvious to anyone who has spent time in Asia over the years since 2000. And in the category of "This time it's different," the fact that most Asian countries are now tightening monetary policy before the Fed, Bank of Japan (BOJ), European Central Bank (ECB), and Bank of England (BOE) must count for something.

To some degree, this is good news as it shows a willingness on the part of Asian central bankers to tackle the continent's nascent inflationary problem. It also shows a certain degree of confidence that Asian central bankers always seemed to lack. So, on a structural basis, it is encouraging. However, the hawkishness of Asia's central banks also means that while OECD yield curves are steep and likely to remain so for the foreseeable future, Asian yield curves are now flattening rapidly all across the board. One amazing development is that the US (and German) yield curves have, since 2009, continued to shift lower in spite of the economic recovery. In Asia, we are seeing exactly the opposite, with yield curves flattening (in Malaysia, Indonesia, China, Thailand, Australia, etc.) or shifting higher (India), a divergence in trend that can only logically be explained by the differences in monetary policy. And, of course, this should logically have an impact on currency markets since steep yield curves often weaken currencies, while flat or inverted yield curves strengthen them (cash becomes harder to find, thereby inviting companies and individuals to repatriate capital from abroad, etc.). In other words, the differences in monetary policies between the East and the West should ensure that Asian currencies remain well bid.

But it also means that most Asian indices face some new headwinds. Indeed, most Asian equity indices are typically comprised of 20–25 percent of exporting stocks (which should struggle as Asian currencies move higher) and 30–35 percent of Asian financials (for whom the flattening yield curves could prove a headwind). In other words, investors into Asia who decide to solely get exposure through benchmark ETFs are likely investing more than half of their money in what should prove to be "dead money." Asia's very different cyclical and policy outlook argues against investing in indices and instead for concentrating on the parts of the market that will benefit from the higher currencies and lower long-term interest rates. This of course includes long-dated Asian government bonds, high-dividend yield-paying stocks (which tend to always outperform when yield curves flatten and/or invert), utility stocks, local consumption stocks, and all the "stable growth" stocks, whether pharmaceuticals, consumer staples, software and tech stocks, and so on. (Figure 6.2).

Take China as an example. The local market peaked in August 2009 and has since given up more than a quarter of its value. Usually, in the midst of such a pullback, almost all stocks would be affected. But what is interesting is that since 2009, stocks linked to local consumption, which one would expect to hold up decently as yield curves flatten, have done precisely that. In a sign of unprecedented maturity for the Chinese market, most of the sectors listed above are actually trading at higher levels than they did when the Chinese market peaked in August 2009!

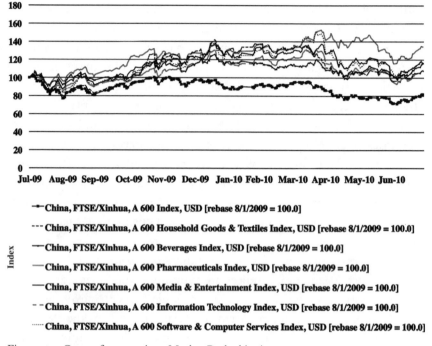

Figure 6.2 Outperformers since Market Peaked in August 2009
Source: Thomson Reuters

The Second Challenge: A Structural Shift?

We would be remiss to mention the outperformers in China's current bear market without highlighting the sectors that have brought the index down. And here, one finds mostly the sectors one would expect to see penalized by a flatter yield curve, whether financials, steel and cement (since there should be less construction), mining, oil and gas, real estate, and so on. (see Figure 6.3). But this underperformance raises the question of whether China's economy (and to some extent Asia's, as China is increasingly the largest motor of Asian growth) is simply going through a cyclical adjustment or whether it is experiencing a structural shift.

There is little doubt that it is the latter for a number of reasons, which include:

- The fact that the momentum of exports to the developed world is unlikely to continue at the blistering pace of 2000–2010, whether because of higher base effects or weaker Western currencies and demand.

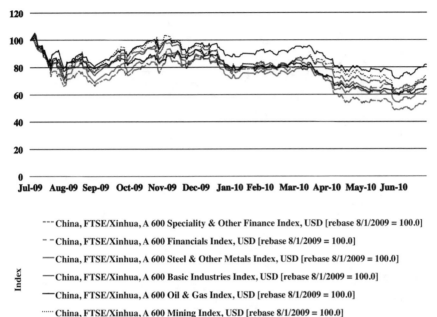

Figure 6.3 Underperformers since Market Peaked in August 2009
Source: Thomson Reuters

- The fact that "hard" infrastructure spending will lose steam, if only because a lot of the obvious infrastructure build-out (for example, China's highways, high-speed rail lines, etc.) will soon be coming to completion.
- Most importantly, the fact that the era of cheap labor is now squarely behind us. This means that, unlike what we witnessed from 2000 to 2010, any future spending on infrastructure, whether by the government or entrepreneurs, can no longer be funded by squeezing labor. In a Marxist world in which added value is split between workers, capital, and governments, the workers are about to get a fairer shake, which is great news for consumption, but bad news for infrastructure spending (Figure 6.4).

And needless to say, when one buys an Asian ETF today, one buys an index that is heavily skewed toward a continuation of the infrastructure spending boom (that is, steel stocks, coal mines, banks, etc.), when what one *wants* to buy into is the unfolding Asian consumption boom.

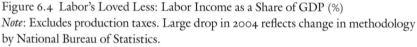

Figure 6.4 Labor's Loved Less: Labor Income as a Share of GDP (%)
Note: Excludes production taxes. Large drop in 2004 reflects change in methodology
by National Bureau of Statistics.
Source: Bai Chong'en and Qian Zhengjie (Tsinghua University)

Higher Labor Costs Are a Genuine Paradigm Shift

In 2007 China's leading labor economist, Cai Fang of the Institute of Population and Labor Economics of the China Academy of Social
Sciences (CASS), published a controversial book arguing that China's
economy was about to reach a crucial turning point: The supply of "surplus labor" from the countryside was on the verge of drying up. Cai built on
the development theory of British economist Arthur Lewis, who showed
that early-stage industrial economies had two distinct sectors operating in
parallel: a traditional agricultural sector with low productivity and a modern capitalist sector with high productivity growth. In the early stage of
industrialization, the impoverished traditional sector provides a large
labor pool for the modern capitalist sector, which offers higher wages. This
pool is at first effectively infinite, because the capitalist sector can continu-

ously raise its demand for labor without raising real wages—or, at any rate, by raising wages well below the rate of productivity growth in the capitalist sector. But at some point—a moment dubbed the "Lewis turning point"—the pool of labor in the traditional sector becomes smaller than the demand for labor in the capitalist sector, and the change in the supply-demand balance requires real wages to rise. In the first Industrial Revolution in the United Kingdom, real wages were static from the late eighteenth century until about 1840; after that they grew smartly. Japan hit its Lewis turning point around 1960 and experienced very rapid wage growth thereafter. Cai's book asserted that China was about to hit the same turning point.

With the supply of young workers entering the labor force set to drop by one-third by 2022, it now seems obvious that Cai was right, and that 2010 may well mark the year in which China hit its Lewis turning point. This is a momentous change because businesses have simply assumed for years that China has an unlimited supply of young people who can be had for modest wages and replaced at will. By 2025 this will cease to be the case. Businesses will have to pay more for entry-level workers and then work harder to retain them for longer because they will not be so easy to replace.

The macroeconomic consequences of the Lewis turning point are large. Before the turning point, the capitalist economy grows mainly through an accumulation of factors—labor and capital. The efficiency with which these factors are used—in economists' jargon, "total factor productivity," or TFP—is secondary. After the turning point, sheer factor accumulation slows down, and efficiency or TFP gains must become the main driver of economic growth. The most important question now confronting Asian bulls such as ourselves is: Can Asia evolve from "growth through accumulation of factors" to "growth through productivity"?

A Structural Rebalancing Toward Consumption

The answer to the above question would require a full book, but regardless of the longer-term trend, one thing now seems obvious: A certain amount of economic rebalancing will occur naturally as households will grab a bigger share of national income, thus increasing their consumption power. This means that the central "imbalance" in China's economy, namely the excess of thrift, could soon start to abate and will not be without consequences (for global interest rates, global currencies, regional growth, etc.).

While it is important for a developing country to have a high national saving rate to finance large-scale investment in industry and infrastructure, China has taken this rule to an extreme: It saves and invests too much, and it consumes too little of what it produces. In their intensive development eras, Japan, South Korea, and Taiwan enjoyed peak national saving ratios of 35–38 percent of GDP. China maintained a similar saving rate in the 1990s and early 2000s, but after 2003 the saving rate soared, reaching 52 percent of GDP in 2009. This enabled China to finance investments totaling 47 percent of GDP, which is ten points higher than the peak ratios in earlier East Asian economies. And while we do believe that these absolute numbers are exaggerated (thanks to the Chinese statistical system's chronic inability to accurately count the consumption of services), the trend of rapidly rising national saving and investment to levels that are almost certainly unsustainable cannot be denied.

The question of why China saves so much has sparked much debate among economists. Some believe the rising saving rate reflects an increased tendency of households to save because of an ever more patchy social safety net or for life-cycle reasons. Others (including ourselves) have argued that the main contributors to national savings have been ever more profitable companies and a parsimonious government. The debate usually boils down to an argument about how to interpret the "flow of funds" data in the national accounts, which track the sources of income in the whole economy. These data are of questionable quality, frequently revised, and hard to square with other economic statistics. Happily, recent careful work by Bai Chong'en and Qian Zhengjie, two economists at Tsinghua University, resolved many of these difficulties and made clear that virtually all of the increase in China's national saving since 2000 has been in the corporate and government sector. Bai and Qian reconciled national data with detailed provincial data and found that the corporate saving rate rose from 16 percent of GDP in 1997 to 23 percent in 2004, after which it remained roughly constant. Government saving (much of which represents investments in infrastructure) exploded from 4 percent of GDP in 2002 to

12 percent in 2007. Household saving remained roughly constant at 15–17 percent of GDP during the entire 2000–2007 period. And over that period, households tended to save a constant share of their income, a bit over one-quarter.

So household saving was roughly constant both as a share of GDP and as a share of household income. But household consumption plummeted from 46 percent of GDP in 2000 to 35 percent in 2008. If household saving was constant but the household consumption share of GDP fell, the only possible explanation is that household income's share of GDP also fell. And this is precisely what Bai and Qian found: From their analysis of national and provincial data, they estimated that the labor income share of GDP fell by 7 percentage points from 1997 to 2007.

Since the mid-1990s, Chinese wages have grown fast, but not as fast as GDP. As a result, household incomes—which are mainly a function of wages—grew slower than GDP. Consequently, household consumption's share of GDP also fell, even though households were not saving any more of their income. So if the government wants to boost the consumption share of the economy, it must try to boost the labor income share of GDP. In order to do so, it must first understand why the labor income share fell so sharply in the first place.

Bai and Qian's answer to this question is straightforward. About two-thirds of the drop in the labor income share can be explained by the economy's structural shift from agriculture, where the labor income share is around 90 percent, to industry, where the labor income share is typically less than 50 percent. Most of the remaining fall in the labor income share can be explained by a fall in the labor share within industry, which is mainly thanks to the restructuring of the state-owned enterprises sector in 1997–2003. This resulted in layoffs for many workers, large new capital investments, and the setting of wage rates more in line with productivity growth.

There can be almost no doubt that the sheer abundance of labor from 1990 to 2010, which made it impossible for workers to bargain for a wage that matched the huge productivity growth being generated in industry, played a crucial supporting role in the processes described by Bai and Qian. But as labor becomes more scarce, wages will have to be raised until they match or exceed the rate of productivity growth. This is what we are now witnessing all along China's coast (for example, at Honda, Foxconn). Once wages grow faster than productivity, the labor income share of GDP will start to grow, and household consumption will begin to assume its rightful place as the main motor of the Chinese economy.

Conclusion

These are not easy times for Asian investors, who are faced with global concerns weighing on markets (US double dip? EMU solvency? etc.), unprecedented cyclical adjustments (Asia now leading the tightening cycle), and a very important paradigm shift (the end of cheap labor in China). In the face of so many changes, one must remain nimble and accept that being stubborn will not pay off. Instead, one has to remain very close to the market, identify where positive momentum is strongest—whether on earnings or share price performance—and question whether the momentum makes macro sense before participating. That being said, a few key trends are already emerging:

- Asian currencies will remain well bid for 2011 and likely thereafter. Long-dated Asian government bonds are increasingly the best hedge against equity risk for any portfolio. After all, if the twin "fat-tail" threats to equity markets today are (a) a double-dip recession in the United States, and (b) a solvency crisis in Europe, then long-dated Asian bonds can immunize the risk from either of these events—at least, this is what happened in the second quarter of 2010!
- Asian indices and ETFs are likely to suffer as the markets adjust to the aforementioned new realities, which are all too often underrepresented in benchmarks. Investors deploying capital in Asia should do so with managers willing to stray substantially from any benchmark.
- Within the Asian equity markets, we would favor high-dividend yield-paying stocks, utility stocks, and stable growth stocks, especially those linked to the consumer.
- Stocks linked to the infrastructure roll-out (steel, commodities, etc.) should be seen as a trade at best, or simply avoided, even if valuations currently appear attractive. Such stocks were the main driver of the

Asian boom from 2000 to 2010. They will not be the leaders from 2011 onward.

- Because of the fall in the euro, every investor is enamored with Europe's exporting stocks, but we need to remember that Europe's machine tool and capital good exporters may not be the top performers in a portfolio of exporter stocks. Investors should focus on the Western world's service exporters instead.

7

JAPAN: RETURN TO NORMAL

Robert Madsen

The surge in GDP growth that Japan experienced from 2002 to 2007 suggested that the country had at last escaped the trammels of deflation and embarked on a period of economic expansion and perhaps even fiscal reconstruction. But then came the 2008–2009 global financial crisis, which eviscerated international trade and industrial output, lowering Japan's rate of economic growth dramatically and pushing it back into its old deflationary mire. Consequently, 2009 was the country's worst year in decades; and while 2010 brought a big improvement, the problems that manifested during the worldwide disaster will continue to overshadow Japan for years to come. It is difficult to overstate the implications of this. Indeed, historians may one day look back on recent events as the catalyst that pushed the country past the point of fiscal sustainability and into an eventual sovereign debt crisis.

The Old Normal and the New Normal

Although most of the debate about Japan's economic malaise since the 1990s focused on the country's structural weaknesses and the efficacy of government policy (or lack thereof), the fundamental problem was actually an unhealthy balance between savings and investment. A big household savings surplus in the 1990s and progressively larger retained earnings in the corporate sector through the middle 2000s combined to depress aggregate demand markedly. For smaller countries facing comparable challenges—Switzerland and Singapore, for example, at different points in time—the solution was lending the surfeit capital abroad and a corresponding expansion in the current account surplus to above a tenth of GDP. In effect, these countries used overseas demand to supplement their insufficient domestic demand. But Japan comprised too big a proportion of world GDP to pursue such a strategy: A current account surplus sizable enough to maintain full employment of the country's capital stock would have imposed enormous costs on the rest of the world. Indeed, other countries objected strenuously when the surplus expanded to just about half of the requisite size. Thus prevented by both diplomatic and economic factors from importing the foreign demand it needed, Japan was in danger of falling into a depression. The predictable, almost mathematically inevitable, outcome was a steady increase in the scale of the fiscal deficit from 1992 until the false dawn of the early 2000s. This governmental largesse succeeded in sustaining a modicum of GDP growth throughout that period, but a chronic negative output gap and year upon year of price deflation indicated that the specter of severe recession had not been vanquished.

It would be wrong to say that Japan did not change in the 1990s and early 2000s, for the regulatory environment and corporate behavior in many industries transformed over those decades. But many of the structural reforms actually aggravated the underlying flaws in the economy. Deregulation, cost cutting, and a more efficient allocation of resources, for instance, translated into stagnant and even declining wages and bonuses, which discouraged growth in consumption and private-sector demand. What was needed, contrary to the confident advice of the United States and other governments, was not supply-side reform, but rather better demand management. Accordingly, the commercial efflorescence of the mid-2000s stemmed more from a sharp increase in overseas commercial activity than from domestic reforms. At the risk of oversimplification, robust growth in the US and Chinese economies enabled Japan to expand its current account surplus and stimulated more capital investment, thereby overcoming the weakness in domestic demand and engendering a few years of strong GDP growth, as well as a tentative return to slight price inflation.

Yet the recovery was fragile and, therefore, vulnerable to international shocks. In the mid-2000s the United States bought many of Japan's exports, and a big chunk of the sales to other Asian nations also ultimately found its way into the North American market. For China was serving as an assembly factory, buying Japanese and other Asian countries' goods and then processing them into more advanced products for transshipment across the Pacific. To that extent, the United States was the critical source of demand for East Asia, and hence for Japan, even more than for the rest of the world. Furthermore, US demand was itself unbalanced, dependent in large measure on a seemingly inexorable increase in leverage that enabled households and companies to spend ever more. The implosion of the subprime mortgage market in 2007 and 2008 triggered a reversal of these trends, with American leverage beginning a long decline and the US appetite for other countries' goods and services suddenly and substantially diminishing. This loss of demand caused global exports to plummet, which did profound damage to Japan's manufacturers and consequently to industrial output and the economy as a whole. The country's GDP shrank by 6.5 percent peak to trough, with 2009 proving to be the worst annual performance in many decades. The outlook brightened with the ensuing worldwide boom in fiscal spending and corporate restocking, which lifted 2010 growth to around 3 percent, but the upturn in those factors reversed toward the end of that year; and 2011 will surely disappoint.

This incipient slowdown reflects the fact that the world economy in 2010–2011 looks much like Japan's economy did in the early 1990s. In both cases the implosion of asset bubbles precipitated a vast deleveraging process that vitiated private-sector demand and employment. The resulting contraction in tax revenues pushed official budgets far into the red, a tendency reinforced by the almost universal governmental determination to provide aggressive stimulus. But again, as in 1990s Japan, the adoption of unprecedented fiscal and monetary policies failed to revivify the corporate, household, and banking sectors in most of the major economies because businesses had not yet achieved their target levels of leverage and therefore insisted on paying down their debts still further. This represents a long-term problem for most of the advanced economies because private-sector deleveraging will require at least another few years and must then be followed by public-sector deleveraging in the form of painful spending cuts and more onerous taxes. The prospect is thus one of subdued growth until perhaps 2020. In the medium term, help will arise from the developing world. China, India, Brazil, and other poor countries are on the verge of attaining enough combined size to counterbalance the sluggishness in the developed world and impart significant positive momentum to global GDP growth, but this effect will not become truly pronounced for several more years.

Having benefitted so considerably from vigorous international growth between 2002 and 2007, and then again in late 2009 and early 2010, the slowdown in Japan's export markets that has occurred since then is an ill omen. The weakening of external demand has predictably aggravated the shortfall in household spending and corporate capital expenditures and led to another period of deflationary stagnation. According to the national Consumer Price Index (CPI), the global recession brought inflation down to −2 percent in the fall of 2009. This caused some alarm, but the Bank of Japan (BOJ) and other observers took heart from the strong recovery that was already occurring abroad and reckoned that the price index would return to positive territory by late 2010. Over the next few quarters the index registered some improvement, but then came a number of additional setbacks. Worries about Greece, Ireland, Portugal, and Spain caused investors to flee to the safe-haven currencies—the dollar and the yen—and then fears that the American recovery was flagging put further upward pressure on the Japanese exchange rate. With the yen's fast appreciation past ¥85 per dollar and ¥110 per euro through the end of summer 2010, the country faced more deflationary danger than perhaps at any point since 1995. Moreover, this precipitous upward movement in the exchange rate could persist for some time unless the Japanese government adopts radically different macroeconomic policies. In the meantime the aberrational nature of the 2002–2007 and 2009–2010 booms has been revealed, and Japan has settled into a "new" normal that strongly resembles the "old" normal that prevailed during the "lost decade" of the 1990s.

The Policy Response

Not only has Japan sunk back into its old deflationary swamp; it has done so in an unusually inclement global environment. The best hope for growth in the short term would be robust international trade, which might bring a return to the favorable conditions of the mid-2000s. But with China refusing to revalue the RMB and Germany benefitting from the export-enhancing effects of a greatly diminished euro, there is once again only a single major engine of world demand: the United States. For the United States to lead the world back to the prosperous days of 2002–2007, however, its households and corporations would need to go on a borrowing binge that appears highly unlikely. For although the global financial imbalances have started to widen again, American banks, mortgage lenders, and other creditors will not be in a position to provide the same volume of credit that they did in the bubble period. Nor is there much chance that the US government will expand its deficit spending, and conversely its borrowing, enough to accelerate global GDP growth anytime soon. Meanwhile, the probability of stronger domestic commercial activity is low given the combination of a weak labor market, constraints on credit creation, and corporations' intentions to restrict the volume of new capital expenditures. Therefore, just as in the late 1990s, the prospects for Japanese GDP growth over the next several years depend heavily on monetary, fiscal, and exchange-rate policy.

Monetary Policy

The return of price deflation in 2009 and 2010 presented a compelling case for aggressive monetary easing, but the BOJ refused to act decisively enough to thwart this danger. Ever since gaining its statutory independence from the Ministry of Finance (MOF) in 1998, the central bank's highest priority has been to assert its autonomy from the elected authorities in fact as well as in name. Since Japan's economy remained weak over the ensuing dozen years and politicians more or less consistently demanded greater accommodation, the BOJ's determination not to be pushed around translated into chronically and inappropriately tight monetary policy. Thus, the BOJ, which pioneered quantitative easing in the early 2000s, never employed those unconventional methods boldly enough to overcome the problem of declining prices. To the contrary, its spokesmen stated on several occasions that the agency had done all it possibly could and that deflation simply could not be defeated through monetary means—a notion eventually belied by the success of the United States, the United Kingdom, and other countries in using quantitative easing to combat intense disinflationary pressures in 2008 and 2009 (and again in late 2010 and 2011). It would be wrong to suggest that the BOJ did not loosen policy in reaction to the crisis. But the magnitude of change it made was not especially impressive; most of the stimulus was channeled into a banking sector that was not "multiplying" credit normally and hence could not transmit increases in base money into comparable growth in the broader aggregates. When criticism of its insouciance mounted in late 2009, the BOJ grudgingly announced a modest new program of ¥10 trillion—an economically negligible sum—in additional lending to the money markets. Then on December 18, 2009, Governor Masaaki Shirakawa held a press conference in which he declared that the central bank really did view falling prices as unacceptable. That such a statement was necessary in the first place was a stark indictment of the BOJ's credibility.

The BOJ's intransigence continued through most of 2010. After several months the ¥10 trillion program grew into a ¥20 trillion scheme whose practical effect was still vanishingly small. After the July 2010 election, Prime Minister Naoto Kan sought a meeting with Governor Shirakawa to discuss the need for coordinated policy regarding both deflation and the precipitous appreciation of the yen, but according to press reports the central bank resisted those requests on the grounds that an interview would give the impression that the government was trying to dictate terms to an independent agency. By late August, however, the slowdown in the United States, Japan, and elsewhere had bolstered the cabinet office's position and rendered the BOJ's recalcitrance conspicuously dangerous—for if the cabinet and Diet grew too angry, they might open parliamentary deliberations over whether to deprive the agency of its statutory powers and subordinate it anew to the MOF. Something spectacular was plainly required. So Governor Shirakawa traveled to the annual central bankers' conference in Jackson Hole, Wyoming, only to declare that he had to return to Tokyo for an emergency meeting on monetary policy. Yet rather than do something fittingly assertive, he and his colleagues merely announced that they would expand the ¥20 trillion program by another 50 percent, which was still macroeconomically trivial. The same was true of the ¥5 trillion in funds the BOJ allocated for purchasing publicly traded assets in the autumn. In the end Shirakawa had no choice but to begin communicating more openly with Prime Minister Kan. This nascent dialogue between the central bank and the government may eventually have a salutary effect on monetary policy, but if history is any guide, change will come a day late and a dollar short.

Exchange Rate Policy

Legally, exchange rate management falls under the aegis of the Ministry of Finance, which may act on its own behalf or instruct the BOJ to buy or sell various currencies. In the past, the MOF has occasionally intervened in exchange markets in order to combat what it terms "disorderly" or "volatile" trends, which empirically means undesired yen appreciation. This is important because of the tremendous upward pressure on Japanese currency, and hence downward pressure on domestic prices, produced by China's unwillingness to revalue the RMB, the euro's precipitous depreciation, and the shrinking interest-rate differential between the United States and Japan. Indeed, by late summer 2010 the yen had strengthened so rapidly that it posed a grave threat to the economy, and the cabinet had pledged to watch the exchange rate "carefully" and consider whether forceful intervention might be necessary. If the MOF chooses to weaken the Japanese currency unilaterally, it would presumably have a moderate effect inasmuch as investors are generally reluctant to bet against such a powerful financial and regulatory actor. But if it wants to influence the exchange rate more decisively and lastingly, the MOF must enlist the support of the central bank in the form of much bolder quantitative easing within Japan as well as in the yen market. In other words, here too the country's economic future depends on whether Prime Minister Kan and his successors can persuade the BOJ to abandon what has proved a remarkably destructive monetary policy.

Fiscal Policy

The remaining macroeconomic tool is of course fiscal policy, on which Japan relied so heavily during the 1990s and 2000s to supplement aggregate demand, stabilize GDP, and attenuate deflationary momentum. The slowdown in Japanese and world GDP that began in the latter half of 2010 would seem to call for the same sort of budgetary expansion, but room for maneuvering in this regard is quite limited. Academic research indicates that difficulties ensue when a country's gross national debt reaches 70–90 percent of GDP. On one hand, taxpayers start to behave in a Ricardian manner—reacting to bigger deficits by curtailing their own expenditures in anticipation of higher taxes in the future—and thereby neutralize much of the effect of new fiscal stimulus. On the other hand, at such elevated levels an eventual sovereign debt default becomes progressively more likely. Japan, with its gross debt of nearly 200 percent of GDP, has already moved well beyond the standard risk threshold.

Optimistic observers contend that the normal rules do not apply to Japan because 96 percent of its outstanding financial obligations are to domestic investors and because the net national debt (what would be left if Tokyo sold off a range of its own assets) is only a little above one year's GDP. Both of these advantages, however, are easy to exaggerate. The calculations used to compute the net debt, for example, make a range of dubious assumptions, including that the government's entire portfolio of marketable securities could be sold at a constant value. That is patently nonsensical. Disposing of a third of annual GDP in bonds would inevitably drive the value of those securities down significantly, thus reducing the volume of capital gains considerably. Equally problematic is the fact that virtually all attempts to translate the gross national figures into net numbers overlook the substantial unfunded pension and health care liabilities for which the government will ultimately be held responsible. If those contingencies are properly accounted for, the actual national debt could prove greater than even the gross figures indicate.

Yet if, for the sake of argument, one ignores these computational mistakes and takes the net estimates as credible, the outlook remains gloomy because a national debt of just over one year's GDP is already extremely high for a country with a shrinking population and limited growth potential. During the halcyon years of 2005–2007, the MOF proclaimed that gradual fiscal tightening could bring the primary budget (revenues minus all expenses other than those necessary to roll over the existing debt) into balance by 2020, paving the way for a later surplus on the overall budget. But that would still leave the net national debt at 125 percent of GDP at the very least. Moreover, the rates of economic growth, and thus the volume of tax receipts, assumed by the MOF were almost Panglossian in their hopefulness. In any event these unrealistic expectations were dashed by the 2008–2009 crisis and the slowdown that began toward the end of 2010. The truth is that the government may need to expand the budget deficit beyond that of fiscal 2010 merely to prevent a relapse into recession and the concomitant collapse in tax revenues. But there is only so far Tokyo can go before additional budgetary largesse triggers a Ricardian contraction in the private sector and the danger of a financial crisis reaches prohibitive dimensions. Clearly monetary expansion and exchange rate intervention are more appropriate tools for a country with Japan's economic characteristics.

Here, however, is where Japan's second putative advantage—the fact that almost all of its debt is held by domestic investors—adds another element of complexity. For although individuals and institutions everywhere have a modest home-country bias, they are not entirely oblivious to risk and return. It may well be that Japanese investors continue to accumulate government debt because they presently earn unusually large profits on it. Assuming deflation of 1.5 percent per annum, for instance, a nominal yield of 1.0 percent on the benchmark Japanese government bond (JGB) translates into a real return of 2.5 percent, which is quite attractive to capitalists who worry about the risks inherent in the alternative strategy of investing abroad. To this extent Tokyo may have inadvertently become dependent on marginal deflation to keep real rates elevated, money at home, and new borrowing easy. For if the BOJ were to increase its quantitative easing aggressively enough to generate inflation of, say, 2 percent per annum, investors might see the value of their bond holdings start to fall and shift a substantial portion of their money into foreign assets. Indeed, by the early fall of 2010 the volume of Japanese purchases of foreign stocks and bonds was already increasing. It could be that this is an early harbinger of an eventual rise in interest rates within Japan that would force the government to roll over its financial obligations at much higher cost. Over time the annual expense of funding the national debt could conceivably rise above the country's potential rate of GDP growth, which would put it squarely in a debt trap. In other words, the bold loosening of monetary policy that is necessary to reinvigorate the Japanese economy could in today's circumstances prove to be the event that destabilizes the country's fiscal balance and leads to an eventual sovereign debt default.

Another Lost Decade

While the acute phase of the worldwide crisis has ended, the chronic phase, driven by deleveraging in most of the major economies, will not reach completion until perhaps 2020. Japan's disproportionate reliance on overseas demand implies the same pattern for its domestic economy: Fast growth in early 2010 followed by significant deceleration at the end of that year and subpar expansion for three to five more years. Since the average rate of GDP growth is unlikely to surpass 1.0–1.3 percent per annum over the medium term, the output gap will not close, and deflation—or at least disinflation—will remain a serious threat even as the budget deficit persists at disturbingly high levels. The most promising way out of this unhealthy situation would be to adopt a much looser monetary policy, which would give some positive impetus to prices, promote exports, and increase tax revenues. Sooner or later the BOJ will be forced to move much further in this direction, although its policy preference will probably stay conservative for some time. Whether this restraint is good or bad depends on one's calculation of the risks. On one hand, a gradual, hesitant loosening of monetary policy may fail to stimulate commercial activity and inflation enough for the country to escape its new stagnation. But on the other hand, the national debt may already have grown so big that it is only sustainable if inflation and interest rates stay abnormally low. The danger of a financial crisis will of course increase with the scale of the national debt, but it is already nontrivial. It may therefore be only a matter of time before some combination of greater debt and higher inflation precipitates a crash in the JGB and yen markets.

8

JAPAN: THE INTERREGNUM GOES ON

Richard B. Katz

No Political Stability without Economic Prosperity; No Prosperity without Structural Reform

The long political interregnum that began in 1989—with the peak of the 1980s financial bubble and the fall of the Berlin Wall—seems destined to continue for at least several more years. In 2009, hopes were raised that the smashing victory of the Democratic Party of Japan (DPJ) in the Lower House elections would usher in at least a few years of political stability and some substantial progress on economic reform. Not only did the DPJ throw out the Liberal Democratic Party (LDP), which had ruled virtually uninterrupted for nearly six decades (making the 2009 election the first time voters had ever affected a change in government in postwar Japan), but it did so in an unprecedented landslide. It captured 64 percent of the seats in the Diet's dominant Lower House, a larger share than the LDP had ever won (the LDP's two-thirds majority in the 2005 election was the result of its alliance with the Komeito Party). Moreover, despite much confusion in its economic program, large parts of the party were committed to some notion of economic reform. Since then, unfortunately, hopes have been dashed by the DPJ's unpreparedness to rule.

This does not gainsay the positive achievement of the 2009 election: the end of one-party rule by the LDP or anyone else. Prior to 2009, Japan was the last advanced industrial democracy without the alternation of parties in power (except for one eleven-month interruption in 1993–1994). Japan is now part of the era of contested elections in which parties will alternate in power. It is a signal achievement, a necessary precondition to political and economic reform.

However, the DPJ has proven itself woefully "not ready for prime time." The DPJ's first prime minister, Yukio Hatoyama, proved so hapless that he fell from power only nine months into his term and ruined his party's chance to win a single-seat majority in the crucial July 2010 elections to the Diet's Upper House. Then, Hatoyama's successor, Naoto Kan, threw away the DPJ's chance for avoiding a big loss of seats by making an early hike in the unpopular consumption tax the centerpiece of his campaign. How long Kan will last remains to be seen.

The fact remains that from 1989 to 2010 only one prime minister, Junichiro Koizumi, has enjoyed a long tenure. Excluding Koizumi's five years, Japan has run through fourteen prime ministers in sixteen years. Contrary to the expectations raised by the DPJ's landslide victory in 2009, this pattern so far shows no sign of changing. Neither the LDP nor the DPJ has strong public support.

The LDP is clearly on the decline and could even disappear altogether within a few years. In the July 2010 Upper House elections, it showed yet another decline in its share of the proportional representation vote, the segment of the election in which voters select a party rather than an individual candidate. Its share fell to 24 percent, down from 28 percent in 2007, and way down from 39 percent in 2001. In the district vote for individual candidates, the only place the LDP picked up seats was in twenty-nine mostly rural districts, from which 30 percent of the nation's voters pick 40 percent of the district seats. In the districts representing the other 70 percent of the population, the LDP did not pick up a single seat.

Like the defunct Christian Democratic Party of Italy the LDP may be the kind of party that cannot survive for more than a few years out of power. Having lost access to the budget trough to feed its support organizations in the traditional manner, this machine-oriented party may, like its Italian counterpart, simply evaporate.

But the DPJ's historical role has simply been to end LDP rule. Opposition to the LDP is the main force unifying this fractious party. As the LDP weakens, and perhaps disappears, the centrifugal forces in the DPJ will grow. The DPJ is further destabilized by the presence of the widely despised former party chief Ichiro Ozawa, who is considered guilty of corruption by more than 80 percent of the public, and who, as of this writing, has been indicted, but not yet tried. It is by no means certain that the DPJ will even exist in 2020. All in all, political turbulence is the most likely course for the medium term.

Some analysts believe that Japan can remain in a state of low growth and weak government as a semipermanent state. That might be the case in the other countries, but not Japan. All of Japan's political institutions require a certain minimum level of real and nominal growth. The current situation is an *unstable* equilibrium. It is precisely the tension between the need for reform and the failure to provide it that has caused the political situation to be so turbulent. Regimes will come and go until Japan finally comes up with a regime that can restore economic vitality. Only then will the political equilibrium be stable. In our view, Japan cannot have political stability without economic vitality, it cannot have economic vitality without structural reform, and it cannot have structural reform without a political regime capable of instituting it.

As of November 2010, there was no party united around a clear, viable plan for economic reform. The LDP simply had nothing to say about economic reform; it is fighting to survive. A new party composed of Koizumi disciples who split from the LDP—known as the Your Party—said its top priority is fighting deflation. In reality, deflation is a symptom of Japan's travails, not the cause. The DPJ is focused on survival and internecine struggles rather than economic reform. Regarding the economy, Prime Minister Kan's main priority seems to be cutting the budget deficit— another symptom—rather than raising economic growth. Others in the party emphasize the need to increase consumer demand, but they ignore the issue of how to pay for their programs or how to raise the economy's potential growth.

There are many individuals within the DPJ, LDP, and other parties committed to reform. There is, however, no consensus on what constitutes reform. We have certainly found quite a few individuals across parties, ministries, companies, and universities who have a good sense of what needs to be done; yet there are no viable institutions through which these people can work. This institutional/intellectual vacuum is the main reason for political instability and economic malaise.

Why the LDP Rose So High Only to Fall So Precipitously

To understand this political and economic interregnum, we need to look deeper into why the LDP ruled by itself for so long and why it fell so disastrously. No matter how well entrenched a political regime may seem, once it loses its raison d'être, it sooner or later loses its être. So it was with dictatorships like the Communist Party of the Soviet Union and the authoritarian "developmental states" of South Korea and Taiwan. So it has been with one-party democracies like Italy under the Christian Democrats and Sweden under the Labor Party. And so it was with Japan's one-party democracy under the LDP.

As noted earlier, Japan was the last remaining one-party democracy among rich countries, and even that was diluted since, in its waning years, the LDP could no longer retain power without a smaller coalition partner. Competition is just as necessary for the political health of a modern society as it is for the economic health of a modern economy. Modern, complex societies need course corrections, and one-party systems in which the same people are in power for decades invariably become rigid, blind, and often corrupt.

The system in Japan was made worse by the fact that so many of the Diet seats were inherited. Prime Minister Naoto Kan is rather unusual in being a self-made man, the son of an ordinary businessman. By contrast, Yukio Hatoyama was more typical. He is the grandson of former prime minister Ichiro Hatoyama, who served as the first prime minister under the LDP when rival Liberals and Democrats merged in 1955. Hatoyama's predecessor, Taro Aso, the last LDP prime minister, is the grandson of yet another prime minister, Shigeru Yoshida, who served as the first prime minister after World War II. Aso's predecessor, Yasuo Fukuda, is the son of former prime minister Takeo Fukuda. Fukuda's predecessor, Shinzo Abe, is the grandson of Nobusuke Kishi, who was not only a prime minister in the 1950s but was also jailed as a Class A war criminal suspect following World War II. Before the 2009 election, nearly 40 percent of the LDP's 303 Lower House members were the sons, grandsons, sons-in-law, or nephews of prior Diet members. The proportion was even greater among senior party members. (These figures do not even take into account cases in which Diet members' aides took over their seats.) So when members of the LDP make excuses for Japan's actions during World War II, or seek to continue its various practices in the succeeding decades, they are not simply defending Japan or their party—they are defending their own fathers and grandfathers. While there are some hereditary seats in the DPJ, the share is far smaller, particularly among those who were elected to the Diet for the first time as part of the DPJ rather than as defectors from the LDP or some other party.

All of this begs the question, If one-party democracy is maladaptive for modern economies, how did the LDP and its precursor parties manage to rule in all but two of the sixty-five years following the end of World War II? The answer is that, for a long time, the LDP served Japan very well. For one thing, it kept Japan in the Western camp during the Cold War. Recall that until the fall of the Berlin Wall and the collapse of the Soviet Union, the primary opposition parties were the Socialists and Communists who, unlike the pro-Western Social Democrats of Western Europe, oriented toward Moscow, Beijing, and even Pyongyang. As long as the Socialists and Communists remained the voice of the opposition, the LDP was safe. Not until the LDP split in 1993, when a nonsocialist opposition emerged, was there a genuine alternative to LDP rule that was acceptable to the typical Japanese voter.

Equally important is the fact that the LDP created the political coalition that not only engineered the economic miracle of the 1950s and 1960s but ensured that most Japanese citizens enjoyed its benefits. It is no wonder voters kept rewarding it with a return to power. For decades, the LDP successfully ruled as a "catch-all coalition" that combined a strategy for rapid development with full employment, equal distribution of income, and a system for compensating those sectors of the population, such as workers in obsolescent industries, who were hurt by rapid development.

On the strategy side, the "industrial policy" of the LDP and allied bureaucracies amounted to an extraordinarily successful "infant industry" policy that used a combination of promotion and protection to nurture future "winners," such as autos, electronics, and steel, until they were ready to compete on the world stage on their own. While some undeserving industries also obtained promotion and protection, the benefits far outweighed the costs. Japan industrialized faster than any country before it and faster than almost any country after it. At the same time, the LDP made sure that it retained political support by spreading the benefits around. This included compensating the losers, including coal miners made redundant by the increased use of oil and small retailers in danger of being supplanted by large stores. While such compensation policies slowed growth from the "first best" situation, they were the political price necessary to keep the overall growth strategy going, hence a good "second best" solution.

Things changed in the mid-1970s when Japan reached economic maturity. Infant industry industrial policy began to hurt more than it helped. Unfortunately, the butterfly, still thinking it was a caterpillar, refused to leave the cocoon. Japan continued its industrial policy, but the policy became more about protecting losers than promoting winners. In the balance between pro-growth strategy and political compensation, the balance shifted to the latter. Japan turned into a "dual economy," a deformed hybrid of superefficient exporting industries—the ones that so impressed the world in the 1980s—and superinefficient domestic sectors that were all too often shielded from competition (either from imports or from domestic newcomers) via informal collusion abetted by protective regulations and anticompetitive business practices.

For a long time, the LDP was able to rule successfully as a "catch-all coalition" that encompassed both the bright and the dark sides of the "dual economy." It mediated the transfer of income from the efficient to the inefficient, and it relied on continuing GDP growth to finance this transfer. As long as growth was high enough, this political formula worked. However, unlike in the high-growth era, the methods that the LDP used to compensate losers killed the goose that laid the golden economic and political eggs. The LDP helped create massive disguised unemployment and inefficiency via regulations, pervasive private cartelization, and high prices that protected the backward sectors. For example, the cosseted food-processing sector (the stage between crops leaving the farm and food arriving on grocery shelves) had productivity at only 40 percent of the US level. Overall, manufacturing productivity is only 70 percent of the US level; it is even worse in the services sector. The 1980s bubble and subsequent bust were symptoms of these deeper processes.

Ultimately, decades of protecting the inefficient sectors of the economy meant that the economic pie was no longer growing fast enough to share a slice with everyone. Hence, conflicts of interest started growing, producing strains in the LDP's catch-all coalition. City taxpayers objected to their tax dollars being used to bail out credit institutions tied to the LDP-allied farmer cooperatives. They objected to the hikes in consumption taxes that were imposed to support the growing ranks of the elderly—tax hikes that the finance ministry demanded because slow growth meant a lower tax base. In turn, the elderly resented the zero interest rates being used to bail out the banks and "zombie" borrowers because they led to drastic cuts in their insurance annuities, pension programs, and savings income. Meanwhile, farmers, retailers, taxi drivers, construction firms, and a host of other interest groups resented losing the traditional protections and subsidies on which they had relied for so long.

In 1989, for the first time in four decades, the LDP lost its majority in the Upper House of the Diet, the weaker of the two houses. It has never since regained that majority. Then, in 1993—amidst economic stagnation, chronic corruption scandals, and popular demand for political reform—the LDP split. In the ensuing elections, it lost its majority in the Lower House and fell from power for the first time in four and a half decades. It regained power a year later, mostly as a result of internal squabbles within the opposition coalition that had temporarily taken power. But in order to return to power, the LDP had to ally itself with its Cold War adversary, the Socialists. Since then, the LDP has not been able to rule except in coalition with one or more of the former opposition parties. In the 1998 elections for the Upper House, the LDP was soundly thrashed by an anxious electorate. It lost seventeen seats, including every single contested seat in the major cities. Thus, while single-party rule continued, the LDP's total monopoly had already ended by the 1990s.

The era of short-lived prime ministers was just one symptom of how economic stagnation undermined political stability.

The Koizumi era was the LDP's last chance to show it could produce the economic reform that is indispensable to prosperity. The problem was that, although some parts of the LDP base would benefit from reform, large parts would be hurt. As a result, the party straddled. Aside from solving the banking problem, Koizumi did far less than advertised on the matter of reform. And once Koizumi departed, the LDP abandoned his efforts at reform. His successors could not turn back the clock so easily, but they refused to let it move forward.

Electoral Changes Pressure Parties to Be More Responsive to Voters

The "lost decade," as the era since 1990 is known in Japan, produced a marked change in voter behavior, which helped bring the DPJ to power but also makes it challenging for the DPJ to hold onto power. In the past, elections centered not on which party and policies should govern the nation, but on whether the local candidate had a strong support organization and was able to deliver enough pork to his district. This mentality has changed, partly because of changes in the election rules in 1994 that raised the importance of parties, and partly because Junichiro Koizumi ran the 2005 election as a referendum on policy. In the 2009 Lower House election, voters told pollsters that they were giving priority to the party that would form the national government and to the performance that they could expect from the party. In the past, it did not pay for parties to be responsive to the broad public. Instead, they had to pay attention to narrow, organized interest groups because voters were very loyal to their party and their local Diet member. This, too, is changing. According to traditional analysis, the LDP enjoyed many safe seats, particularly in rural areas. Of the total 168 single-member-district (SMD) seats that the LDP won in 2003—the last pre-landslide election—it won 107 by a margin of more than 10 percent, including 51 by a margin of more than 25 percent. Yet in 2009 it only won sixty-four SMD seats in total. In that election, the DPJ won 221 of the 300 SMD districts (74 percent). Of these, it won 120 by a margin of more than 10 percent, including 71 by a margin of more than 20 percent. Yet these seats may be no more "safe" for the DPJ in 2013 than the LDP's "safe" seats proved to be in 2010. Voter volatility—that is, willingness to switch from party to party—was higher in the 2005 and 2009 Lower House elections than ever before. Three hundred of the 480 Lower House members are elected in SMD elections while the other 180 seats are chosen via a proportional representation vote in which voters select the party that they prefer.

The increase in voter volatility was evident in the Upper House election of 2010, where, less than a year after the DPJ's landslide victory, it suffered a devastating defeat. Both the LDP and the DPJ lost support in the PR segment of the election to an LDP split-off known as the Your Party.

The practice of prioritizing national parties over local candidates, combined with voter volatility, has big implications for how the DPJ or any party will have to rule from now on if it wants to stay in power. Ruling parties will have to become more sensitive to voter opinion and broad national interests than in the past. Mandates may be short-term affairs. The era of one-party rule is over. The DPJ will continually have to convince the voters of its right to govern, and to be convincing it will have to deliver good performance. It will have to address structural reform of the economy since that will affect growth, the tax base, returns on savings, the need to raise taxes, the ability to provide for the elderly or students, and so many other factors that impact the livelihood of the populace. It will need to have a reasonable security policy. Successful policy and effective politics will have to intersect more than in the past. Thus, the things that the DPJ had to say to win power in 2009 may not be good predictors of what the DPJ will have to accomplish by 2013 and beyond in order to stay in power.

The DPJ faces the same political-economic dilemma that brought down the LDP. Part of the DPJ's base would be helped by reform; part would be hurt. The DPJ's task is to find ways to square the circle, to achieve the reforms it needs to stay in power while keeping the loyalty of the constituencies that it needs to stay in power. If it does not do so, it will go the way of the LDP. As of November 2010, the Kan administration had not articulated a coherent policy to restore economic vibrancy. Its "growth strategy" document offered little growth and even less strategy.

What Can Bring Meaningful Reform to Japan?

Two areas in particular—agriculture and labor—highlight the political complexities of economic reform.

Agricultural protection is a major drag on the Japanese economy. For decades, the LDP had a deal with the major agricultural cooperative, Japan Agriculture (JA), to limit imports (albeit with increasing difficulty) and to subsidize production. In return, JA ran get-out-the-vote efforts for the LDP. Many farmers are thus kept dependent on JA for supplies and marketing, and some resent it. One reason farms are so small and inefficient in Japan—1 percent of the average size in the United States and 10 percent of the average size in the European Union—is that their purpose is not to produce cheap food but lots of LDP voters. Moreover, most nominal farmers do not really do much farming, earning a mere 15 percent of their income from farming, the rest coming from other jobs and government subsidies. Rather, they earn their income elsewhere while enjoying tax breaks as farmers. Sixty-one percent of male "core farmers," who own a farm and make a substantial portion of their income from farming, are older than sixty-five. Many of these part-time farmers rely for their income on public works projects, many of which have been wasteful (hence the nickname "bridges to nowhere"). Property taxes and land-use laws make it difficult for small, inefficient farmers to sell their land to firms that could make better use of the land by building larger, more efficient farms, let alone homes, offices, stores, and factories.

These practices do serious damage to the overall economy. About 30 percent of the non-forest land in the three metropolitan areas of Tokyo, Osaka, and Nagoya is zoned as farmland. Liberating this land would create a lot of cheap land that could be put to better use, thereby lowering the costs of doing business and owning homes. Secondly, the high price of food effectively reduces real consumer purchasing power. In 2008, the typical household had to spend 23 percent of its budget just on food, leaving less money to spend on other items. Thirdly, history has shown that countries with higher trade:GDP ratios tend to grow faster, one reason being that the force of global competition compels domestic firms to be more efficient. However, the farm lobby and its supporters in the Diet have limited Japan's ability to form high-quality free trade agreements (FTAs).

Some in the DPJ want to break the logjam in agriculture. Far from being beholden to JA, they want to break JA's power by going over its head and appealing directly to farmers. Instead of subsidizing production, the DPJ would subsidize income for the shrinking ranks of farmers. They would make up the difference between the market price and a certain set price per unit of output. The tax cost to pay this income subsidy would end up being less than the cost of high-priced food to consumers and the general economy. Rival South Korea has managed to couple income support for farmers with growing FTAs with some of its biggest customers who are also farm exporters—including one with the European Union that is set to go into effect in 2011 and one with the United States that was signed in 2007, but, as of November 2010, faced resistance in the US Congress. Some in the DPJ have called for emulating South Korea's practice.

In practice, however, that effort was diluted by electoral calculations—especially by Ozawa—that the rural districts were the key to victory. Instead of limiting the income subsidy to farms above a certain size, all farmers became eligible. Despite some talk, genuine movement on FTAs that would further open up imports and lower food prices has stalled. There is little movement on changing either land-use laws or property taxes that give farmland special breaks, even when there is little real farming.

An even bigger problem is labor rigidity, and this problem shows both the great need for reform and the great political obstacles that have so far blocked it. Having strong ties to the labor movement—including Rengo, the major labor union federation—many DPJ leaders support Rengo's preference for job security. Japan has a very thin social safety net for those who lose their jobs, and it is very difficult for people who lose their jobs mid-career to acquire an equivalent new job at another firm. This is because, as part of Japan's "lifetime employment" system, firms do not "poach" a competitor's employees. Instead, a person's current job at their current company is their main safety net. Thus, there is incredible pressure to avoid layoffs or downsizing, and incredible pressure to keep "zombie" firms alive. This was one of the factors in the nonperforming loan crisis. Many firms were so moribund that their products were not worth what it cost to make them. They built up unpayable debts. Yet, these "zombie" firms were propped up for years and allowed to accumulate even more unpayable debt, lest their bankruptcy cause big job losses. The rigidity in the labor market has produced rigidity in the entire business world. As a result, Japan has one of the lowest rates of labor mobility and firm turnover (births and deaths of firms) in the OECD. Since the births and deaths of firms are key to productivity, this mutually reinforcing rigidity in the labor and firm markets is a major cause of Japan's low growth.

Since the 1990s the LDP has been helping firms increase their share of "irregular" workers (part-timers and temporaries) to one-third of the entire labor force in the name of injecting labor flexibility into the economy. But the irregulars get lower wages per hour—40 percent lower per hour for part-timers—and few of the benefits that apply to regular workers, including the twice-yearly bonuses that can amount to as much as a third of income, company-provided portions of health insurance, and pensions. The increase in irregular workers was not a display of flexibility—it was wage austerity that has resulted in declining real wages in every year but one since 2000.

For much of the DPJ, the answer is to end flexibility and restore lifetime employment as much as possible. But there is no going back. The DPJ needs to learn from Sweden and Denmark, which have combined the best of market flexibility with security. Companies rise and fall. Jobs come and go. But people receive help transitioning from job to job via generous unemployment compensation and training. Income security is high, equality is high, wages are high, unemployment is low—and growth is high. In the early 1990s, the Scandinavians went through the same sort of structural crisis as Japan, but they have come out the other side in much better shape.[1]

Growth requires creative destruction. But if the destruction is too destructive, it will be politically intolerable. The Scandinavian use of a well-designed, pro-growth social safety net has made those countries politically safe for creative destruction. Rather than suffering a trade-off between its social safety net and growth, the Scandinavians enjoy a synergy: good growth finances the social safety net, while the safety net makes workers tolerate the creative destruction that generates good growth. Some reformers in Japan want the creative destruction without a proper social safety net. Others want to preserve Japan's traditional, antigrowth social safety net and avoid creative destruction. That is why Japan has so far failed to come up with the needed solution.

The DPJ's handling of the financial crisis at Japan Air Lines (JAL), which involved major concessions from labor as well as loss to stock- and bondholders, is a test case of whether the DPJ can handle the problem of moribund firms better than the LDP. As of this writing, there are some encouraging signs on this front. JAL has been put through formal bankruptcy so that it can be reorganized; it is downsizing its staff and cutting out unprofitable routes. However, the needed reforms cannot be accomplished one firm at a time. It is hard to force firms to let go of unneeded workers if other firms are unwilling to hire them mid-career. So far, the DPJ has failed to exhibit any vision of a more comprehensive overhaul of the country's labor and business institutions.

The LDP was incapable of making changes in either itself or Japan that were needed to restore prosperity. Whether the DPJ can do much better remains to be seen. If it does not, its reign—perhaps its very existence—could prove to be short-lived. Its failure would probably not spark a return of the LDP, however, but further party splits, realignments, and coalitions. Fasten your seatbelts. It's going to be a bumpy ride.

Note

1. Richard Katz, "A Nordic Mirror: Why Structural Reform Has Proceeded Faster in Scandinavia Than in Japan," Center on Japanese Economy and Business, Working Paper Series No. 265, October 2008, http://academiccommons.columbia.edu/item/ac:100544.

PART

IV

SOUTHERN HEMISPHERE ECONOMIES

9

PROSPECTS FOR SUB-SAHARAN AFRICA IN 2010–2011

Keith Jefferis

The global economic and financial developments that unfolded from mid-2008 to 2009 had a dramatic impact on Sub-Saharan Africa (SSA). The continent escaped the direct impact of the global financial crisis—outside of Nigeria there have been no serious banking crises—but has felt the indirect impact of global recession and, in particular, the dramatic slowdown in world trade. Many SSA economies are highly export dependent, and they have been affected by weak demand in key industrial country markets and lower prices for many exports, especially commodities. This has been compounded by a drop-off in tourist arrivals, reduced remittance inflows from the diaspora, a slowdown in inflows of foreign direct investment, and uncertainty over the availability of donor funds. The general trend has been reduced GDP growth, widened balance of payments deficits, and increased budget deficits. Only a few SSA countries have direct access to international capital and financial markets, but those that do experienced problems in accessing funds or had to pay higher prices as global risk appetite diminished.

However, conditions improved by the end of 2009, and prospects for 2011 are moderately optimistic. Global recovery is under way, and it is being led by emerging markets. The worst fears of a prolonged global depression have not been realized: Commodity prices and export volumes are recovering; global risk appetite is recovering; and perhaps most important, SSA economies are much more resilient due to a long process of macroeconomic, and to a certain extent microeconomic, reform.

Key Themes

A number of key themes are likely to dominate in Sub-Saharan Africa in 2011. These include:

1. the playing out of the global recovery, with improving exports and commodity prices;
2. accessing finance, both through international markets and domestic reforms;
3. the challenge of fiscal consolidation and sustainability;
4. the pursuit of economic integration at both a regional and continental level;
5. changing external influences, with the rise of China;
6. persistent problems of conflict and fragile states.

The Impact of Global Recovery

Having been hit hard by the global downturn and contraction in world trade, African economies are beginning to see some light at the end of the tunnel as global growth recovers; this trend is expected to continue in 2011. Commodity exporters such as Zambia (copper), Botswana (diamonds, nickel), and, of course, the various oil exporters (Angola, Nigeria, Equatorial Guinea, Gabon, Chad, Cameroon, the Democratic Republic of the Congo) saw a significant improvement in demand and prices in the second half of 2009. The fact that the possibility of a deep and prolonged global recession seems to have passed is a relief. Nevertheless, consensus expectations are that recovery in developed markets will be fragile and weak, with global growth remaining below trend, even with stronger recovery in many emerging markets. Sub-trend growth implies that export demand may remain below previous levels, and commodity prices are unlikely to return to previous highs. Industries such as manufacturing are likely to be characterized by global overcapacity for the foreseeable future, which will squeeze producers in SSA who are often not very competitive by global standards. Tourism should pick up, but capacity and prices will remain under intense competitive pressure.

On the positive side, SSA has made huge strides in improving the economic environment, with policy reforms at both the macro and micro levels. Prior to the crisis, growth in SSA was good by global standards, surpassing 6 percent a year from 2004 to 2007. SSA economies are much more outward oriented, flexible, and adaptable, with improved fiscal positions and lower debt burdens, than they were in the 1990s and early 2000s, and they should be well placed to benefit from global recovery. Furthermore, China and other emerging markets are increasingly important in SSA exports, and the anticipated higher growth rates in emerging markets will also help to boost growth.

Accessing Finance

Most SSA economies are dependent on external sources of finance to meet savings-investment imbalances and hence require capital inflows to finance current account deficits. The drying up of international flows to emerging markets in late 2008 and early 2009 hit many African economies hard, at least those middle-income and "frontier" markets that were in a position to raise capital from international markets. Financing South Africa's large current account deficit, which had previously been largely reliant on portfolio inflows, became very difficult. Countries such as Kenya and Zambia, which had been planning debut eurobond issues, had to postpone issuance plans. And the price of existing eurobonds, such as those issued by Ghana and Gabon, collapsed as risk appetite evaporated. Countries that were unable to access international markets became even more dependent on remittances from the diaspora, which started shrinking as jobs in developed countries dried up, and on the international financial institutions (IFIs), which suddenly found their resources inadequate. As a result of reduced export earnings and financing difficulties, currencies such as the South African rand, Zambian kwacha, and Nigerian naira fell sharply in value.

Conditions did, however, improve significantly in 2010. The combination of improving risk appetite and low returns in developed markets prompted a resurgence of capital flows to emerging markets, and African frontier markets are well placed to benefit from this. The IFIs have benefitted from increased resources, and, combined with relaxed lending conditions, have enabled increased flows from the IMF and World Bank;

this progress should continue in 2011. FDI flows are also likely to pick up, although they will do so slowly until there is more clarity in commodity market developments and while excess capacity persists.

SSA countries will also continue to develop domestic capital markets. This initiative is partly driven by governments' immediate need to issue bonds for the purpose of financing budget deficits. But in the longer term, equity and bond markets are needed to provide alternatives to the bank-based financial systems that characterize most of SSA. Nevertheless, banking systems are better run, and better capitalized, than in the past, which goes some way toward explaining their resilience in the face of the global financial crisis. Interestingly, the crisis and associated developments in the banking systems of major industrialized economies has not led to any backlash against privatization and financial-sector reform in African economies.

One uncertainty relates to the impact of global regulatory reform on financial flows to emerging markets. The regulatory reform agenda is still in flux. However, any changes in capital requirements that lead to higher charges for risk may make it more difficult or expensive for African markets to access finance. There will also be pressure on African banking systems to adhere to new regulatory requirements, which will impose demands on regulatory authorities and banks that they may find difficult to meet.

The Challenge of Fiscal Consolidation and Sustainability

Many SSA economies have implemented wide-ranging fiscal reforms over the years since 1990, and budget deficits have generally been contained to manageable levels, albeit with a high level of donor financing in some cases.

As in developed countries, the crisis has led to intensified fiscal pressures. Tax revenues have fallen, especially in countries that are dependent on the taxation of commodity exports. Import duties have also declined as trade volumes have fallen. At the same time, given the demands for social spending, public expenditures have gone up to cushion the impact of the global slowdown. Several countries have deliberately chosen to use fiscal policy in a countercyclical manner to offset the impact of external developments. There is scope for this in the countries that had favorable fiscal positions when the crisis began.

Compared to the situation in late 2008 and early 2009, there is now more space for financing fiscal deficits. Financial flows to emerging markets have resumed, the IFIs have more resources, and there is opportunity for tapping domestic capital markets. However, governments will have to be very careful not to amass excessive debt. As the recovery gathers pace, the emphasis will have to shift from stabilization to the more traditional emphasis on debt sustainability, and countries will need to plan the transition back to lower deficits. Nevertheless, it is likely that there will be some reversal of the gains of debt reduction that have been made as a result of the Highly Indebted Poor Countries (HIPC) and Multilateral Debt Reduction Initiatives (MDRI).

The Pursuit of Economic Integration at Both the Regional and Continental Level

The African Union has set some very ambitious targets with regard to regional and continental economic integration. Although some of these targets may be unrealistic—such as those relating to a single African currency—regional integration will nonetheless continue to be an important theme in SSA in the coming years. There are many positive reasons for supporting regional economic integration. Not least of these reasons is that integration helps counter some of the problems that result from excessive fragmentation of the continent (which results in some nation-states being too small to be economically viable, and limits their ability to benefit from economies of scale). However, the process will not be painless. Progress has generally been limited to the establishment of free trade areas (FTAs), which are the easiest and least complex component of regional economic communities (RECs). Beyond this, African states in general have not shown a willingness to forgo national sovereignty and hand over powers to regional bodies, which is necessary if subsequent stages of meaningful regional economic integration (customs union, common market, monetary union) are to be achieved. Similarly, African states have been unable to make the political choices necessary to unravel the "spaghetti bowl" of overlapping regional agreements. Once RECs move beyond FTAs, it will only be possible to belong to one REC.

This problem is perhaps most acute in Eastern and Southern Africa, where overlaps between the Southern African Development Community (SADC), the East African Community (EAC), and the Common Market for Eastern and Southern Africa (COMESA) prevail. Instead of dealing with the issue by requiring countries to decide which single REC they wish to belong to, governments have proposed combining all three RECs into one giant REC, comprising twenty-six countries, from Libya to South Africa. Such a solution is likely to prove unworkable. It is no coincidence that the REC that has made the fastest progress toward integration is the EAC, which has only five members. Until politicians are willing to make hard choices, progress toward regional economic integration will be slow.

A third problem with regional economic integration is that RECs are obsessed with creating common currencies. All RECs have common currencies as their final objective, typically with very optimistic timescales. There is insufficient understanding of the prerequisites for making common currencies work and the compromises that are entailed along the way. And unlike trade integration, which is almost always beneficial, monetary integration may well not be a positive move for the countries involved.

Monetary integration may make sense for some groups of countries, such as those surrounding South Africa and the EAC, but even in those smaller groups the challenges are substantial. The problems faced by Greece in particular and the eurozone in general illustrate the difficulties involved in making monetary integration work in the absence of political and fiscal integration. More generally, excessive focus on monetary integration is likely to detract attention from much more pressing issues and decisions that are required to make less sophisticated forms of regional economic integration work.

The Rise in Chinese Influence in Africa

Chinese growth has been highly resource intensive, and the country has made concentrated efforts to ensure security of supply. African countries are among the top global suppliers of several industrial minerals, as well as oil. China has shown a willingness to invest in Africa, with perhaps less concern with risk than traditional Western mining companies. China has capital to invest, and a combination of state-owned and privately owned firms has provided mining investment, infrastructure investment, and other loans, sometimes as part of barter deals. In some cases, China has taken advantage of the global financial crisis to acquire assets relatively cheaply. One of the results has been a reorientation of SSA exports toward China, especially commodity exports. Given rapid Chinese growth, this is helping some SSA countries to quickly recover from the impact of the global crisis.

Chinese investment in Africa is not without controversy. The lack of conditionality associated with Chinese capital has undermined Western efforts to link investment and aid with governance reforms. Within Africa, a demanding Chinese presence has sometimes caused resentment, especially as it is often associated with high levels of Chinese labor inflows. Furthermore, the Chinese interest in large infrastructure and mining projects has been supplemented by smaller-scale investment in trading activities. In some places this has encroached on the activities of African entrepreneurs, and has led to calls for restrictions on Chinese investment and immigration.

Nevertheless, the Chinese presence in Africa is likely to grow, as Chinese companies and the state look to achieve further security of supplies. African countries will benefit from capital inflows, expertise, and the Chinese ability to handle complex engineering projects, as well as the supply of cheap goods. However, it is likely that China will make efforts over time to comply with broadly accepted international standards.

Persistent Problems of Conflict and Fragile States

Africa has long been plagued by problems of conflict and fragile states. While several conflicts have been resolved in recent years (for example, Liberia, Sierra Leone, Rwanda), others have proved more intransigent, with either persistent conflict and instability (Democratic Republic of the Congo [DRC], Somalia) or a seeming inability to reach a lasting peaceful solution (Sudan, Côte D'Ivoire). And there is also the risk of new conflicts breaking out (Guinea). These conflicts have a variety of causes: fighting over natural resources; ethnic, regional or religious tensions; and the unwillingness of incumbent leaders to relinquish power, with one or more of these factors present in all of the current or recent conflicts.

The IMF classifies nearly one-third of the continent as fragile states (most of the above-listed countries plus Burundi, Central African Republic, Comoros, Eritrea, The Gambia, Guinea-Bissau, Sao Tome, Togo, and Zimbabwe). It is difficult to be optimistic about any resolution of the major conflicts in the DRC and Somalia in the next couple of years, and there is a danger that others could become worse, especially in the Sudan following the referendum on independence for South Sudan in early 2011. There is also a possibility that ongoing tensions in SSA's second largest economy–Nigeria–could erupt into something more serious.

Key Regional and Country Developments

Southern Africa is of course very much tied to events and developments in South Africa. There, the dominant event of 2010 was the FIFA World Cup that was held mid-year. The event put immense strains on public services, transport, infrastructure, and police and security services, but contrary to some expectations that it would prove to be somewhat chaotic, it ran smoothly and turned out to be a great success. The World Cup brought many first-time visitors to Africa, and it should provide a long-term boost to tourism. It also showed that South Africa can host a major complex event and meet the highest international standards of service and delivery.

However, Southern Africa will continue to face power supply problems through 2011. While the economic slowdown temporarily reduced the pressure on power supplies, the recovery of growth will quickly erode any margin of comfort. The South African power utility, Eskom, has been unable to bring sufficient new generating capacity online to meet demand, and the policy framework has also stymied the potential contribution of independent power producers. A new power supply policy framework for South Africa announced late in 2009 should eventually help to resolve these issues. In the near future, however, other countries in the region that are dependent upon South Africa for power—notably Botswana, Namibia, Swaziland, and Zimbabwe—will also face power supply constraints that may reduce economic activity. Looking further ahead, most power-generation potential in Southern Africa lies with coal, which is out of favor internationally and may struggle to attract sufficient investment. Longer term, there is huge potential in hydropower and solar energy, but most of the former is located in the conflict-ridden DRC and is probably at least two decades away from being an effective power source, and technology for large-scale, cost-effective solar power generation is still at the developmental stage.

More generally, South Africa is lagging the economic recovery in emerging markets. This will hold back recovery in partner countries in the Southern African Customs Union (Botswana, Lesotho, Namibia, and Swaziland).

As for Zimbabwe, prospects for 2011 are uncertain. According to the trilateral agreement signed in 2008, a new constitution should be established in 2011 and would then be followed by fresh elections. Most observers agree that the ruling ZANU-PF party would be routed in anything resembling a free and fair election in Zimbabwe. This, along with a fear of losing control of patronage and rent-seeking activities, explains ZANU-PF's reluctance to abide by the spirit of the unity agreement. Unless the Southern African Development Community (SADC) in general, and South African president Jacob Zuma in particular, are willing to apply real pressure to ZANU, there may be a prolonged period of political impasse. The economy has recovered somewhat since the abolition of the Zimbabwean dollar and the reining-in of the central bank's power to print money (which is another reason for ZANU's reluctance to face an election–the central bank printed money to finance ZANU-PF's previous election campaign and various related patronage schemes, which was one reason for the dramatic money supply growth that caused hyperinflation; now that the economy is [US] dollarized, the central bank can no longer do this). However, until the political logjam is broken, investment will be discouraged and the economy will only show slow growth.

Elsewhere in the region, Zambia has bright prospects for a recovery of growth as the international demand for copper picks up. Similarly, recovery of growth is likely in Angola as oil production continues to expand and a high level of investment takes place in infrastructure to deal with the legacy of thirty years of civil war.

In East Africa, growth should be reasonably robust in Tanzania, Uganda, Rwanda, and Ethiopia. Growth in Kenya will continue to be hobbled by political problems and the spillover from instability in Somalia. Uncertainty is likely to persist at least until the next elections, which are due in 2012. Oil has been discovered in Uganda, and although the magnitude of commercially viable deposits is still to be clearly established, the investment required to bring this industry onstream will underpin growth. Rwanda is positioning itself as a services and IT hub aimed at linking anglophone East Africa to francophone Central Africa.

Prospects for Central Africa are mixed. The massive potential in the DRC will continue to remain unexploited while low-level civil war persists, and there is little prospect of the conflict ending anytime soon. The large UN peacekeeping force in the DRC can do little more than contain unrest. Mining companies were piling into the DRC in the mid-2000s on the basis that the massive potential returns outweighed the huge risks of operating there, but the global recession caused a major pullback from the country. As commodity markets recover, exploration and mining companies are starting to return.

Elsewhere in Central Africa (Gabon, Cameroon, Republic of Congo, Equatorial Guinea), the dominant factor will be oil market development, with a rise in prices helping to restore balance of payments and fiscal surpluses. However, growth may prove elusive, in part due to the constraint imposed by the need to preserve the common currency's peg (the Central African franc) to the euro.

West Africa continues to be the most diverse and complex region of Africa. Nigeria remains the dominant state. It has the largest population in Africa and the second-largest economy after South Africa. Recent developments have been promising, with signs of stability in the Niger Delta following an amnesty agreement with rebels. This progress should allow Nigeria to restore oil production to full capacity, and a more conducive security environment should encourage renewed international investment in the industry. Deregulation of petroleum product prices should also help to encourage investment in downstream activities. Outside of the oil sector, 2009 was a challenging year for Nigeria's banks. The banking system was the only one in Africa to be badly affected by the global financial and economic crisis, as loans to the oil industry and margin lending for stock purchases fell victim to falling oil and stock prices. These problems were compounded by corruption and lending to insiders and cronies. A major rescue and clean-up exercise launched by the central bank required the takeover of several banks and the removal of many bank executives. Further restructuring and consolidation will take place as these banks are privatized, and these efforts, combined with improved regulation and supervision, should provide the basis for a more stable banking system in the future. However, with the run-up to the 2011 elections being a time of potential instability, politics will remain a key issue in Nigeria, especially as many regional, ethnic, and religious tensions remain.

Elsewhere in West Africa, Ghana is gearing up for the commencement of large-scale oil production, which is expected to transform the economy from 2011 onward as oil revenues reach an estimated $4 billion a year. In the meantime, however, Ghana has large fiscal and current account deficits that need to be carefully managed, notwithstanding the prospect of significant oil revenues in the future. The partial stability achieved in Côte D'Ivoire could not survive the much-delayed presidential election—finally held in November 2010—and further civil strife looms. Liberia should continue to experience a robust recovery after years of civil war, as should Sierra Leone, where there is also the prospect of oil production in due course. The West African members of the Communauté Financière Africaine (CFA) zone (Senegal, Côte D'Ivoire, Togo, Benin, Mali, Burkina Faso, Niger, and Guinea-Bissau), which, unlike the Central African franc zone, are not oil producers, will need to ensure that fiscal and monetary policy are consistent with the exchange rate peg to the euro. This means paying close attention to maintaining adequate levels of international reserves. They will also need to undertake structural reforms to boost growth, which has been insipid in recent years.

Overall, prospects for Sub-Saharan Africa are good now that the worst of the global financial and economic crisis has passed. Although several countries continue to face major problems, the region as a whole has proved resilient, and should be well placed to benefit from global economic recovery.

10

SOUTH AFRICA AFTER 2010

Iraj Abedian

The End of the Second Golden Age Exposes
Structural Shortcomings

South Africa's political economy took a remarkable turn in 2008. On one hand, the country's nascent democracy was subjected to a momentous shift of political forces within the ruling African National Congress (ANC) Alliance, culminating in the recall of Thabo Mbeki from the office of the presidency. He was replaced by President Kgalema Motlanthe as a caretaker president until the national elections in April 2009. In May 2009, President Jacob Zuma took office after a conclusive victory in a highly contested, widely supported, and peacefully conducted election. On the other hand, the economy was battered by the prevailing global "great recession" that had engulfed all regions the world over. The projected growth rate of nearly 6 percent plummeted to a mere 1.3 percent in the third quarter of 2008, followed by a negative growth of 0.7 percent and 7.4 percent during the last quarter of 2008 and the first quarter of 2009, respectively. The recessionary conditions prevailed with −2.8 percent growth in the second quarter of 2009, and recovery returned in the third quarter of 2009 when the economy registered a quarter-on-quarter annualized growth of 0.9 percent. This growth momentum increased to 3.2 percent during the fourth quarter of 2009. Overall, the 2009 GDP registered a negative growth of 1.8 percent—its first negative performance since 1992. However, by the end of the first quarter of 2010, the economy had its third successive quarterly growth, recording an impressive 4.6 percent quarterly annualized GDP increase. As of the fourth quarter of 2010, the projected annual GDP growth for 2010 was 3.0 percent, and is expected to increase to 3.4, 4.1, and 4.5 percent in 2011, 2012, and 2013, respectively. In part, this sharp turnaround is technical: it was driven by the poor performance of the economy in the first quarter of 2009. As is the case the world over, the prospects for sustained economic performance remain tentative. South Africa's major trading partners are bedeviled by a blend of substantial pan-European public debt, Anglo-Saxon capital and financial market problems, and tectonic shifts in the structure of the global economy. As a small open economy, South Africa is affected by these global economic-financial forces.

For much of the early 2000s, South Africa's macro-financial and fiscal indicators compared favorably with those of many of its peer countries. This was, to a large extent, the outcome of a consistent and ambitious fiscal reform program over the 1994–2007 period. The Aparthied regime had left the country's macroeconomic and fiscal configuration saddled with high public debt, excessive budgetary deficits, double-digit inflation, and a vulnerable currency. When combined with interest rates hovering in the mid-20 percent range, this configuration led to a GDP growth rate of 1.2 percent in 1992–1993. The country faced a classic case of severe macroeconomic instability. Given its precarious point of departure in 1994, South Africa's fiscal policy reform has achieved a great deal at the macro-financial level. Such progress helped underpin the country's much-needed macroeconomic stabilization goal during the critical period following the birth of the country's democratic era. Not only were inflation and interest rates brought down, but there was also a considerable reallocation of resources in favor of the poor and lower-income households. Thanks to the South African Revenue Services' (SARS) consistent success in improving its collection capability and restoring tax morality, the additional fiscal resources enabled both reallocation of revenues to the poorer segments of society and a lowering of personal income taxes and company taxes, particularly for small and medium enterprises. Over the same period, the democratic government invested a great deal of political and technical capital in the modernization and systemic design of the new fiscal architecture. The fiscal reform program and the government's political leadership were further enhanced by rising local and domestic economic performance.

Despite remarkable achievements from 2000 to 2010, South Africa's "second golden age" (after its acclaimed 1960s boom period) has come to an end, leaving behind some obdurate structural shortcomings. It is now widely acknowledged that policy from 2000 onward has had some critical inadequacies and outright failures. Unless the root causes of the prevailing shortcomings are identified and remedial actions are taken, the sustainability of economic growth and attainment of further socioeconomic development remain at serious risk.

Past Policy Failures Will Determine Future Growth Prospects

The single greatest setback to socioeconomic development is the prevailing inadequacy of the national education and training system. The widespread shortage of skills within society is but one of its manifestations. The modernization and technological upgrading of the economy since 2000 has increased the economy's skill intensity greatly. This in turn has accentuated the systemic unemployment problem. Meanwhile, the country's human capital accumulation has proved wanting. Although much has been achieved in promoting access to the public school system, little has been achieved with regard to quality improvement of the education offered. Consequently, "unemployability," widespread vacancies, and a huge skills gap have emerged concurrently. As a result, the income and wealth inequalities within society have worsened. The most recent projections suggest that South Africa may well have overtaken Brazil as the country with the most unequal distribution of income.

Another crucial policy failure has been the absence of a well-defined industrial strategy that is rooted in the country's comparative advantages and enhanced by an appropriate mix of factor prices and implementation institutions. In particular, some of the country's sources of comparative advantage are either neglected or markedly eroded. The mining sector, which has been a cornerstone of the economy for decades, has experienced major setbacks. Agriculture and agribusinesses have received little, if any, attention. Moreover, a poorly managed land redistribution policy has caused much uncertainty in the farming sector. Although many factors have been at play, attempts to develop industrial strategy have suffered primarily from one major shortcoming: The strategies have been partial in their perspective. The country's key sectors, including agriculture and mining, have been left out of the purview of the industrialization strategy. The golden rule of any industrialization strategy is to begin with the country's "initial endowment." This has been lacking thus far. A general lack of effective implementation capacity within the various spheres of the public sector is another evident shortcoming.

Perhaps one of the most damaging failures has been the absence of medium- to long-term planning for socioeconomic infrastructure. This problem most poignantly manifested itself in the recent electricity crisis. In the first quarter of 2008, the national electricity utility (Eskom) experienced serious generation failures, subjecting the country to blackouts and causing severe socioeconomic damage. The trouble resulted from years of neglecting to create an appropriate energy policy as well as inadequately investing and maintaining Eskom's electricity generation capabilities. A number of other areas of infrastructure planning and investment were equally neglected. In general, as Figure 10.1 illustrates, there has been a growing gap between private and public investments dating back to the mid-1980s. This gap has narrowed marginally since 2004 when the new national public infrastructure investment plan was launched, estimated at R800 billion (approximately US$110 billion) over a seven-year period.

The sudden "Eskom blackout" in the first quarter of 2008 was the first sign that the country's growth faced a real obstacle in the form of electricity shortage. As of the third quarter of 2010, there was growing public debate about a similar shortage in water resources. In particular, the debate focused on the quality of existing water sources and the actual and potential risks it posed for growth in business activity and public health of urban communities going forward. The status of the national road network is yet another major area of weakness. Years of neglect and underinvestment have created real bottlenecks for growth and rural development in almost all provinces. Last but not least, the country's aging urban infrastructure has been largely ignored. Even key metropolitan centers suffer from basic symptoms of decay in urban utilities, poor institutional performance, and weak financial management capability. Local government

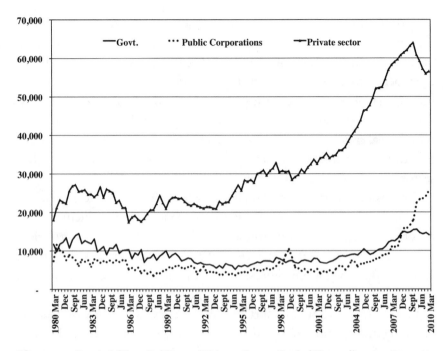

Figure 10.1 South African Public- and Private-Sector Capital Expenditure, 1980–2010
Source: South African Reserve Bank

institutional infrastructure has generally been left to falter. Such prolonged neglect has both developmental and growth consequences. Beyond a certain point, no further private-sector investment can become viable unless and until the complementary public-sector investment is implemented first.

The country's failures have in turn led to its declining global competitiveness. While South Africa's competitiveness rose markedly during the 1997–2004 period, the country has been losing its edge in a number of areas since 2005. These factors combined to culminate in South Africa's sharp fall in rank by nine positions between the 2006–2007 and 2009–2010 Global Competitiveness Reports. Falling global competitiveness has led to exports' declining contribution to GDP. These declines have worsened the growing balance of payments deficit, which has surged due to rising imports.

Improving Infrastructure and Productivity Are South Africa's Key Tasks

The South African economy needs an appropriate mix of macro- and microeconomic policies to help increase its global competitiveness and achieve its socioeconomic development goals. Significantly, the conceptualization of such a policy mix and its successful implementation require a skillful state. The success of economic policy henceforth rests on the capabilities of the state infrastructure and its effectiveness in policy development, coordination, integration, and implementation. Transforming the modus operandi of the state, therefore, is indispensible if some of the failures of the recent past are to be reversed.

Just as important, increasing public-sector productivity is necessary if the economy is to raise wage levels for the working classes. Ironically, the logjam between organized labor and the government from 2000 to 2010 has been one of the key contributors to declining productivity in the public sector. The inability to create a public service working environment that is conducive to performance has resulted in the deepening of the culture of mediocrity and bureaucratic formalities within the public sector. This is inimical to the sustainability of growth and social development. At the same time, the longer it persists, the more complex effective macroeconomic management becomes.

Operationally, public service delivery is inherently labor intensive, and labor-intensive production processes more readily lend themselves to systemic inefficiency and x-inefficiency syndromes. Such processes are typically far more management and system intensive, and they require effective capabilities for ongoing monitoring and performance assessment as well as the ability to take remedial actions.. Yet these are the very attributes that the South African public sector operations lack at present. Furthermore, since 1994 the social imperative for black economic empowerment has deepened the politicization of public service. This is not to say that prior to 1994 public service was not politicized; indeed, it was heavily populated by the protégés of the ruling National Party. Political change since 1994 transformed the racial composition of public service, but it did not transform the managerial culture of its operations. Thus, it is not surprising that the abuses of public resources that existed in the dying years of apartheid have continued. Managerial ineptitude, misapplication of public resources, and corruption are rife across the three spheres of government. It is this managerial culture that generates inordinate amounts of wasteful inefficiency and exacts a heavy welfare loss, particularly on the poor.

Such government failures cannot be allowed to persist. In this light, President Zuma's intention of tackling the gaps within the cabinet structure is a welcome initiative. Both from a political economy perspective and for reasons of short-term economic stimulation of the economy—given the cyclical downturn—President Zuma's policy has to fulfill a two-fold objective. First, government operations have to become a great deal more efficient so as to be able to "do more with less." Second, the government structure has to undergo a tectonic shift in order to be able to plan and implement a well-coordinated public-sector investment program with a view toward expanding productive capacity and stimulating economic performance.

Zuma's New Cabinet Structure Has Produced Polarizing Reactions

The composition of President Zuma's cabinet has raised a mix of excitement and anxiety. At first glance, the structure seems set to deal with the above-mentioned glaring gaps within the macro-policy domain that have haunted the economy for years. There is, however, widespread anxiety regarding the workability of the cabinet structure insofar as socio-economic policy and timely policy implementation are concerned. Interestingly enough, the increase in the cabinet's size by more than 20 percent is almost entirely due to the creation of new economic policy ministries. By increasing the ministerial posts, the new cabinet facilitates the inclusive participation of all key ANC tripartite partners. Politically, this is smart. Operationally, however, this has created considerable challenges in regard to consistency, timeliness, and effectiveness. What was missing at the start was a "business strategy" and an "operational directive" for the newly created ministries. These are the elements that would bridge the gap between the proposed "structure" and the "promised output" of departments.

Anxiety arose from the assumption that collaboration, coordination, timeliness, and policy consistency were expected to emerge automatically with the creation of the ministries. In effect, much is left to "interpersonality" and "leadership" dynamics. Experience shows that any new organization takes three to five years to establish its management team and operational culture, fine-tune its policies, and aim at effectiveness. Within public-sector organizations, the process is further bedeviled by a mix of political considerations, procedural delays, change of leadership guards, and budgetary constraints. Exogenous global factors, a rapidly shrinking domestic economy, rising unemployment, falling fiscal revenues, and heightened expectations for service delivery with their resultant socioeconomic vulnerabilities add to the anxiety. Such circumstances do not favor experimentation, and they effectively leave President Zuma's government with little if any freedom with regard to time and policy procrastination.

Comparable global experience shows that changing the operational culture of a complex and varied organization such as public service takes time and perseverance. At the same time, in the absence of such behavioral and managerial transformation, the promise of better public service delivery and/or cost-effective fiscal management is bound to remain a mere slogan.

Private and public finances have been shaken to the core across the world, and nearly all governments are in search of remedial policies and effective governance modalities. President Zuma's variation is no exception. Ultimately it is not the form per se, but rather the consistency of the principles and the spirit that animates the operational culture that will ensure the success or the failure of the new administration.

Meanwhile, with regard to the direction of macroeconomic policy, much debate and controversy rages both within the ANC Alliance as well as throughout broader society. Key components of the macroeconomic policy such as inflation targeting, liberalized international trade, and free-floating foreign exchange policies have been particularly questioned. In part, this is a reflection of the "coalition nature of the ruling party." Over the years since 2000, and under President Mbeki, the "ANC Alliance coalition" demonstrated political tension, but operationally economic policy was dominated by the ANC, with little direct control exercised by the other "coalition partners"—COSATU (Congress of the South African Trade Unions) and the SACP (South African Communist Party).

Since May 2009, however, the workings of the government have been materially different under President Zuma. In operational terms, when it comes to economic policy formulation and implementation, the ANC Alliance increasingly resembles a European-style "coalition government." So the "behind-the-scene issues" are out in the open, and differences of opinion are made clear in public forums. As such, interinstitutional and interministerial differences and contradictions have increasingly surfaced. So far, however, the policy debate in the country has been confined to ministerial "turf battles." While the economy has been on the slide, and over one million jobs have been lost since October 2008, the government has yet to provide a credible countercyclical solution to the problem of job losses and economic stress. In particular, the macroeconomic policy framework is kept intact as if it is business as usual. The government, and in particular the newly appointed governor of the Reserve Bank, Gill Marcus, have made it clear that they will adhere to a free-floating foreign exchange policy.

Despite such assurances, the prevailing structural changes within the global economy and the growing ineffectiveness of the macro-policy configuration, with its adverse effects on the structure of the South African economy, mean that it is unlikely that the policy framework can persist without major changes. Two areas in particular require urgent attention. The first area is the composition of the fiscal expenditure, namely the growing dominance of welfare expenditure and its attendant crowding-out effects on other education, health, and infrastructure budgets. The second is the rising concern over the strength and volatility of the rand. Unlike the early years of South Africa's democratic dispensation, when currency volatility was caused primarily by domestic sociopolitical factors, ever since the collapse of the Lehman Brothers in September 2008 the sources of rand strength and its above-average volatility are mostly exogenous. In effect, fundamental shifts in the dynamics of the global capital markets, together with marginally high domestic interest rates, lead to sustained strength and volatility of currency. This in turn leads to ongoing deindustrialization and the gradual emergence of the so-called Dutch Disease. The negative economic, fiscal, and employment consequences of this process are too severe for South Africa. The underperformance of South Africa's export sector, despite the prevailing super cycle of commodity prices, is, to a large extent, attributed to the currency factor, which is operating within a free-float regime. Increasingly, there is a case for a shift from a free float to a "managed float" for the currency, with a view to moderate foreign exchange volatility and its socioeconomic impact.

Meanwhile, in an attempt to reverse the sagging and tentative growth performance of the economy, a new growth strategy (the "new growth path") was endorsed for the country in a special cabinet meeting convened by President Jacob Zuma on October 25, 2010. This is seen as a major step by the government in addressing the serious structural constraints that are embedded in the economy. The strategy aims at reducing unemployment from 25 percent to 15 percent in the long run. The new growth path is set to unlock the economic potential of the country through a considerable investment in infrastructure, agricultural industries, mining value chain, green economy, and the manufacturing and tourism sectors.

Rising Deficits and Public Expenditures Are Triggering Fear

The most tangible changes to macroeconomic indicators have resulted from the impact of the global economic recession and its associated international financial dynamics. Not only has the rand shown a sustained appreciation bias that has exacted pressure on export earnings; most seriously, government revenues have been affected markedly, leading to a drastic fall in tax revenues and a concurrent rise in public-sector borrowing requirements. Whereas in 2008, the actual public-sector borrowing requirement (PSBR) was 3.8 percent of the GDP, it is estimated to have risen to 9 percent in 2009 and 10.1 percent in 2010. Consequently, public debt-to-GDP ratios are set to rise sharply from 22.6 percent in 2008 to 27.4 percent in 2009 and beyond, reaching well over 36 percent by 2013.

Meanwhile, rising unemployment has placed additional pressure on the government's welfare expenditure. The government's expenditure mix is bound to continue in favor of welfare spending. Notably, welfare has been the fastest-growing expenditure category since 2000. The child support grant is set to rise sharply as a result of the October 2009 extension to the age of sixteen. It is a matter of time before welfare expenditure exceeds expenditure on education, which is the largest budgetary allocation within the national budget. From 2013 to 2015, a growing level of fiscal stress is likely to emerge primarily as a result of the trade-offs between "welfare expenditure" and "socioeconomic infrastructure expenditure."

Unlike the period 2000–2006, the financing of the budget deficit is bound to receive increasing attention. Not only are the days of tax cuts gone; there is a growing likelihood that the national tax burden may rise. Given South Africa's relatively narrow tax base, this is likely to become a looming concern over the medium term. In this regard, the Minister of Finance's Medium Term Budget Policy Statement, delivered to the Parliament on October 27, 2010, introduced some relatively strict fiscal measures to bring down the budget deficit to a 3 percent level by 2013. Whether this will be achievable will depend entirely on the pace of economic growth in the medium term.

In the short term, the recent global recession will cause macroeconomic and fiscal changes in South Africa that are in line with similar developments worldwide. In the fourth quarter of 2010, South African macroeconomic policy was reconfigured to a mix of tight fiscal policy alongside a much looser monetary stance. Interest rates were cut by a cumulative 650 basis points from the prevailing level in 2008, leading to the lowest interest rate in thirty years. Fiscal policy meanwhile is tightening, and aims to reduce the budget balance from −5.3 percent in 2010–2011 to −3.2 percent in 2013–2014.

However, in the medium term, prospects will be defined more by the policy responses of the government that are driven by the dynamics of the ruling ANC Alliance. Judging by political economy developments in 2009 and 2010, it is evident that substantive change will take time, and the structure of the economy as well as global financial factors will be significant considerations in the process.

11

IT DIDN'T HAVE TO BE THAT BAD—THE COUNTEREXAMPLE OF AUSTRALIA

Saul Eslake

The series of financial shocks that has come to be widely known as the "global financial crisis" is, in truth, better understood as a "North Atlantic financial crisis," albeit one with much larger global ramifications than those of earlier crises afflicting Mexico, Asia, Russia, and Argentina during the 1990s and early 2000s.

Over and above the waves of euphoria and panic (or greed and fear) that are common to all speculative bubbles and busts, the financial crisis of 2007–2009 was largely the result of failings in the management and supervision of American and British financial intermediaries, flaws in the structure and operation of the American mortgage market, and macroeconomic policy errors by the US Federal Reserve (in particular) in the years preceding the onset of the crisis. Of the $2.2 trillion in write-downs that the IMF expects to have been incurred by global banks between 2007 and 2010 on their holdings of loans and securities, 49 percent will be attributable to American and British banks. Most of the losses that will be sustained by banks domiciled elsewhere among advanced economies will result from their operations in American or British markets, or from their exposure to American mortgage-backed and corporate securities.

Given the importance of the US and, to a lesser extent, British economies and financial systems to their global counterparts, it was inevitable that the North Atlantic financial crisis would have serious global consequences. In particular, the collapse of Lehman Brothers and AIG in September 2008 triggered an abrupt decline in business and consumer confidence and, via their impact on share prices, a sudden and substantial loss of household and corporate wealth. The ensuing financial turmoil triggered a sharp contraction in the availability of finance for, among other things, international trade. Given the United States' position as the world's largest importer (by a wide margin), and with the United States and the United Kingdom running the world's largest and third-largest current account deficits, respectively, the abrupt decline in American and British domestic demand (and their associated inventory cycles) was bound to be mirrored in sharp economic downturns for countries whose growth had become increasingly dependent on exports.

The inherently North Atlantic nature of the financial crisis of 2007–2009 is also born out by the surprisingly contrasting experience of the Australian economy during this period.

Through most of the postwar period, Australia's financial and business cycles have been closely aligned with those of the United States. And although Australia's political cycles have not always mirrored those in the United States and Britain (indeed, it is striking how Australian and British electorates have swung in opposite directions since the 1980s), Australian policymakers have been significantly influenced by political and intellectual fashions and trends emanating from Britain and America. In particular, since the 1980s Australian government have for the most part been committed to the so-called Washington consensus of trade liberalization, privatization, and deregulation of financial and other markets. Moreover, most of Australia's major financial institutions have been managed by executives originally from, or with substantial experience gained in, the American or British markets for at least part of the 1990s or early 2000s. And there are other parallels.

Australian households have substantially increased their borrowing since the early 1990s—much more rapidly than their British or American peers. Australian residential real estate values have risen significantly over the same period. And Australia, like the United States and Britain, has persistently incurred large current account deficits since the 1990s; indeed, in the years leading up to the onset of the financial crisis, Australia's current account deficits had typically been the fourth or fifth largest, in absolute terms, in the world. Moreover, these deficits were financed predominantly by the overseas borrowings of the Australian banks.

Hence, it was widely expected that Australia would also experience a severe economic downturn once the financial crisis entered its darkest phase in the final months of 2008. This view intensified so much during the first half of 2009 that the Australian government's budget for the 2009–2010 financial year, presented to Parliament in mid-May 2009, was the first ever to have been predicated on a forecast of recession.

Yet, contrary to widely held expectations, Australia did not experience a recession, at least not in the commonly defined sense of consecutive quarters of negative real GDP growth. The Australian economy contracted only in the fourth quarter of 2008. And although unemployment rose by nearly two percentage points from its precrisis low, it remained below 6 percent—well short of official forecasts that it would peak at 8.5 percent.

Australia's resilience during the financial crisis and the global recession reflects a combination of good luck and good management. Australia's experience also provides some lessons for other countries in managing a financial crisis and its economic consequences. That said, the particular features of the 2007–2009 crisis also include some warnings for Australia against any complacent self-belief that it is intrinsically immune from financial or other shocks emanating from other sources.

Australia's Banking System Was Managed and Regulated Differently

Australia's banks had minimal exposure to the "toxic assets" that crippled the balance sheets of, and public confidence in, many American and European banks. None of the four major Australian banks had their credit rating downgraded during the financial crisis, with the result that they are now among fewer than a dozen banks worldwide that are rated AA or better. And no Australian financial institution required a taxpayer-funded bailout.

Australian banks managed the asset side of their balance sheets more conservatively than many of their American and British peers, in part because of the institutional memory of the difficulties that many of them experienced in the early 1990s. The Australian banking system was opened to foreign competition and substantially deregulated during the 1980s. This prompted a period of rapid and in many cases injudicious growth in lending, which ultimately led to the collapse of a number of "second-tier" financial institutions (including several banks owned by Australian state governments) and "near-death" experiences for two of the four major banks in the early 1990s. These experiences, together with some subsequent smaller ones (including those arising from the Asian financial crisis later in the decade), imparted a greater degree of caution on the part of Australian bank managers than turned out to be the case in the United States or Britain.

Australian banks were also arguably under less pressure than their peers in other countries to adopt lower credit standards in pursuit of higher shareholder returns. Nor was there as much pressure to add riskier but higher-yielding assets to their securities portfolios, because they were achieving improvements in profitability from the consumer and funds management sides of their businesses.

The Australian banking system was also, for the most part, more effectively supervised and regulated from the standpoint of avoiding the risks that precipitated the North Atlantic financial crisis. In the late 1990s Australia's system of prudential supervision and regulation of financial institutions was reconfigured along the lines of the Canadian system. The new system established a single regulator for all approved deposit-taking intermediaries, thus limiting the scope for "regulatory arbitrage" that the US system of multiple regulators provides. In 2001 the collapse of HIH Insurance, the largest Australian insurance company, prompted the Australian Prudential Regulation Authority (APRA) to take a more skeptical and assertive approach to its task. Following the HIH collapse, the APRA could in no sense be described as "light-handed" after the fashion of the UK Financial Services Authority.

The Australian banking system did have an Achilles' heel in the form of a relatively low deposit-to-loan ratio and, correspondingly, an unusually high level of dependence on "wholesale funding," especially from offshore. This rendered Australian banks potentially vulnerable to the drying up of international liquidity. As such, the Australian government's prompt extension of a guarantee of banks' wholesale borrowing after the collapse of Lehman Brothers was critical in preventing the loss of liquidity.

Australia's Residential Property Market Rested on Firmer Foundation

House prices in Australia's major cities rose by about 150 percent over the twelve years preceding the onset of the financial crisis—more than in the United States or Canada, but less than in a number of European countries, including the Netherlands, Norway, the United Kingdom, Spain, and especially Ireland. The rise in Australian house prices was paralleled (and in large part driven) by a significant increase in household borrowing, which, scaled against household income, was somewhat larger than in most other advanced economies. Nonetheless, the Australian residential property price boom had more solid fundamental underpinnings than the contemporaneous booms in many other countries.

In particular, the rise in Australian house prices owed almost nothing to temporarily higher rates of home ownership, as turned out to be the case in the United States. Although Australian governments of both political persuasions have proclaimed higher rates of home ownership as a policy objective since the 1950s, the means by which they have sought to achieve it—for the most part by providing first-time homebuyers with cash grants or relief from taxes on real estate purchases—have been spectacularly unsuccessful. These efforts have served more to increase house prices than to increase home-ownership rates, which reached 71 percent in 1966 but have remained in a range of 68–71 percent ever since.

Australian policymakers (unlike those in the United States) have never put pressure on lending institutions to relax their credit standards in order to increase home-ownership rates, either in general or among specific segments of the population; and while competitive pressures resulted in some relaxation of credit standards in the 1990s and 2000s, the practice never went as far as it did in the United States. "Nonconforming" mortgages (as subprime mortgages were known in Australia) never amounted to more than 1 percent of all mortgages outstanding, while "low-doc" and "no-doc" mortgages (the Australian approximation of "Alt-A" loans) peaked at about 8 percent of all mortgages.

More generally, very few Australian households took out mortgages that they were unable to service as interest rates rose. Lending at very high loan-to-valuation ratios did not become as commonplace as it was in the

United States or Britain, partly because a much smaller proportion of mortgages are securitized in Australia than in the United States (thereby giving Australian loan originators greater capacity and more incentive to satisfy themselves as to the ability of borrowers to meet their commitments—an incentive that is reinforced by Australian consumer credit laws). Furthermore, Australian interest rates were not left as low for as long in the early 2000s, as was the case in the United States and Britain. The Reserve Bank of Australia began tightening monetary policy in 2002, and the initial increases in interest rates in 2002 and 2003 were accompanied by explicit "jawboning" from Reserve Bank officials about the risks involved in debt-funded speculative investment in real estate.

Moreover, although the typical Australian mortgage is for a term of twenty-five years, most mortgages are paid off much more quickly, partly because the Australian tax system, which does not allow interest on owner-occupier mortgages as a deduction, provides a strong incentive to do so. Hence, although the ratio of Australian household debt to income is relatively high by international standards, the ratio of debt to assets is not.

The upshot has been that, even though Australian standard variable mortgage rates peaked at just under 10 percent in mid-2008, the proportion of Australian mortgages classified as seriously delinquent peaked at less than three-quarters of one percentage point, compared with 9.7 percent (at last count) in the United States. The rapid decline in (variable) mortgage interest rates between October 2008 and April 2009, combined with the relatively small increase in unemployment, also helped to significantly reduce "mortgage stress." This, in turn, has meant far less downward pressure on house prices from "distressed sellers" or foreclosures.

The other fundamental factor differentiating the Australian residential property market from its US counterpart (in particular) is that since the 1990s it has been characterized by an excess of underlying demand over supply. The former has been driven by relatively high and (until 2000) rising levels of net immigration, while the latter has been constrained (despite what might appear to foreign observers to be an almost limitless supply of land relative to Australia's population) by restrictive land use (or zoning) policies of urban local governments and high "up-front" charges that are imposed on developers by some state and local authorities for the provision of suburban infrastructure. The persistent "excess demand" for housing in Australia has, together with the absence of a material volume of forced selling, helped to keep a floor under house prices, even in circumstances where would-be buyers have been constrained by relatively high interest rates or by the uncertainty created by the financial crisis.

The resilience of the Australian housing market has been an important factor differentiating Australia's experience during the financial crisis from that of other advanced economies. It has contributed to the relatively benign bad debt experience of the Australian banks, and has limited the erosion of personal wealth incurred by Australian households.

Contraction in Global Manufacturing-Trade Had Little Impact on Australia

As noted earlier, one of the principal channels through which the North Atlantic financial crisis was transmitted to the global economy was via the dramatic contraction in trade, particularly in manufactured goods, that was prompted by the abrupt decline in discretionary spending in the United States and Britain, and by the associated fierce inventory cycle that followed the collapse of Lehman Brothers.

However, this sharp trade downturn had very little impact on Australia as a result of the unusual (for an advanced economy) composition and orientation of Australia's exports. North America and Western Europe account for only 15 percent of Australia's merchandise exports, with Asia taking 70 percent (within that total, non-Japan Asia makes up just over 50 percent); thus, the sharp contraction in American and European imports had little direct impact on Australia's exports.

From a different standpoint, manufactures represent only about 16 percent of Australia's total exports; hence, although Australia's export of manufactures fell by as much as those of most other advanced economies, the decline had far less impact on Australia's overall export performance than it did on that of most other advanced economies.

Australia's commodity exports, which account for around 60 percent of the total, were among the major beneficiaries of China's massive stimulus program that was launched in November 2008. China takes over 20 percent (by value) of Australia's total exports, including over 70 percent of Australia's iron ore, nearly 50 percent of its nickel, and 30 percent of its copper exports. These commodities are, for the most part, inputs into China's domestic demand, not semi-processed items that are used in China's exports to advanced economies (which make up much of the exports sold by many of China's other Asian trading partners). China in effect sets the price that Australia's other markets pay for these and other commodities, and in particular for coal, which is Australia's largest export (of which China takes 14 percent).

The prices of Australia's key export commodities, as well as its volume of iron ore and coal exports, began declining sharply from their mid-2008 peak as the extent of China's economic slowdown became clear. However, prices began to recover through 2009 as China's stimulus measures started to have their intended effect. By late 2010, the 38 percent decline in Australia's export commodity prices between July 2008 and May 2009 had been completely reversed.

Australia's relatively mild experience with the downturn in international trade was also aided by a decline of more than 25 percent in the trade-weighted value of the Australian dollar between mid-2008 and the first few months of 2009, although this decline has since been more than entirely reversed. This echoed the role that large swings in the value of the Australian dollar had in cushioning the impact of the Asian financial crisis on Australia's trade in the 1990s.

There is little doubt that if China's response to the downturn in its economy had been less effective, Australia's experience with the financial crisis would have been less benign. It also follows that if China were to experience a more sustained downturn at some point in the future, the impact on Australia may be greater than that of the North Atlantic financial crisis turned out to be. Australia could also suffer "collateral damage" if any serious trade frictions emerge between China and major Western economies.

Australian Macroeconomic Policy Responses Had a Substantial Impact

The final reason for Australia's relatively benign experience during the financial crisis was the scale of the policy response to the crisis by Australia's monetary and fiscal authorities. After the collapse of Lehman Brothers, the Reserve Bank responded to the marked deterioration in financial conditions and economic prospects with large and rapid reductions in interest rates. It was well positioned to make such cuts because it had been steadily tightening monetary policy up to April 2008. Over four consecutive board meetings, the Reserve Bank slashed its cash rate by a total of 375 basis points. Reflecting the variable-rate structure of most of Australia's mortgages, the bulk of these reductions in official interest rates were passed on to homebuyers (although businesses benefitted to a rather lesser extent). As noted earlier, the sharp decline in interest rates contributed significantly to the resilience of the Australian housing market. Indeed, Australian house prices rose by nearly 18 percent between the end of 2008 and the second quarter of 2010, although they have since flattened out.

Australia was also well placed to implement a large fiscal policy response to the downturn as a result of the string of budget surpluses that had been accumulated by the previous conservative administration led by John Howard. Together with some large asset sales, these surpluses resulted in the Australian government being a net creditor to the tune of 4 percent of GDP immediately prior to the onset of the financial crisis. Thus, although the succession of fiscal stimulus measures announced between October 2008 and May 2009 amounted to 5.8 percent of GDP (the largest of any advanced-economy member of the G-20, other than South Korea), the Australian government's net debt is expected to peak at 6 percent of GDP in the 2011–2012 fiscal year (well below the peak of 94.2 percent expected for the major advanced economies in 2015). This makes Australia one of only five (of twenty-nine) advanced economies that will, according to the IMF, require little or no medium-term adjustment in order to achieve fiscal sustainability.

Two other features of Australia's fiscal policy response to the crisis are worth noting for the purpose of making comparisons to other countries. First, the response was unusually timely. The first stimulus package was announced in early October 2008, at the beginning of what turned out to be Australia's only quarter of negative real GDP growth, while the second was announced in February 2009 before it had been confirmed that the economy had indeed contracted in the final quarter of 2008. This stands in marked contrast to Australia's previous experience with discretionary fiscal policy. During the recession of the early 1990s, the fiscal response came too late to prevent a contraction and lingered after the recession was over, which contributed to upward pressure on interest rates during the recovery phase (an experience that consciously informed official advice flowing to the Australian government in late 2008). It was also in marked contrast to the timing of fiscal policy measures in most other advanced economies during the 2008 downturn, which was in most cases already underway before governments began to implement significant fiscal measures. Of course, Australia had more warning of the impending downturn than countries at the epicenter of the financial crisis, where the initial downturn came on with inherently less advance notice.

Second, Australia's fiscal measures were intentionally crafted with a view toward maximizing their short-term impact on economic activity and employment. Australia eschewed cuts in income or sales taxes. Instead, the Australian federal government channeled money to households through what were described as "bonuses" to recipients of age and disability pensions and family benefit payments; in a second round, money was directed to low- and middle-income taxpayers through a "tax bonus," on the grounds that such payments were more likely to be spent than conventional tax cuts (the subsequent buoyancy in consumer spending lends support to this contention).

Another major element of Australia's fiscal stimulus was a series of "small-ticket" infrastructure spending programs, including the construction of new libraries or assembly halls at almost every elementary school across Australia, an expanded social housing program, and subsidies for the installation of ceiling insulation and solar hot-water heating in homes. The goal of these programs was to ensure that the stimulus flowed into the economy broadly and quickly, by obviating the time-consuming planning and approvals processes associated with more traditional "big-ticket" infrastructure projects. However, the efficacy of some of these programs was compromised by inadequate design, poor administration and supervision, cost overruns, and project delays, leaving the overall stimulus package open to accusations of being larger than required, representing poor value for money, and continuing to provide stimulus when it was no longer needed.

Despite these flaws, the announcement of the succession of fiscal measures, combined with the large reductions in interest rates, had a larger-than-expected indirect positive effect on consumer and business confidence. And as business confidence improved, employers became more willing to use the greater flexibility provided by the labor market reforms of the 1990s and early 2000s to manage their overall labor costs by reducing average hours worked—a switch from the more traditional means of mass retrenchments— which contributed to containing the rise in unemployment.

Lessons from Australia's Experience

Australia's somewhat benign experience during the North Atlantic financial crisis and the "Great Recession" of 2008–2009, especially when compared with that of other advanced economies, owes something to good fortune. Australian policymakers cannot take the credit for the fact that Australia is well endowed with mineral and energy resources, and thus stood to gain substantially from the efficacy of China's stimulus measures; nor can policymakers claim responsibility for Australia's minimal exposure to the global downturn in trade in manufactured goods.

However, current and previous Australian policymakers can be credited with having done more to safeguard Australia's financial system from many of the excesses that, as we now see all too clearly, characterized the bubble that preceded the onset of the crisis. These policymakers created a more comprehensive and effective system for the supervision and regulation of financial intermediaries. They proved themselves willing to learn from earlier mistakes, and their system was more pragmatic and less influenced by intellectual fashions than those developed in many other countries.

Australia's central bank was more willing to use the instruments at its disposal to "lean against" the emergence of destabilizing speculative pressures than many of its peers—although the extent to which it should do so remains a subject of intense and unresolved debate, including within the Reserve Bank itself. Previous Australian governments, unlike their contemporaries in most other Western countries, were willing to run budget surpluses during cyclical upswings, thereby allowing the government of then Prime Minister Kevin Rudd much greater room—which it was willing to use—to deploy fiscal policy aggressively to cushion the impact of the most recent global downturn.

More broadly, since the mid-1980s Australian government has pursued a reform agenda that has enhanced the capacity of individual businesses, and the economy as a whole, to absorb shocks more readily than had been the case throughout much of the twentieth century. Pursuit of this reform agenda has required Australian government to resist pressure from industries and constituencies with strong vested interests in the established order of things—pressure to which governments in many other countries have perhaps been more sensitive.

Shocks of a different nature or provenance than the North Atlantic financial crisis of 2007–2009 may well have produced more severe outcomes for Australia. As acknowledged earlier, Australia stands to be more significantly buffeted by an abrupt economic downturn in China, especially if a downturn were to occur before Australia has rebuilt its fiscal resources and while the memory of the most recent shock is still prominent in people's memories.

But Australia's experience during the North Atlantic financial crisis suggests that it is possible for "good policy" to reduce the risks an economy faces and to respond effectively to the risks that it cannot eliminate or avoid within the framework of a market-oriented economic system.

A somewhat ironic lesson from Australia's experience is that success in avoiding recession does not necessarily guarantee political success. In June 2010, Prime Minister Kevin Rudd was removed from office by his own Labor Party after a sharp decline in his (and his government's) previously very high standing in opinion polls. He lost popularity as a result of his inability to "sell" his resistance to a carbon emissions trading scheme and a complex and controversial supertax on mining company profits. His successor, Julia Gillard, proved unable to capitalize on Australia's relatively benign experience during the global financial crisis or to counter Opposition Leader Tony Abbott's effective campaign, which focused on government deficits and debt. The Labor Party lost its parliamentary majority in the August 2010 elections, and was obliged to forge agreements with two independents and a newly elected member of the Green Party in order to ensure its ability to pass a budget and survive "no confidence" votes.

12

THE FUTURE OF THE US DOLLAR AS A RESERVE CURRENCY

John Greenwood

Two topics that are widely discussed in the media and among investors are the possible displacement, or even demise, of the US dollar as an international reserve currency within a few years, as well as what currency might replace it. However, in order to comment sensibly on the prospects for the international reserve role of US currency, and to answer the question about what might replace it, we first need to set out the essential characteristics of an international reserve currency. This chapter will first review the historical process by which the US dollar emerged as the preeminent international reserve currency, drawing from that experience a list of the prerequisites for reserve status. Having established these necessary conditions, we can then proceed to ask which existing national currencies could replace the US dollar, and whether a synthetic currency could fulfill the necessary conditions. Finally, the chapter will look at the conditions that the Chinese renminbi (RMB) must fulfill in order to become a candidate for international reserve currency status.

The Decline of Sterling and the Rise of the US Dollar as the Leading Reserve Currency

During the nineteenth century under the gold standard and into the early years of the twentieth century, the British pound sterling was the preeminent international currency. Its importance is illustrated by traders' and financiers' tendency to denominate and finance trade and capital transactions in sterling—even for transactions that may not have involved a British counterparty. For example, textiles exported from Japan to the United States were often financed by means of bills drawn on British banks in London. This role in the financing of private transactions did not automatically make sterling "the" international reserve currency. Gold being the primary international reserve, and the Bank of England being at the center of the gold standard, credits on London were thought to be as good as gold. The key reason for sterling's preeminence was the fact that Britain was the largest economy in the world and was also a major creditor nation. However, during the early decades of the twentieth century, several factors caused sterling to lose its dominance.

First and foremost, the United States gradually began to replace the United Kingdom as the leading global economy between roughly 1890 and 1920 in terms of GDP, trade volumes, and so on. Importantly, the Federal Reserve was created in 1913, and by the 1920s bills or acceptances on New York (in US dollars) used as a means of financing international trade were as important as bills or acceptances on London (in sterling) had been before World War I. Second, the United Kingdom ceased to be a creditor nation due to the financial burden of the two world wars (1914–1918 and 1939–1945). Third, when the postwar monetary system was planned at Bretton Woods in 1944 and launched with the IMF and the World Bank as its core institutions, the system was built around the US dollar—not the pound sterling—as the key currency, with the dollar convertible to gold at a fixed price. Moreover, sterling's reputation suffered significantly from the 30 percent devaluation of 1949 (although a number of other nations also devalued in line with Britain) and the subsequent exchange controls imposed within the sterling area. Years of dismal economic performance, characterized by the stop-and-go policies of the postwar years and the devaluations of 1967 and 1972, did nothing to restore sterling's pre-1914 supremacy.

Consequently, in the post–World War II era, most currencies—with some exceptions, including the currencies of the remaining British, French, and Belgian colonies—were pegged to the US dollar. The dollar, therefore, became the key "intervention" currency of most nations, and in turn the main currency in which other economies held their reserves.

Domestic Currency Characteristics

From this brief historical sketch we can derive the essential characteristics of domestic and international currencies. The classical requirements for domestic money are that it should fulfill three functions:

1. Unit of account
2. Medium of exchange
3. Store of value

But clearly an international reserve currency that is used outside its domestic market (for example, for trade invoicing, capital remittances, reserve holdings, or as an exchange rate anchor for other currencies) must fulfill more than these three functions. The additional attributes necessary for a currency to perform international functions are listed below.

International Currency Requirements

In order for a currency to be an international currency, it must clearly fulfill the three basic requirements listed above. It needs to meet at least two additional conditions to be an international currency:

4. It must be available beyond the borders of the home economy. This means more than simply being available for small transactions (for example, for conversions by tourists or business travelers). The currency must have the capacity to be deposited, loaned, and widely acceptable in large-scale transactions such as remittances, trade, and capital payments beyond local borders—the same way sterling was used in the nineteenth century by traders and investors not connected to Britain.
5. It must be fully convertible. An international reserve currency must be convertible for both current and capital account transactions, and it is desirable, though not imperative (as evident in the case of sterling before exchange control was abolished in 1979), that there be no restrictions—explicit or implicit—on such activity.

These two characteristics do not automatically make an international currency an international reserve currency, however. To highlight the difference between the two, consider the Hong Kong dollar and the Singapore dollar. Both are used outside of their own domestic economies, but neither currency qualifies as having the status of an international reserve currency. It is true, however, that the Hong Kong dollar is the currency to which the Macau pataca is pegged, and the Singapore dollar is the currency to which the Brunei dollar is pegged. Both currencies meet conditions 4 and 5, but these conditions are clearly not sufficient for international reserve status.

International Reserve Currency Status

To be not only an international currency, but also an international reserve currency, it must satisfy four additional requirements:

6. Creditor status. Creditor status is essentially an extension of the store-of-value concept, except that it is derived primarily from the strength or weakness of the management of the government's fiscal accounts, as well as the economy's net international balance of assets and liabilities, rather than from the monetary discipline of the central bank. Creditor status is arguably required for both international currency status and reserve currency status. However, there are numerous examples of currencies being used for long periods outside their own territory when the government's creditor status was questionable, as was the case with the French franc and the Spanish peseta. In addition, the British pound continued to be used internationally long after the country lost its position as the world's major creditor nation in the aftermath of World War I. Nevertheless, Britain's deteriorating credit status significantly contributed to the displacement of the pound sterling and its replacement by the US dollar.

7. Economic size. The size and international role of the economy issuing a particular currency plays an important role because a large economy will naturally have a large number of transactions—both current and capital—with other economies. The emergence of the US dollar and its replacement of the pound sterling were closely associated with the growth of the US economy, which gradually approached and overtook the United Kingdom in terms of GDP. As a corollary, it seems unlikely that there will ever be more than a handful of major international reserve currencies, and that in general these select few will normally com-

prise the currencies of the leading economies. For example, there are currently four major reserve currencies: the US dollar, the euro, the Japanese yen, and the UK pound sterling. These currencies represent, respectively, the first-, second-, third-, and fifth-largest economies or economic zones in the world when ranked by 2008 GDP.[1] The country missing from this list—the fourth-largest economy—is China.

8. Developed financial system. Partly by virtue of the size of its economy and its advanced state of technological development, and partly by virtue of its legal and regulatory systems, the United States has a sophisticated and highly developed financial system. Consequently, the US dollar benefits from a large market of low-risk and highly liquid securities. Foreign central banks are able to utilize these securities as investment vehicles for their reserves, particularly US Treasury bonds and bills, as well as agency securities. The liquidity of US dollar instruments also benefits from network externalities (see 9 below). US government and agency securities are easy to hold, there are minimal restrictions, and they are easy to buy and sell, even on a large scale. In short, US dollar security markets are highly convenient for individual, corporate, and official or government users around the world. These attributes largely explain the role of the US currency as the primary vehicle for holding foreign exchange reserves, as the most widely traded currency in international private trade and capital transactions, and as the leading currency in global foreign exchange transactions.

9. Network effects. As explained earlier, the US dollar did not start out as the world's reserve currency. Much as English did not intentionally become the world's most widely spoken language, the dollar did not become the world's leading reserve currency by deliberate policy. The supremacy of the dollar is, like the supremacy of the English language, the result of gradual usage and experience. Like a common language, the US dollar enjoys what economists call "network externalities"—the greater the number of people who transact using dollars, the more beneficial this is to users, and the more dominant it becomes. Consequently, the US dollar deposit, loan, and funding markets outside the United States are far larger than those of any other currency traded outside its home borders; this effectively underwrites the continued financing of trade and capital transactions in dollars around the world.

To undermine these network effects and simultaneously create a truly viable alternative reserve currency would therefore require both a dramatic shock to the dollar and the ready availability of a realistic alternative. However, a major erosion of any of the nine conditions listed above could undermine confidence in the US dollar, threatening its role as a currency for international transactions and as a reserve currency.

Feasible Alternatives to the US Dollar

Having established the nine characteristics required of an international reserve currency, we may now ask what alternatives there might be to the US dollar, either now or in the medium-term future. Two broad categories are possible: (1) another existing national currency in widespread use, such as the euro, the Japanese yen, the British pound, or even the Chinese RMB; or (2) a synthetic currency designed for such a purpose, of which the Special Drawing Rights (SDR) would be the leading candidate, as was hinted at in March 2009 by Governor Zhou Xiaochuan of the People's Bank of China.[2] We will review the three main candidate currencies in turn, followed by the SDR, before considering the RMB.

Existing National Currencies

The euro has been available for payments and deposits since 1999, and it has been in circulation as a physical currency since 2002. By the end of 2009, sixteen countries had adopted the euro in place of their former national currency. It is also widely used in European Union economies that have not yet formally adopted the euro but are likely to do so. It is also used by a number of prospective members of the European Union, such as Scandinavia and the Eastern European and Balkan states.

Despite its youth, the euro meets most of conditions 1–9, except perhaps 8 (that is, it is not quite a developed financial system). Euro capital markets are still fragmented despite the rapid evolution and large size of the eurozone economy (around 300 million people). Depending on the particular financial instrument, liquidity varies widely. This is important because holders of international reserves cannot simply hold euros (that is, deposits at private commercial banks); they need to hold highly liquid, euro-denominated securities that are preferably issued by governments.

As shown in Figure 12.1, the largest single issuer of euro-denominated government securities is the Italian government, with $2.61 trillion outstanding in 2008. Since Italian public debt is 114.5 percent of GDP, many central banks would hesitate to hold such securities. The Italian population is aging rapidly, which implies its pension and health care obligations are rising rapidly, threatening its credit rating, and the Italian government lacks a reputation for budgetary discipline.

The next largest issuer is Germany with $2.54 trillion in government debt outstanding. But German government debt is predominantly long-term debt, with only about 10 percent of the outstanding stock having

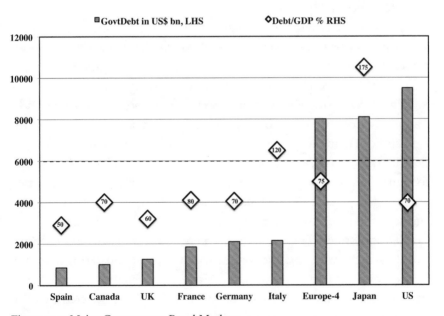

Figure 12.1 Major Government Bond Markets
Note: The chart compares major European government issuers of debt with government debt issues by the United States, Japan, the United Kingdom, and Canada. The bars show the outstanding government debt on the left-hand scale in US$ billion, while the diamonds show government debt as a percent of GDP on the right-hand scale. The horizontal line marks the 100 percent debt-to-GDP ratio.
Source: OECD and Invesco Calculations

maturities of less than one year. In addition, German institutional buyers tend to hold to maturity, so the secondary market is much less developed than its counterparts in the United States or the United Kingdom, which means that German bonds are less liquid than US Treasuries or UK gilts.

Figure 12.1 also shows the smaller amounts of euro-denominated government debt issued by France ($2.18 trillion) and Spain ($0.75 trillion), which are the next two largest issuers. While the total outstanding euro-denominated government debt issued by the four largest European economies (Germany, France, Italy, and Spain) is $8.08 trillion, in practice the market is more fragmented and much less liquid than the market in US government securities—essentially because there is no federal European government issuing sovereign debt for the area. In contrast to the $8 trillion issued by the four largest European issuers, US government debt totaled $10.1 trillion in 2008, including about $2 trillion of short-term debt (20 percent).

Japan has a very large government debt at $8.4 trillion—only slightly less than that of the United States—of which about one-third is short-term debt. However, there are several problems with Japanese securities as a basis for the leading international reserve currency. First, the extremely low yields on Japanese government bonds and short-term debt since the mid-1990s are a major drawback for investors. Second, the tendency of the Ministry of Finance to engage in "guidance" of the Japanese currency and debt markets also acts as a deterrent to prospective holders. As a result, foreigners are minority holders of Japanese government debt, accounting for only 5–6 percent of outstanding issues. Third, Japanese government (gross) debt is approaching 200 percent of GDP, the highest among the OECD economies. The low level of interest rates in Japan, the high national savings ratio, and the low demand for credit in Japan have prevented any financing problem so far. However, foreign official holders of yen securities would wish to be confident about the future creditworthiness of the Japanese government. The slow growth rate of the Japanese economy combined with the rapid aging of Japanese society would be distinct negatives in any assessment of the attractiveness of Japanese government securities.

Finally, the UK government had a total outstanding debt of only about $1.5 trillion in 2008, although it has grown rapidly since then. The market is therefore significantly smaller than that of the larger eurozone countries, and less than the current size of China's foreign exchange reserves. However, the secondary market in UK government bonds (gilts) is much better developed and more liquid than that of the eurozone or Japan. Nevertheless, another problem for sterling is that it has tended to be viewed as a volatile currency, which makes it unreliable as a store of value.

Given these shortcomings, a provisional conclusion is that despite the recent depreciation in the US unit—which may lead to some temporary diversification of reserves away from the US dollar—there is no other existing major national currency that is currently in a position to dislodge the US dollar from its preeminent role as "the" international reserve currency.

Synthetic Currency: SDR or Other "Basket"

The leading synthetic currency candidate is the Special Drawing Right issued by the IMF. The SDR is essentially a synthetic "basket" of currencies that is comprised of four existing currencies: the US dollar, the Japanese yen, the euro, and the British pound sterling.

There are many problems with the use of a composite currency as an international reserve currency, and these problems apply to the SDR or any basket arrangement. They are as follows:

1. In international trade and financial transactions, settlement or payment is normally specified in an existing single, mutually agreed-upon currency, not in a synthetic currency. Few sellers will want or agree to receive payment in a bundle of currencies, and few buyers will find it convenient to assemble all the component currencies. Normally they will settle in dollars or euros that are converted at the appropriate rate against the composite or basket currency. If such is the case, why not just stick with the preferred currency and hedge the value of the transaction in the forward foreign exchange markets?

2. Baskets are invariably subject to changes in composition (changing weights, changing methods of computation, etc.) or even manipulation.

3. Interest rates are hard to compute in synthetic currencies because they must be computed from all the constituent currencies at all the relevant maturities.

4. Futures markets in the composite currency, or commodities (such as oil) priced in synthetic currencies, will not be as efficient because the interest rates that permit arbitrage between spot and future values will themselves be a composite of interest rates in all the constituent currencies. This is a major reason why Hong Kong adopted a peg to the US dollar rather than pegging to a basket of currencies.

Ultimately, participants in international trade and financial transactions would rather transact with a single, convertible, widely traded currency with deep and active domestic money markets than with a synthetic currency. For these reasons I suspect that proposals to replace the US dollar with the SDR will simply run into the sand.

Specific Problems with the SDR

The quantity of SDRs issued is not tied to the quantity of the SDR's underlying component currencies; it is essentially a unit of account for trading obligations in the constituent currencies. At the end of 2008 there was SDR 21 billion outstanding that had been issued by the IMF, but the United States and the European Union have an effective veto on new issuances through their voting rights in the IMF. However, in 2009 the G-20 agreed to authorize a general issuance of SDR 161.2 billion (US$250 billion), and a special issuance of SDR 21.5 billion that was first proposed in 1997 was also approved. These issuances involved distribution to new members such as China and Russia, as well as existing members such as Brazil, India, and South Korea.

The SDR is currently only used by national monetary authorities, the IMF, the World Bank, and the Bank for International Settlements. Most transactions in SDRs are in fact between national monetary authorities and the IMF itself. In order to become a meaningful international currency, the SDR needs to be widely used by private-sector firms and individuals.

The SDR is priced daily,[3] and could be priced continuously, but the fact that it is not widely used suggests that there are good reasons not to use a synthetic currency. Most holdings of US dollars outside the United States are by private parties, and financial markets are operated largely by and for private parties, with governments and central banks taking advantage of market arrangements. If the SDR were to become a truly international currency, it would need to become a vehicle of choice by private parties.

The RMB as a Potential International Reserve Currency

Turning to consider future possible reserve currencies, what would have to happen for the Chinese RMB to emerge as an international reserve currency?

Viewed in terms of the nine criteria for an international reserve currency, China and the RMB currently meet only five (unit of account, medium of exchange, store of value, economic size, and creditor status), while the remaining four (availability beyond home borders, full convertibility, developed financial system, and network effects) have yet to be met. In terms of its government debt market, China's government and central bank bond market combined is still relatively small, with approximately $1.4 trillion outstanding in 2008, of which about half (mainly the central bank's sterilization issuance) was short term. Fiscal policy has generally been conservative, and the debt-to-GDP ratio is low, but the Chinese capital markets, including those for government securities, are still underdeveloped. Liquidity among domestic holders is limited as most purchasers hold until maturity. Foreign exchange controls mean that, other than for tourists' needs, the RMB is only available on a very limited basis to nonresidents. Access to domestic, onshore RMB equity and debt markets by foreigners or by foreign entities is subject to qualified foreign institutional investors quotas, while onshore RMB deposit accounts at banks are simply not available to nonresidents. Liberalization does not appear to be imminent for the onshore RMB markets. Thus, the RMB does not currently meet the criteria for becoming an international reserve currency.

However, in the offshore arena, the market for RMB has seen some significant developments, and there could be further substantial changes in the next decade. Numerous experiments are currently under way, including bilateral swaps between the Chinese central bank and foreign central banks (one side of which is RMB), and reciprocal invoicing of trade transactions between a number of partner economies and the People's Republic of China (again involving RMB).

But the main test-bed for gradual liberalization of the RMB is Hong Kong. For several years Hong Kong residents have been able to accumulate RMB deposits (at a limited rate), and since July 2010 several RMB investment products such as RMB-denominated bonds or money market funds have become available in the territory. Also since July 2010 Hong Kong banks have been allowed to offer settlement facilities for trade transactions (but not capital transactions) denominated in RMB, together with limited deposit and lending facilities. For example, loans to companies–whether resident in Hong Kong or not–are permitted if related to trade transactions, but not loans to individuals. These opportunities are important for Hong Kong's banks, but the overall market in offshore RMB will remain restricted in terms of size and type of transactions permitted. These transactions will not place the RMB in the same league as US dollar transactions in London or Frankfurt where there are no such restrictions.

The gradual internationalization of the RMB must be understood in the broader context of the limited convertibility of the currency. The RMB is convertible only on current account (for trade and certain service transactions on production of the underlying documentation), while all capital transactions are subject to strict and detailed scrutiny and control. Consequently these tentative steps to create an offshore market in RMB are on a small scale and are far from allowing the RMB to become an internationally traded currency in the full sense of the term. Nevertheless, China's government is plainly intent on achieving both a more developed domestic capital market and a more internationalized currency. In summary, China's financial system will require many fundamental reforms and an extended period of development before the currency can become a serious contender for the role of international reserve currency. In order for the RMB to compete with—let alone replace—the US dollar as the world's primary international reserve currency, it is clear that the Chinese authorities still have a long march ahead of them.

Conclusion

It is clear that none of the other leading currencies in the world today are in a position to replace the US dollar as an international reserve currency. On the contrary, the US dollar is likely to remain the dominant international currency for many years, both for private transactions and for official uses such as intervention and reserve currency holding. In private-sector transactions, the US currency has enormous advantages over other currencies, such as global usage that is supported by network externalities and a leading role in commodity markets. The international role of the euro will surely expand, but the lack of a federal European debt market means that the euro-sovereign debt markets are likely to remain relatively small and fragmented. This constitutes a significant barrier to the euro replacing the dollar. The Japanese yen and the pound sterling are even less likely to challenge the dollar.

We can also conclude that synthetic currencies or basket arrangements such as the SDR will not displace individual national currencies due to all the inherent problems of pricing, trading, and settling in composite currencies in private-sector markets. The practical difficulties to be overcome when introducing such a composite are huge, and they should not be underestimated. The SDR is therefore likely to remain restricted to a unit-of-account role among a limited number of supranational or official financial institutions such as the IMF and central banks.

Finally, notwithstanding the current phase of weakness in the value of the US unit, and the recent experiments in creating a limited offshore market for RMB in Hong Kong, the RMB and Chinese authorities have a mountain to climb before there is any possibility of the RMB becoming an international currency, let alone an international reserve currency on a par with the US dollar.

Notes

1. The World Bank, "World Development Indicators 2008," http://data.worldbank.org/indicator/NY.GDP.MKTP.CD (accessed August 5, 2010).

2. Zhou Xiaochuan, "Reform the International Monetary System" (speech, March 23, 2009), http://www.bis.org/review/r090402c.pdf (accessed November 28, 2010).

3. The International Monetary Fund, "SDR Valuation," http://www.imf.org/external/np/fin/data/rms_sdrv.aspx (accessed August 5, 2010). The SDR interest rate is determined weekly and is based on a weighted average of representative interest rates on short-term debt in the money markets of the SDR basket currencies.

1 3

WILL THE GOLD RALLY CONTINUE?

David Hale

Investor Uncertainty and New Investment Vehicles Drive
the Price of Gold to All-Time Highs

The price of gold recently reached new highs against all the
world's leading currencies. The enthusiasm for gold has been buoyed
by the creation of new investment vehicles such as exchange-traded funds
(ETFs) and investor apprehension about the global economy. The majority of G-7 countries are running unprecedented fiscal deficits. Central banks
have slashed interest rates to record lows while engaging in quantitative
easing to provide more liquidity for the financial markets. Many investors
fear that the combination of large fiscal deficits and central banks accommodation will ultimately set the stage for higher inflation. A few also fear
that the monetary stimulus will fail and set the stage for deflation instead.
At the beginning of the third quarter of 2010, the price level was falling in
some troubled European countries, such as Ireland and Greece. The core
inflation rate in the United States has dropped below 1.0 percent. If the
recent upturn in the G-7 countries is followed by a double dip, the deflation that has gripped Japan since 1996 could spread to other G-7
countries.

Gold has long been a magnet for investors who are confronting uncertainty. As the global financial crisis of 2008–2009 has bequeathed
unprecedented levels of fear and doubt, it is not surprising that gold should
rally. Nor is there any reason to expect the rally to end.

There will be no simple solution to the fiscal deficit problems in the G-7 countries. Political gridlock in the United States will make it impossible to achieve any breakthroughs without a bond buyer's strike and large rise in long-term bond yields. Japan's public debt will soon exceed 200 percent of GDP. The Ministry of Finance has long advocated a large increase in the value-added tax, but such a large tax hike could drive the economy into recession. Japan would then have to pursue a major devaluation of the yen in order to bolster exports. The eurozone has been offering emergency financial assistance to its troubled debtor countries, such as Greece, Spain, and Portugal, but many fund managers remain skeptical that Greece can avoid a debt restructuring. They also have doubts about whether the Germans will be prepared to keep propping up the monetary union with large fiscal transfers. As a result, there are now serious doubts about whether the monetary union itself can survive. Such doubts will make it difficult for the euro to rival the dollar as a reserve currency. If investors also have concerns about the dollar, gold will be a natural alternative.

Supply-and-Demand Factors Are Bolstering the Price of Gold

In 2005 exchange-traded funds were launched in Australia and the United States, opening the door to gold investment by a whole new range of investors. ETFs allow investors to buy the precious metal without having to take actual delivery of it. ETFs now own nearly 2,000 tonnes of gold, and could easily own more than any central bank in the next ten years. As a result of ETFs, investor demand for gold rose to 1,893 tonnes in 2009 from 973 tonnes in 2008 and 612 tonnes in 2007. In the first quarter of 2010, investor demand was 349 tonnes. The rising investor demand for gold helped to compensate for a slump in jewelry demand as prices rose. The jewelry demand for gold fell to 1,759 tonnes in 2009 from 2,418 tonnes in 2007.

Despite the success of ETFs, there has been a surge of direct gold purchases by retail investors. At the Chicago Mercantile Exchange COMEX, investors took delivery of 39 percent more gold in 2010 than in 2009. The World Gold Council announced in June 2010 an investment of more than $9 million in BullionVault, which is a five-year-old London firm that stores $835 million of gold for clients. Sprott Asset Management in Toronto added about 250,000 ounces to its holdings at the Royal Canadian Mint in the first half of 2010. The fund allows investors to take possession of the metal by redeeming shares. Ex Oriente Lux AG, a German company, introduced vending machines for gold purchases in 2010. There has been a surge of German gold-buying this year because of unhappiness about the European Central Bank's decision to support the debt markets of Southern Europe. German retail investors own 7,500 tonnes of gold, which is more than the Bundesbank. The Austrian Mint sold 1.6 million ounces of gold in 2009 compared to 137,000 in 2007. The Rand Refinery expects to have sold one million Krugerrands in 2010. The current boom in retail demand for bullion products is not unprecedented, however. From 1974 to 1984 the Rand Refinery sold 2–6 million ounces of Krugerrands every year.

The supply of gold is also slowly declining. In 2008, global mining output of gold fell to just below 2,300 tonnes from 2,600 tonnes in 2001. It declined further in 2009. South African output has declined from 32 million ounces in 1970 to only about 6 million ounces. China has replaced South Africa as the world's leading gold producer, followed by the United States and Australia. South African output has suffered from an exhaustion of easy-to-mine reserves near the surface as well as power shortages. There have been many new gold discoveries in Africa since 2000, including in Mali, Tanzania, Burkina Faso, and Ghana, but they have not been able to compensate for the decline of South Africa. The rising demand for gold in China, India, and other developing countries will require gold prices to rise in order to encourage more exploration and development in the frontier countries of Africa and Central Asia. The Australian Bureau of Agriculture and Resource Economics estimates that Australia's gold output could have risen by 10 percent in 2010 to 239 tonnes. It projects a further rise to 269 tonnes by June 2011. Such output gains would make Australia the world's second-largest gold producer after China. China increased gold production by 11.3 percent in 2009 to 313.9 tonnes, and accounted for 13 percent of total gold output. In the first half of 2010, Chinese gold output was increasing at a 6 percent annual rate.

China has only a modest 4 percent share of global gold reserves (1,900 tonnes), and many of its mines are small, so there are limits to how it can expand output. The world's largest reserves are still in South Africa (6,000 tonnes), Australia (5,800 tonnes), Russia (5,000 tonnes), the United States (3,000), and Indonesia (3,000 tonnes). It is important to remember that 80 percent of the world's total gold stock of 165,000 tonnes has been mined since 1900. Two-thirds of that total has been mined since 1960. Gold production has doubled since 1980 despite the decline of South Africa. But the cash costs of producing gold have increased from nearly $200 per ounce in 2003 to over $500 in 2010. The rising cost of gold output will require a rising gold price to generate further gains in output.

Central Bank Demand Is the Most Bullish New Factor for Gold Strength

The most bullish new factor in the gold market is potential central bank demand. In 2009 and 2010, India, China, and Russia announced the purchase of several hundred tonnes of gold after a long period in which European central banks were regular sellers. Central bank gold holdings peaked at 38,347 tonnes in 1965 and declined to 29,726 tonnes in 2008. The United States has the largest reserves with 8,134 tonnes. Germany has 3,407 tonnes, and Italy and France each have just over 2,400 tonnes. The Netherlands has only 612 tonnes, but it is equal to 55 percent of the country's foreign exchange reserves compared to 65–68 percent for the other leading European holders.

UBS conducted a survey in mid-2010 that suggested that the central bank demand for gold could increase further. In the survey, UBS asked central bankers what the most important reserve asset would be in the future. Half of the officials said the US dollar would be, but 22 percent said gold. Bullion ranked well above the European currency and Asian currencies. UBS surveyed more than eighty central bank reserve managers, sovereign wealth funds, and multilateral institutions with over $8 billion of assets at its annual seminar for sovereign institutions. In the run-up to the G-20 summit in Korea in November 2010, World Bank President Robert Zoellick suggested that the world should move toward a multipolar currency system with some form of anchor in gold. He did not ask for a return to the old gold standard, but rather acknowledged that gold could play some role. The fact that many central banks in developing countries now plan to buy gold suggests that it could be gradually re-monetized.

The most important new player could potentially be China. China announced in 2009 that it had increased its gold reserves from a long-standing figure of 600 tonnes to 1,054 tonnes. Some government officials have called on the central bank to increase its gold holdings to 10,000 tonnes by 2020. In early 2010 China Investment Corporation, Beijing's newest sovereign wealth fund, revealed a $155 million investment in the SPDR gold trust—an ETF. As China has over $2.3 trillion of foreign exchange reserves, it could expand its gold holdings three or four times, and they would still represent less than 10 percent of total reserves. The same is true of other Asian nations. They now have collective foreign exchange reserves of nearly $5 trillion that are invested overwhelmingly in dollar securities. Gold accounts for only 1.4 percent of Malaysia's foreign exchange reserves, 2.2 percent of Thailand's, 2.4 percent of Singapore's, and 3.9 percent of Indonesia's. Only the Philippines has gold holdings in excess of 10 percent of the country's forex reserves (13.7 percent).

Asian central banks have significantly increased their commitment to the euro since 2007, but now that there are doubts about the survival of the single currency, they will probably want to find alternatives. Some are buying the Canadian dollar and the Australian dollar, but both countries have very modest financial markets compared to the US dollar or the euro. Gold is likely to become an alternative, especially if sentiment again turns negative toward the US dollar.

Chinese Gold Market Liberalization Will Also Help Bolster the Price of Gold

China moved to liberalize its gold market in order to facilitate more private investment in gold in the second half of the 2000s. The central bank increased the number of banks that were allowed to trade bullion internationally, and said it would permit the development of gold-linked investment products. It also hinted at changes in the tax on bullion. The Chinese gold market could also open up further because of the launch of the Hong Kong Mercantile Exchange in late 2010. The first product on the exchange will be a gold futures contract with a delivery in Hong Kong. In 2009, Chinese private investors purchased seventy-one tonnes of gold compared to eighteen tonnes in 2007. Their demand could easily double or triple as more investment products are created to facilitate gold investment. China's jewelry gold demand is only about 0.27 grams per capita. This number is about half of the US demand and only a quarter of Taiwan's demand. As Chinese incomes rise, the per capita jewelry demand could converge with Taiwan's. Before 2002, the Chinese gold market had been a monopoly of the central bank. The Shanghai Gold Exchange was launched that year, but there was not a significant expansion of trading in the early years. Its turnover value in 2009 was equal to only about one-seventh of the gold turnover on COMEX.

The *Wall Street Journal* reported in late July 2010 that China is importing more gold than it currently reports. The article cited a variety of deals in which China purchased Canadian and Australian gold for use in its own smelters. In 2009, China's gold demand reached 442 metric tonnes while output was only 411 tonnes. This gap suggests that imports were thirty-one tonnes.

China will be attracted to gold because of its reemergence as a great economic power. The distribution of world gold reserves in the early 1900s illustrates the relationship between gold and power. In 1913, the United States was rapidly emerging as a major new power and had 2,293 tonnes of gold, which was more than any European country had. Britain had 248 tonnes, compared to 439 tonnes for Germany, 378 tonnes for Austria-Hungary, 1,030 tonnes for France, and 1,233 tonnes for Russia. In 1930, the United States displayed its new preeminence by having 6,358 tonnes of gold compared to 1,080 tonnes for Britain, 794 tonnes for Germany, and 3,160 tonnes for France. (See Figure 13.1) France was then on the gold standard, but it could not sustain the link, and its gold holdings plunged to only 1,772 tonnes by 1940 while US gold holdings rose to 19,543 tonnes. In 1948, the United States had 21,682 tonnes of gold, or 72 percent of the world total. Gold was a clear proxy for US power.

The Price of Gold Is Still Far from the All-Time Real High of 1980

The previous peak in the price of gold at approximately $800 per ounce came in 1980 when the Dow Jones Industrial Average was also

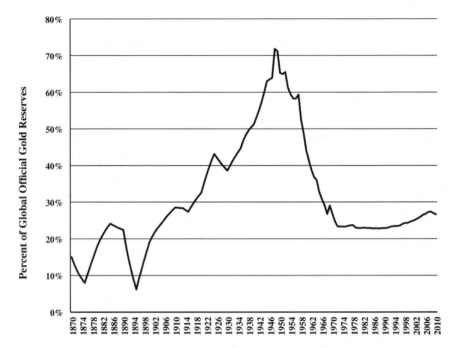

Figure 13.1 US Gold Holdings as a Percent of Global Central Bank Gold Reserves
Source: World Gold Council, International Monetary Fund

about 800. In 2010, the Dow Jones was 11,150, or nine times the price of gold. John Hathaway of Tocqueville Asset Management estimated that gold was worth approximately 6 percent of global financial assets in mid-2010 compared to 22 percent in 1980 and 20 percent in the mid-1930s. Ronald Peter Stoferle produced a report for Erste Bank around the same time with even more provocative numbers than Hathaway. He estimated that all gold assets (bullion, ETFs, equities, etc.) were equal to only 0.8 percent of global financial assets compared to 26 percent in 1980, 30 percent in 1948, and 28 percent in 1921. He said that the value of gold equities is only about $200 billion, or an amount equal to 1.9 percent of the market capitalization of the S&P 500. Stoferle stated that if gold holdings were to rise to a level equal to 2 percent of all financial assets, investors would have to purchase 85,000 tonnes.

There is no way to predict exactly how far the price of gold will rally. Gold surged amid concerns about the stability of the European monetary system in May 2010. There was an unusual rally in both gold and the dollar in July 2010 when Southern European countries succeeded in once again selling government debt to private investors. Investors slightly reduced their positions in the gold ETFs. The market was also startled by the announcement that several European commercial banks did a gold swap with the Bank for International Settlements (BIS) for 346 tonnes. Some European banks were experiencing funding problems at the time, so they turned to gold as a source of liquidity with the BIS. The fact that gold could play such a role is further confirmation that it retains a quasi-monetary function. China's announcement that it would liberalize its domestic gold market gave a boost to the price of gold in early August, but as the central bank did not make any further purchases for its own account, the rally was limited.

Three Key Factors Will Influence the Price of Gold in the Medium Term

There will probably be three major factors influencing gold prices during the next five years. The first factor will be how long central banks pursue highly accommodative monetary policies in the G-7 countries. Gold is sensitive to the level of interest rates, so the highly accommodative monetary policies that have been in place since late 2008 have been positive for the metal. The slow pace of recovery in the US, European, and Japanese economies suggests that interest rates will remain low well into 2011, so monetary policy is unlikely to pose a challenge to gold in the short to intermediate term. In fact, the Federal Reserve has announced a program of quantitative easing to purchase $600 billion of government securities through June 2011 because of its impatience with the inability of low interest rates to revive the US economy.

The second important factor will be the dollar. It rallied during the first half of 2010 because of Europe's financial problems, but the rally faltered when European conditions improved and there was evidence of sluggish growth in the US economy. The great uncertainty about the dollar centers on when investors will demand higher bond yields to compensate for the inflation risk posed by America's large fiscal deficits. The fear of deflation has driven ten-year bond yields below 3.0 percent. There is no sign that investors will care about the fiscal deficit until the economy is much stronger and private credit demand revives. This factor could restrain bond yields through the early months of 2011. But when the economic recovery proceeds further and the Fed decides to raise interest rates, there will be greater concern about the deficit, and bond yields will rise. The foreign exchange market could also start to focus on the deficit and the fears that it will ultimately be inflationary. In such a scenario, gold could have a traditional rally as the dollar falls.

The third factor will be China. There is no way to predict when China's central bank will purchase more gold for its official reserves. As in 2009, it may not disclose any transactions until long after they have been completed. Private Chinese demand will increase, but it will be modest compared to potential central bank purchases. Chinese official purchases could easily give a significant boost to the confidence of the gold market in 2012 or 2013, but the market will not know what is happening until the central bank makes an announcement.

The price of gold has reached a new high in nominal terms, but it will not regain the inflation-adjusted peak it had in 1980 until the price rises to nearly $2,400 per ton. The price of gold began to rally in 2001 when the world economy was recovering from the collapse of the technology bubble. The price gains occurred against a backdrop of low US interest rates, record current account imbalances, and the emergence of China as a major economic power. The current economic environment will be conducive to further price gains. Interest rates are at record lows. Central banks will have to maintain accommodative monetary policies in order to protect their banking systems. The dollar benefitted from problems in Europe, but the United States is also confronting unprecedented fiscal deficits. The most important new factor in the outlook for gold is the reemergence of central banks as gold buyers. After selling gold from the 1970s to the 2000s, central banks are once again adding gold to their reserves. During 2009 and 2010, China, India, Thailand, Russia, Sri Lanka, Bangladesh, and South Korea either purchased gold or announced plans to do so. The nations with the largest foreign exchange reserves in East Asia also have only modest gold holdings compared to the older industrial countries of Western Europe. They have traditionally pegged their currencies to the dollar and held dollar reserves because of their trade links to the US economy, but the United States now represents a diminishing share of their trade, and there are many reasons to be concerned about the dollar's status as a secure asset.

If central banks want to diversify their reserves away from both the dollar and European currency, they will have to give serious consideration to gold as an alternative. China's reemergence as a great economic power is also likely to create a political dimension for the country's foreign exchange policies. China will want to hold more gold in order to demonstrate its new wealth and independence from the United States. These economic and political factors are creating potential new sources of gold demand that never existed before. They guarantee that the gold price will remain on an upward trajectory far into the future.

PART

VI

THE GEOPOLITICS OF ENERGY

14

IN THE SHADOW OF PEAK OIL, PEAK CARBON, IRAQI NATIONALISM, AND PAPER BARRELS: THE OIL MARKETS OF THE 2010s

Albert Bressand

So many factors combine to influence oil markets—from international tensions to environmental regulations, and from hundred-billion-dollar investments in the Arctic to flavor-of-the-week trading bets—that oil prices sometimes appear to defy common wisdom. In the year 2010, three paradoxes illustrated the gap between the "flat earth" view of a perfectly arbitraged, globalized economy and the realities of oil markets.

Most obvious was the disconnect between oil prices in the $70–$90 per barrel range—high numbers compared to those of the 1980s and 1990s—and the recession of 2008–2009 that has been widely heralded as the fiercest economic downturn since the Great Depression. Most observers were caught by surprise by how well oil prices weathered the first significant drop in demand in decades. The second noteworthy disconnect was between the price of oil and the price of natural gas, the latter of which plummeted by more than $10 per million British Thermal Units (mbtu) to around $4 per mbtu at Henry Hub, the bellwether for the North American natural gas market. While this could suggest that oil prices are currently levitating above the fundamentals captured in other energy sources, the disconnect also reflects the regional dimension of natural gas markets, with North America as the only market where prices are the result of full-fledged gas-to-gas competition. The third disconnect is the upward slope of the futures market curve. Again, this "contango" may reflect the markets' capacity to price a worrisome combination of accelerated field depletion, geopolitical turmoil, and self-inflicted political constraints in key producer countries, or it may merely illustrate the irrelevance of "future prices" in predicting the future price of oil.

While the near-term economic horizon is currently dominated by an uneven economic recovery process and a reduced appetite for commodities as an asset class, a longer-term time horizon is needed to make sense of market behaviors that fail to be fully determined by the present supply-demand balance. Let us reflect, therefore, on what has been learned since the financial crisis of 2008–2009 regarding the longer-term market determinants. We shall begin with the move toward a post-oil economy that some think could be imposed by geological limits—"peak oil" and the assumed twilight in the desert[1]—or by concerns for climate change. We shall then turn our attention to the energy investment scene and its implications for spare production capacity, and conclude with an examination of the short-term determinants of energy prices, including investment in "paper barrels."

Peaks on the Horizon: Wall or Mirage?

Is "peak oil" a reality that should inform today's investment decisions and prices, as the three-digit oil prices of mid-2008 seemed to suggest, or is the depletion of oil reserves a mirage that is likely to remain, for many years, a couple of decades away as it has been in the past? Peak oil scenarios could materialize as a result of two very different causes. Under the most extreme scenario, as popularized by the Association for the Study of Peak Oil,[2] the world may be on the verge of running out of the reserves needed to prevent oil production from declining—or at best from plateauing for a while before collapsing. Alternatively, in a softer version of peak oil, a large share of "oil in place" may not be accessible due to "aboveground" geopolitical constraints.[3] On both accounts, the recent period has provided important information on the plausibility of both types of causes.

The year 2009 may be remembered in the history of the oil industry as the period during which the stronger, geology-defined peak oil scenario lost its recently acquired cachet. Oil reserves are now growing after two decades of decline, and a whole new class of gas reservoirs is adding a massive amount of recoverable reserves to those that are already known. As we shall see, a number of positive signals have also suggested that above-ground obstacles may be less insurmountable than many had come to believe. A look at the major expansion of Iraqi oil and gas production under way suggests, however, that political obstacles can only be removed at the cost of major changes in the role and rights of international investors, with worrisome implications for company valuations if changes seen in Iraq are part of a broader pattern. Paradoxically, the largely positive signals regarding resource availability and the rethinking under way in the industry coincide with another first-order game changer—namely a global awareness that we live in a carbon-constrained, and therefore hydrocarbon-constrained, world. An interesting question then is whether the politically correct "alternative energy" sources that absorb hundreds of billions in subsidies can bridge the gap between a reduced role for hydrocarbons (which a carbon-constrained world seems to call for) and the expanding hydrocarbon reserve base (which technology and new approaches to relations with producers may well be in the process of creating).

Technology and the New Hydrocarbon Frontier

In 2009 and 2010, ExxonMobil covered airport walls and magazine pages with algebraic equations and pictures of white-clad engineers under the one-word banner of "Technology." It would be wrong to dismiss the campaign as merely reasserting the fundamental American belief that human ingenuity can deal with any challenge and simultaneously save the planet, provide secure and affordable energy for all, and protect the "American way of life." Indeed, the campaign coincided with spectacular increases in natural gas reserves and with continuing progress in hydrocarbon recovery rates that illustrate the power of a continuous stream of innovations. The recent development of shale gas reservoirs, which already account for one-tenth of total North American production, illustrates how natural resource basins once widely considered past their peak can find a new lease on life thanks to horizontal drilling and intensive reservoir fracturing.[4] The Marcellus shale play that covers a large part of the northeastern United States may hold more gas than the much-talked-about Russian or Central Asian gas reservoirs, even if the environmental impact of recovering them is still hotly debated. The innovations behind these increases in supply lack the appeal and glamour of solar power plants—few people dream of horizontal drilling—but their impact can be of an altogether different order of magnitude, as can be seen from the very high recovery rates that Saudi Aramco achieves by combining "giga-cell modeling" of its giant reservoirs with "smart well" technology, "geo-steering" of horizontal drills, and remote "intelligent field" management.

Similarly, technological progress has made it possible to turn deepwater and ultra-deepwater hydrocarbon provinces into a major source of oil production—accounting for six million barrels per day (mb/d), almost 8 percent of the world's total, which according to Cambridge Energy Resource Associates (CERA) should rise to 10 mb/d by 2015. As a reminder that Latin America and Africa were once joined as part of the same continent, the geologic formations that hold Brazil's presalt deposits and put the country on its way to a 5.7 mb/d production level in 2020[5] also hold massive resources off the coast of Western Africa. Recently discovered fields such as Jubilee (Ghana), which is expected to produce as much as 120,000 b/d in late 2011, and Venus (Sierra Leone) are seen as only the first in a series of major discoveries to come. Africa, therefore, is host to a major exploration drive. Middle-sized oil companies such as Tullow and Heritage have captured the limelight through discoveries in Uganda and other "frontier" oil provinces. Majors and supermajors are preparing to enter the fray, as ExxonMobil has now done in Madagascar and as ENI failed to do in Uganda.

Oil-peakers will be watching carefully to see how these new resources fare beyond the recent spectacular successes. Geologists will be the first to admit that the glass is only half full, and it is emptying fast. The International Energy Agency (IEA) keeps drawing attention to the increasingly rapid rate at which newly discovered fields are being depleted, with 7 percent and 8 percent annual depletion rates being common[6] and the headline-making offshore and unconventional fields depleting even faster. By 2030, production of the currently producing oil fields will have decreased by two-thirds and that of currently producing gas fields by close to half.[7] Many producers are experiencing the need for a sustained stream of investment to enhance oil recovery and develop new fields simply to sustain production levels. Nevertheless, some of the world's largest and most economically attractive hydrocarbon reserves are still to be properly explored. How much oil is available in the Arctic, in Western Iraq, or, for that matter, how much gas lies in the Turkmen underground, is still largely unknown. The Joint Oil Data Initiative (JODI), under which Saudi Arabia and the United States cooperate to shed some light on reserve data, is a reminder of the task ahead. That being said, recent developments have been pointing toward upward revisions of ultimately recoverable reserves.

Some Timid Improvements in the Aboveground Constraints

For new discoveries to lead to sustained increases in oil production, today's frontier basins cannot fall victim to a disease unfairly named after the Dutch, as its modern form also includes patronage, corruption, disenfranchised local communities, armed rebellions, and gunpoint "bunkering" in oil fields that make macroeconomic distortions look like the benign part of the oil curse. With aboveground constraints also in mind, Christophe de Margerie, the chairman of Total, has asked his audience not to trust production forecasts above the 100 mb/d mark and to "keep candles at hand."

On this account, the recent period also saw some favorable developments pointing toward higher production levels to come. While Venezuela continues to experiment with twenty-first-century socialism and electricity shortages, Umaru Yar'Adua and Goodluck Jonathan, who replaced Yar'Adua as president of Nigeria after his premature death, have succeeded in launching preliminary discussions with armed groups that compete with the federal government to capture economic rent in the Niger Delta in the name of the local population. The possibility that Nigeria will use most of its energy revenues in support of its own sustainable economic development has improved, and so have the prospects for a resumption of the 400,000 barrels per day in lost Nigerian production. At the same time, however, after thirty years of one-family rule, citizens of Equatorial Guinea— whom statistics tell us "enjoy" the same GDP per capita as the United Kingdom—are still waiting to see some of the fruits of the country's newly found oil wealth.[8] Oil sectors that develop as enclaves in economies where they disrupt, rather than promote, development suggest that the "disease" Nigeria is attempting to conquer remains a threat in countries where social justice, respect for human rights, and diversified development are compromised. The United Nations Development Programme (UNDP) has initiated an effort to give new producers and international investors an opportunity to learn from past experience.[9] The Extractive Industry Transparency Initiative (EITI) continued to make progress in 2009 and 2010 when three countries were certified to have put in place all EITI rules and safeguards. Meanwhile, oil funds that are entrusted with the interest of future generations have met in Baku to consolidate their own forum, also with the goal of promoting transparency in the management of oil wealth. However, the high hopes placed in these initiatives have begun to be reassessed as their momentum has begun to subside and as the sources of the oil curse are understood to go well beyond the relatively technical agendas of these organizations. It is indeed clear that greater transparency is only one element in the more comprehensive reform and strengthening of governance that is needed to prove the CEO of Total wrong—as he would be pleased to be.

Even in pacified countries, the lack of domestic political consensus can keep investment at bay. Witness Project Kuwait, which would double the Emirates' production if only it could be launched. Witness also the more intrusive manner in which oil-producing countries are intervening in decisions by private companies and investor groups on matters that used to be considered part of the normal management and investment process. The most striking example is in the Russian Federation. A new set of laws on deposits of natural resources deemed to be of strategic importance and on all offshore resources now impose constraints on investing exploration and development strategies. The new laws set strict limits on foreign participations and affect the Russian companies' ability to make decisions about trading shares in non-Russian exchanges and more generally on the role and right of foreign investors.[10] Even a country such as Ghana, which is considered very investor friendly, wanted to prevent Kosmos (the company that discovered the Jubilee field) from selling its interests in the field to ExxonMobil, even though the latter would probably be able to bring the higher level of financial and technical resources that the very large deepwater field requires. The Ghanaian government was concerned that Kosmos and the private equity groups backing it (Blackstone and

Warburg Pincus) were going to profit handsomely from the sale.[11] Such decisions are worrisome because they jeopardize a whole set of business models whereby smaller companies focus on the initial risk-taking in the investment value chain, and deep-pocketed companies take over when successful discoveries call for the type of large-scale developments they are better equipped to handle. In this case, the Ghanaian government designated the Chinese company CNOOC as the preferred buyer. Kosmos could not accept this decision, which left the Blackstone Group in the uncomfortable position of having to run an oil company rather than take the fruits of their successful risk-taking to another part of the world.

The Gulf of Mexico Oil Spill and Its Implications for Deepwater Oil and Shale Gas

Restrictions on investors' freedom of operation do not result only from what tends to be summarily labeled "resource nationalism," as can be seen from the reassessment of regulations regarding hydrocarbon exploration and development in the Gulf of Mexico in 2010. The explosion of the Deepwater Horizon platform (operated by Transocean for BP) on April 20, 2010, resulted in the death of eleven crewmen and a spill of 4.9 million barrels of oil before the well could be sealed. This exposed a clear case of regulatory capture by the industry of the US Department of the Interior's Mineral Management Services (MMS), now renamed the Bureau of Ocean Energy Management, Regulation, and Enforcement. MMS was simultaneously in charge of collecting royalties from companies and giving them permission to operate, often waiving many of its own rules.

Although one of several official reports solely placed the blame on the crew of the Deepwater Horizon platform, most analysts have concluded that BP had "cut corners" and used needlessly risky technical solutions for the sake of minor cost savings relative to the cost of the accident. The Deepwater Horizon oil spill has spurred a significant revamping of the applicable US regulations and the manner in which they are enforced. It has also raised more fundamental questions about the capacity of even the largest and most respected companies to fully master and manage the technical and environmental risks associated with state-of-the-art exploration and development in challenging environments. Advocates of sustainable

development strategies have seized the opportunity to call for an accelerated switch away from an oil-based economy. The reassessment that will
follow could be of special significance for deepwater exploration and for
the role that host countries may want to see their national oil companies
(NOCs) play in these developments to the detriment of international investors. A similar regulatory tightening can be observed in the European
Union (EU), where a moratorium on offshore drilling has been put forward both by Energy Commissioner Günther Oettinger and by Jo Leinen,
chair of the European Parliament's Committee on the Environment,
Public Health, and Food Safety. A special worry for EU countries is that
an oil spill in the Mediterranean would be devastating due to a low exchange of water with surrounding water masses. However, it is unlikely
that the EU can regulate nonmembers such as Libya, where BP is to develop resources in the Gulf of Sirte at 1,900 meters below sea level, 200
meters lower than the infamous well at the Macondo Prospect in the Gulf
of Mexico. In the fall of 2010 it began to look as if the oil industry was
getting ready for a return to normal in the Gulf of Mexico, although the
true impact of the large amount of oil (70 percent of the spill) still floating
at various depths under water had not yet been properly been assessed.[12]
The reassessment may also have significant implications for development
of shale gas in the United States, at least in the more heavily populated and
more environmentally conscious parts of the country (witness the debate
raging in the state of New York regarding the pollution of groundwater by
chemicals used during hydro-fracking to ease the flow of shale gas).

Iraqi Auctions and the per-Barrel Service Fee

Of all the good news suggesting that peak oil is not around the
corner, the most important was probably that, by taking advantage of a
relative peace before US combat troops left in August 2010, Iraq has been
taking steps toward a quadrupling of its production to the 10 mb/d level
in the 2020s. This would place the country in the same league as Saudi
Arabia and the Russian Federation—at the probable cost of some major
tensions within OPEC. While the Kurdish region and the central Iraqi
government are still far from agreeing on how that region's resources
can be legitimately developed, there is enough oil in the Shiite southern

region and enough unexplored yet promising regions in the country for production levels of that order to be realistically envisioned. Yet the manner in which Iraq, one of the five OPEC founders, is returning to its historic role suggests that aboveground obstacles to production will only be relieved at the cost of major changes in the oil industry structure, probably to the detriment of the Western majors and in favor of the NOCs from the producing countries, as well as a handful of globalized NOCs (Asian ones in particular). In addition, tensions may rise within OPEC if a rapid increase in Iraqi production does not happen to coincide with an even larger increase in world demand in oil and gas.

Involuntarily disproving the common opinion that oil had been a key reason for the invasion of Iraq, the American occupation will be remembered as the time when production sharing agreements (PSAs) were most spectacularly abandoned in favor of service agreements, and when US and Western international oil companies (IOCs) had to settle for a much less prominent role and retribution than they were accustomed to. To producing countries, service agreements are the modern substitute for the nationalization of energy resources that they cannot develop themselves for lack of technological and/or financial capacities. Under US Securities and Exchange Commission (SEC) criteria, however, companies cannot "book reserves" if their risk-taking is not remunerated in volumes of hydrocarbon—in other words, if they do not bear the full technical and market risks on both sides of their balance sheet. After delays due to complaints by the company in charge of developing southern Iraqi fields that the Iraqi central government was giving foreign companies undue and unnecessary access to Iraq's natural resources, the government conducted two auctions under the service agreement rules. Bidding companies competed on the levels of production increases they would guarantee and the per-barrel service fee to which they would limit themselves above and beyond the cost of developing a given field. The first auction in June 2009 concluded with only BP and China's China National Petroleum Corporation (CNPC) accepting the $2-per-barrel service fee imposed by Iraqi authorities and committing to invest $15 billion to increase production at the Rumaila field. Yet, by December 2009 not only had most international companies reconciled themselves with service contracts; they were engaged in cutthroat competition to cut service fees well below the $4-per-barrel level they had held as a strict minimum only six months earlier. In order to make such cuts, Western IOCs had to follow BP's lead in relying on the lower-cost NOCs' supply chain. This has made CNPC, Petronas, and other Asian NOCs the real winners in what Fareed Mohamedi and his colleagues at PFC Energy[13] call the creation of the Pan-Asian energy grid. As observed by Chatham House's Valerie Marcel, in addition to raising doubts about the sustainability of contracts that will net almost no return to investors beyond the joy of "being present in Iraq,"[14] these actions will likely have implications for the long-term profitability of international energy companies.

For all their talk about developing resources nationally, Iraqi companies could not extract more than 46,000 b/d out of the Majnoon field (which Shell and Malaysia's Petronas partnered on to develop to the 1.8 mb/d level), which suggests that the oil industry remains a two-tier one, even if the first tier is profoundly changing. A small number of NOCs—Norway's Statoil, the Chinese NOCs, Malaysia's Petronas, Brazil's Petrobras, India's Oil and Natural Gas Corporation (ONGC), and a few others—have joined the Western majors in the technology-savvy, capital-rich league. How the newcomers will capitalize on their major successes (such as the Iraqi auctions) to increase their role among the majors, and how a second group (including Algeria's Sonatrach and Angola's Sonangol) will work to become full participants, are important aspects of the evolving oil industry structure.

Iraq's restored status as one of the world's largest producers of hydrocarbons has been widely anticipated to provide a solution to what would otherwise have been a growing discrepancy between rapid growth in world demand and a limited capacity by other OPEC members to meet such demand. In this rosy scenario, the plateauing of non-OPEC production and the continuation of a rapid increase in world demand will be relatively easily accommodated by OPEC. The timing, however, may not be as propitious, and Iraq could find itself in a much fiercer competition with Saudi Arabia if an economic slowdown or a rapid transition to a low-carbon economy were to put a lid on demand growth.[15]

From recent conversations in Saudi Arabia, my impression is that the other key OPEC countries anticipate that Iraq will not be able to achieve the ambitious ramp-up in production that it has announced. Iraq lacks a proper planning and administrative capacity at the national level, and in-security may increase with most American and coalition troops gone. It is one thing to plan for the rapid rise in production in a given project and another to successfully plan and oversee a dozen large projects simultane-ously. In any case, while the IEA was among many that expressed doubts on Iraq's capacity to reach these targets in its November 2010 *World Energy Outlook*, Iraqis as well as Saudis seem to concur that some serious discussions between the two countries regarding the division of labor and the production quotas will be hard to avoid after Iraqi production goes over 4 or 5 mb/d.

Climate Negotiations and the Move to a Lower-Carbon Energy Mix

With peak oil concerns alleviated until at least 2020 (subject to the quadrupling of Iraqi oil production, and therefore to peace in the Iraqi Shiite region), the other long-term consideration for the global supply-demand balance is about the implications of the transition to a low-carbon energy economy. For a brief period, considerations of energy security, peak oil, and climate security converged to make the transition to a new energy mix appear inevitable. As we have seen when assessing peak oil realities, 2009 spelled the end of this convergence, depriving climate ne-gotiators of the broad-based consensus that this convergence could have fostered.

Oil producers, notably Saudi Arabia, are calling attention to the slightly schizophrenic US and European attitudes toward the oil industry. Eu-rope counts on oil producers to develop production and spare capacity while heralding oil as a major pollutant. Meanwhile, the United States endeavors to stop importing oil from the Middle East. Saudi minister Prince Turki Al-Faisal denounced the US "energy independence" motto as "political posturing at its worst—a concept that is unrealistic, misguided, and ultimately harmful to energy-producing and -consuming countries alike," calling to focus instead "on acknowledging energy interdepen-dence."[16] Similarly, oil producers have seized the opportunity of the De-cember 2009 Copenhagen climate summit to present themselves as "victims of climate change" and to protest policies to reduce demand for oil. They should be reassured that even the alternative, lower-carbon scenario presented by the IEA in its World Energy Outlook of November 2009 (the "450 scenario" in which the level of CO_2 in the atmosphere is kept below 450 ppm) foresees a 68 percent share for hydrocarbons in 2030, a $90 per barrel price for oil (in 2008 dollars), and an increase in the production of all energy sources except coal.[17] Oil production in this scenario still grows by 0.2 percent per year on average, reaching 89 mb/d in 2030. Assuming that non-OPEC production will peak in 2010, as the IEA forecasts, this implies an additional 11 mb/d draw on OPEC resources. The IEA's "reference scenario," under which climate policies would not go beyond those agreed to before the Copenhagen summit, implies a growth in oil production of 1 percent per year on average over the projection period, from 85 mb/d in 2008 to 105 mb/d in 2030. This implies an additional 27 mb/d draw on OPEC resources, for which one is at pain today to indicate a reasonable source, except by assuming profound transformations in countries such as Venezuela and Nigeria. Perspectives presented in the 2010 World Energy Outlook are even more encouraging for oil producers, as the 450 scenario appears less plausible than it did before the semi-failure of the Copenhagen climate conference. The commitments entered into by countries either nationally or collectively will translate into a higher share of the energy mix for hydrocarbons in the 2030s.

Oil producers are taking comfort that the Copenhagen climate summit has delayed the introduction of carbon prices into the global economy through taxes and/or obligations to purchase fully auctioned emission rights. Indeed, as observed by Christian Egenhofer and Anton Georgiev, the world at the 2009 Copenhagen COP did not agree to the European proposal regarding "the final sharing-out of the remaining carbon budget of cumulative GHG emissions of around 1,550 billion tonnes of CO_2eq that are left until 2050."[18]

Nevertheless, the industrial electric power users in developed countries can expect to obtain some of the longer-term visibility that it needs to protect billion-dollar investment decisions from the vagaries of policies to come. This will be the case most notably in the US and European utility sectors, even if they are outside of the UN framework. This should translate into a continuing slowdown in projects for coal-fired power generation in the OECD countries and continuing costly support for alternative energy investments. These alternative energy sources will continue to be subsidized compared to hydrocarbons, with subsidies justified to reduce carbon emissions, to speed up the learning process, and, to a growing extent, to cater to the interests of companies that have begun to accumulate political as well as financial capital above and beyond their greatly appreciated contribution to carbon emission reductions. While some realistic assessment of what is possible has begun to emerge, only a few countries have reached the stage where wind energy accounts for a large enough share of total electricity production to create highly visible problems of grid management and generate major new environmental concerns.[19] Similarly, the competition to develop electric cars is intensifying while utilities still have to ponder the profound transformations that will be needed if cars are to recharge their batteries from the grid in ways that do not call for massive new peak-production investment, and that dovetail with the load curves of an electricity production system reshaped by alternative energy sources. Altogether, the semi-failure of the December 2009 Copenhagen climate meeting and the lack of progress on the way to the next climate meeting (held in Cancun, Mexico in early December 2010) should not obscure the fact that low-carbon energy sources will continue to develop, even if they do so more slowly than expected. Limited as it is, the Copenhagen Accord does give legitimacy to the objective of keeping temperature increases less than two degrees Celsius above preindustrial levels, and commits countries to setting national emission targets to 2020 and working toward levels of assistance to developing countries of as much as $100 billion in 2020. Another important development is the commitment made by the G-20 countries at their 2009 Pittsburgh meeting to rationalize and phase out inefficient fossil fuel subsidies that encourage wasteful consumption over the medium term.[20]

Investment and the Missing Trillions

With climate considerations and a revised assessment of peak oil prospects in the background, the post–financial crisis period also saw important changes in the investment patterns that will influence oil and gas markets over the medium term. The total investment needed to expand the world's energy system between 2008 and 2030 is estimated by the IEA at no less than $26 trillion[21] ($1.1 trillion per year), which represents about 1.4 percent of global GDP. For natural gas, the IEA estimates that the world needs to develop additional capacity of around 2,700 billion cubic meters, or four times the current Russian capacity—half of which will serve to offset the decline at existing fields, and half to meet the increase in demand. At first sight, the financial crisis of 2008–2009 has made these objectives harder to attain, although there are also reasons why, in practice, investors may have used the recession for productive purposes.

One could have expected the global economy to go through one more cycle of boom and bust whereby sharply curtailed investment in oil and gas would pave the way for a large rebound in prices. One might indeed worry that upstream investment, excluding acquisitions, likely decreased by $82 billion in 2009,[22] from $524 billion in 2008 to $442 billion in 2009.[23] In early 2009, OPEC announced that its members had delayed completion of 35 of 150 upstream projects because of falling oil prices, which postponed the planned addition of 5 mb/d production capacity until 2013 at the earliest.[24] Looking forward, the IEA carried out a detailed survey of the capital spending plans of fifty leading oil and gas companies. While this survey identifies at least 1 mb/d of deferred investment, it also shows that investment by energy supermajors retrenched only about 7 percent against 16 percent for all companies in 2009, and that the supermajors will keep their investment flat while NOCs will reduce spending by 7 percent and other international investors will reduce spending by 33 percent.[25] While Gazprom, the Russian national gas company, is readying for no less than a 47 percent reduction, China's 53 percent of this total is for the power sector up to the year 2030, requiring 4,800 gigawatts (GW) in new power generation capacity—almost five times the existing capacity of the United States—of which 80 percent is in developing countries.[26] More than half of the total energy demand increase is predicted to take place in developing countries. IEA dollar numbers are in year-2008 dollars.

CNOOC and Mexico's Pemex[27] are planning to increase their investment. The capacity of the energy industry to self-finance is strong compared to other sectors, and a large part of the reduction in investments can also be explained by the anticipation of lower input prices. Thanks to a planned $10 billion investment, Saudi production capacity is set to have risen to 1 mb/d in 2010 to 12.8 mb/d, which will provide the country with enough spare capacity to keep prices from rising to levels that would threaten oil market stability—and excessively facilitate the international ambitions of Iran, Venezuela, and Russia.

Yet these decreases in actual and planned investment levels will not impact the oil and gas industry in proportions similar to what the aggregate nominal decreases would suggest. First, the bulk of deferred capacity is in the power sector—in line with the fact that electricity demand has decreased for the first time—and in Canadian tar sands, for which a pause in an overheated sector in search of its ecological balance has a clear silver lining. Indeed, in Edward Morse's words, "strategy," rather than reduced cash flow, is the "most significant [factor] that [is] delaying projects today," as companies "believe that they can negotiate better terms with contractors the longer they wait."[28] Costs had risen to incredibly high levels,[29] and the ability to build capacity (for example, increasing the number of drilling vessels) needed to be expanded to tame this source of inflation. Therefore, despite the $170 billion in deferred capacity investment documented by the IEA,[30] there are good reasons to believe that the industry is able to avoid the stop-and-go business environment of the mid-1980s and 1990s. The modified investment pattern may not be far from what was called for in response to assist (1) the slump in demand that followed the global economic and financial crisis of 2008, (2) the gradual rise that will follow, and (3) the return to a growth path somewhere between the 0.2 percent and 1 percent annual rates for oil demand forecasted by the IEA in its 450 low-carbon scenario and its reference scenario,[31] respectively.

Another important question related to medium-term investment is whether the recession and slow recovery are hampering the transition to a low-carbon energy mix. One remarkable feature of 2008 and 2009 was governmental effort to protect investments in alternative energy sources from the potentially devastating impact of lower oil and gas prices and of reduced demand forecasts. No less than $250 billion has been earmarked for investment protection in stimulus packages worldwide. In the United States, for instance, the Obama administration has set aside $70 billion for so-called green energy jobs. More generally, investment in energy alternatives has enjoyed significant protection from the stop-and-go approach that resulted from previous drops in oil prices. The ensuing, relatively limited 20 percent reduction in nominal investment levels is not necessarily a bad thing considering that the rapid development of wind farms and solar installations seems to have run ahead of funders' and regulators' ability to properly vet the manner in which billions in subsidies are being used.

Entering the Gas-Glut Decade?

Judging by Henry Hub prices, the gas glut is already a reality in North America. Almost one-tenth of current US production of natural gas comes from shale rocks that were known to hold large reserves but that could not be exploited before a stream of incremental technological improvements made horizontal drilling and large-scale fracturing economically possible. While concerns for the environmental impact of large-scale shale drilling and the US penchant for litigation have the potential to slow these developments, North America seems poised for a prolonged period of natural gas abundance. Interestingly, although some geologists still express doubt, the core areas in large shale gas fields seem to be able to sustain production economically, with relatively low gas prices, which is clouding the prospects for liquefied natural gas (LNG) imports.

In this context, a key source of uncertainty for natural gas is the commercial conditions under which Europe will procure gas from a small number of producers outside of the EU and European Economic Area. Shale gas exists in Europe, but not on the scale that is available in the United States. Therefore, it is likely that with British and Dutch gas production continuing to decline, more gas will have to be procured from the global LNG market and/or from Russia and Algeria. LNG sources include Qatar and Trinidad as well as Libya, Egypt, Nigeria, and some newcomers. In addition, one interesting question will be whether the United States is ready to develop a large-scale LNG export capacity, which would be at odds with its subjective definition of energy security as "energy independence." Russian gas is now very expensive compared to spot prices as a result of the oil-product indexation clauses in take-or-pay Russian contracts. European companies failed to import as much Russian gas as was called for under these contracts. It was all the more intriguing, therefore, to see the Paris-based European electric utility EDF join the South Stream consortium that was put in place by Gazprom and commit to large volumes of Russian gas imports.

Prices, Bands, and Consensus

Having looked at the long-term determinants of supply and at the medium-term investment path for oil, gas, and renewables, let us now look at the short-term factors that will come into play in the early 2010s.

The essential idea of "stability" was put forward explicitly by Saudi Minister Ali I. Al-Naimi. Speaking at the annual CERAWeek energy industry gathering in Houston, Minister Al-Naimi began by stressing the unsustainable nature of the wave of rising commodity prices, asset values, and wealth creation that preceded the financial crisis. He highlighted four conditions that future oil prices should meet for oil market stability to be within reach. The first two conditions are restatements of the classic beliefs that prices should be "low enough to facilitate economic growth" and "high enough to provide sufficient return to producers that ensure adequate and timely investment." The third condition, interestingly, is that prices should be "high enough to provide an incentive for consumers to use oil efficiently" (though one might note that Middle Eastern producer countries provide some of the most inefficient energy subsidies). The fourth condition is even more interesting in light of previous Saudi opposition to alternative energy. Minister Al-Naimi suggests that prices should be "sufficient to encourage production from marginal fields, non-conventional sources, and renewables."[32] Taken together, the four conditions are quite bullish. Saudi high officials made statements in early December 2009 suggesting that, at close to $80 per barrel, oil prices were at what Saudi Arabia sees as the upper limit of the acceptable band. The Algerian minister of oil made similar observations at the March 2010 OPEC meeting.

Based on preliminary estimates, the year 2009 registered a 2 percent decline in global energy use, including an expected 2 percent decline in oil consumption and a 3 percent decline in natural gas demand.[33] Part of that decrease is likely to be offset in the near future as energy consumption will grow 2.5 percent annually until 2015, at which point growth is expected to slacken. On the way to more sustained global economic growth, the first question mark will be the evolution of the huge inventories of oil that were 120 million barrels above the five-year average for OECD countries at the end of 2009. These inventories could decline by as much as 150 million barrels in 2011 if OPEC members succeed in maintaining a relatively satisfactory level of adherence to the organization's 2010 output quotas, which were left unchanged at the organization's meeting in Luanda in December 2009 and in Vienna in March 2010. Whether these conditions will be met is still ambiguous: While the IEA saw global demand for oil increasing by a relatively robust rate in 2010, traders such as Vitol and Trafigura saw only 1 mb/d at the beginning of the year, and OPEC's forecast at the time was even weaker.[34] So far, the IEA view seems to have been the most accurate, and while the prospect of a faltering recovery cannot be ruled out, the demand forecasts for 2010 kept being revised to reflect an increase. In particular, on the basis of stronger GDP assumptions, the IEA predicts that global demand can increase the growth rate in 2010 to 2.2 percent, or 1.8 mb/d.[35] Yet in many ways supply will be the variable to monitor most closely in the early 2010s in order to know whether the increase in demand—itself the result of rapid growth in the emerging countries and of stagnating or declining OECD demand—begins to make a dent in record-level inventories.

In addition to outright increases in supply and demand, a number of business decisions are coming into play that help explain why massive inventories have failed so far to depress the market entirely. These decisions include tanker owners' determination to extract some value from their oversized and growing tanker fleets by using more than one hundred vessels—about 8 percent of VLCC and product tanker fleets in November 2009—as floating storage. Not only did this translate into a significant firming of chartering rates until the summer of 2010 (above what would otherwise have been very depressed prices), but it also met traders' objectives to benefit from the future appreciation of oil as captured in the forward curve.

For the IEA, 2010 was supposed to have been the year when non-OPEC oil would peak; it is plausible, however, that Russian production keeps increasing,[36] and that total non-OPEC production will in fact increase slightly from 52.56 mb/d in 2010 to 52.90 mb/d in 2011.[37] In addition, a significant part of the OPEC production of liquid—which includes crude oil and other sources of liquid hydrocarbons—now comes in the form of natural gas liquids (NGLs), which are expected to rise to about

5.6 mb/d in 2010, up 20 percent from 2008.[38] (IEA has downgraded the forecast to 5.26 mb/d in 2010 but sees an increase to 5.86 mb/d in 2011.) NGLs are not subject to OPEC quotas.

Reflecting on these fundamentals and on the many complicating parameters, the IEA and, with more reservation, the industry seem to agree on a gradual increase that would take oil prices a little above the band of $70–$80 per barrel that persisted for a significant portion of the second half of 2010 on the way to a return to $100 per barrel oil in the not-too-distant future. The two IEA scenarios that we have referred to are associated with respective oil import prices of $90 and $100 in 2020 and $90 and $115 in 2030 (in 2008 dollars). A Reuters poll of twenty-five leading crude oil analysts that was taken at the end of November 2009 foresaw an average price of $75.40 per barrel in 2010, and forecasts for the early spring of 2010 did not differ by much.[39]

As Harvard's Kenneth Rogoff observed, the price range at which oil prices had stabilized for half a year by spring 2010 could be seen as a "sweet spot" for both the oil markets—providing incentives to invest—and for the global economy as a whole, as they did not threaten a still-fragile OECD recovery or discourage investment in alternative energy sources.

Paper Barrels

The forecasts above assume that the speculative demand for oil will not get out of hand one way or another. Demand for "paper barrels" will continue to exercise an autonomous influence on oil prices. In the recent past, this took the form of massive investments in the futures markets in pursuit of large-scale gains as oil, and commodities more generally, turned into a major asset class for hedge fund and other investment fund portfolio managers. The sum of open interests on the NYMEX and ICE futures market jumped from 950,000 contracts (equivalent to just under 1 billion barrels of oil) in 2004 to 2.7 million contracts (2.7 billion barrels of oil) in 2008. According to LCM Research, adding exchange-traded options and futures contracts to the latter figure represents no less than seven billion barrels of oil. The deleveraging that took place in the second half of 2008 reduced this amount to about 1.7 billion barrels. Over-the-counter crude oil contracts exacerbated this speculative spike, adding a full 120 percent to the peak figure as opposed to a fraction (on the order of 80 percent) before and after the spring 2008 episode. Similarly, passive investment into index funds also rose and fell spectacularly, from about $75 billion in 2006 to $280 billion by mid-summer 2008, and back to the 2006 level six months later.[40] The Goldman Sachs–fed allure of $200-per-barrel oil has faded, and it is unlikely that the next couple of years will see an episode of exuberant investing comparable to the year 2008 that is still remembered for oil at $147 per barrel. Nevertheless, the fourth quarter of 2009 saw sustained investment in oil futures, and there may be other reasons why paper markets may not remain neutral for long. In particular, oil recently became a major instrument in efforts to hedge against a fall in the dollar. As observed by LCM Research, the spike in oil prices of late October 2009—during which time oil prices crossed what had been for five months a firm upper limit of $75—can only be explained by the weakening in what had been a negative relationship between gold and the dollar and by the role that oil played, at least for a few months, as "an asset class of choice for dollar refugees."[41] If sustained for a long enough period, a significant weakening of the dollar could test not only this emerging coupling of currencies and oil markets, but possibly the manner in which Saudi Arabia defines what is presently an upper limit of $80 for the range of acceptable oil prices.

Altogether, many trends will converge to significantly change the parameters behind the "sweet spot" that oil markets found in late 2009 and that it still enjoyed in the summer of 2010. These trends include the rate of increase in demand, the date at which non-OPEC production peaks, the relative role of Saudi Arabia, Iran, and Iraq, and the time it takes for the share of alternatives to increase from minuscule to globally significant.[42] These different variables will have major implications for policies and, to some extent, for prices. However, the bottom line remains that in 2030 (notwithstanding the thinking triggered by the Deepwater Horizon oil spill), ours will still be a hydrocarbon-powered economy, and enough oil and gas resources will be available to meet the huge energy demand that cannot be met by alternative energy sources, however rapid their development. Lessons learned in 2009 and 2010 highlight the importance of better governance of energy as well as climate issues.[43]

Notes

1. Matthew R. Simmons, *Twilight in the Desert: The Coming Saudi Oil Shock and the World Economy* (Hoboken, NJ: Wiley, 2005).

2. Kenneth S. Deffeyes, *Hubbert's Peak: The Impending World Oil Shortage* (Princeton, NJ: Princeton University Press, 2001). For an opposing view, see Robin M. Mills, *The Myth of the Oil Crisis: Overcoming the Challenges of Depletion, Geopolitics, and Global Warming* (Westport, CT: Praeger, 2008).

3. "Our data confirms that the world has enough proved reserves of oil, natural gas and coal to meet the world's needs for decades to come. The challenges the world faces in growing supplies to meet future demand are not below ground, they are above ground. They are human, not geological." Tony Hayward, "Group Chief Executive's Introduction," *BP Statistical Review of World Energy*, June 1, 2009.

4. Investment in reservoir exploration and development technology remains relatively concentrated in the hands of the major and supermajor oil companies. Russia's Rozneft, for instance, was recently scolded for investing only 0.3 percent into research and development.

5. Alexei Barrionuevo, "Brazil Seeks to Maximize Gains from Newfound Oil," *International Herald Tribune*, August 18, 2009, 1 and 5.

6. On average the eight hundred fields covered in a 2008 IEA survey exhibited a 6.7 percent depletion rate, to be contrasted with rates of 3 percent or less for giant fields discovered in the postwar decades. The decline rate for the largest gas fields is currently 5.3 percent, and the weighted depletion rate for all gas fields is 7.5 percent. International Energy Agency, *World Energy Outlook 2009* (Paris: IEA Publications, 2009), 11 (hereafter cited as WEO 2009).

7. WEO 2009.

8. Human Rights Watch, *Well Oiled: Oil and Human Rights in Equatorial Guinea* (New York: Human Rights Watch, 2009), http://www.hrw.org/sites/default/files/reports/bhr0709web_0.pdf.

9. See, United Nations Development Programme: South-South Unit, Proceedings of the first Oil and Gas Management Forum, Doha, 2008. Prepared in light of the first Oil and Gas Management Forum, Doha, 2008.

10. Albert Bressand, "Foreign Direct Investment in Natural Gas: Recent Trends and Strategic Drivers," in *Yearbook on International Investment Law and Policies*, ed. Karl Sauvent (New York: Oxford University Press, May 2009).

11. Carola Hoyos, "Exxon Abandons Bid for Ghana Stake," *Financial Times*, August 18, 2010, http://www.ft.com/cms/s/0/9a4f5f8e-aaf1-11df-9e6b-00144feabdc0.html (accessed on August 27, 2010).

12. James Kanter, "Oil Spill Creates Hard Choices for the E.U.," *International Herald Tribune*, August 1, 2010, http://www.nytimes.com/2010/08/02/business/global/02iht-green.html (accessed on August 28, 2010). Clifford Kraus, "BP Oil Spill Has Little Impact on Global Drilling," *New York Times*, August 25, 2010, http://green.blogs.nytimes.com/2010/08/25/bp-oil-spill-has-little-impact-on-global-drilling (accessed on August 28, 2010).

13. Stephen Glain, "Rigging the Game: National Oil Companies and the Future of Energy Consumption," *The Majalla*, January 25, 2010, http://www.majalla.com/en/cover_story/article14606.ece (accessed on August 26, 2010).

14. Quoted in James Kanter, "Iraq Signs Oil Deal with European Companies: Firms Accept Thin Profits to Secure Future Access to Country's Vast Reserves," *International Herald Tribune*, December 30, 2009, 14.

15. See, for instance, Steven Cohen, "We Need a Real Discussion of the Impact of Tighter Offshore Drilling Regulation," *Huffington Post*, August 17, 2010, http://www.huffingtonpost.com/steven-cohen/we-need-a-real-discussion_b_684564.html (accessed on August 29, 2010); and John Broder, "Drilling Permits for Deep Waters Face New Review," *New York Times*, August 16, 2010, A1.

16. Prince Turki Al-Faisal, "Don't Be Crude, Why Barack Obama's Energy-Dependence Talk Is Just Demagoguery," *Foreign Policy*, August 17, 2009, http://www.foreignpolicy.com/articles/2009/08/17/dont_be_crude (accessed on March 20, 2010).

17. WEO 2009, 193 and 204. In the 450 scenario—in 2020 and 2030, respectively—the price of oil is 10 percent and 22 percent lower than in the reference scenario.

18. Christian Egenhofer and Anton Georgiev, "The Copenhagen Accord: A First Stab at Deciphering the Implications for the EU," *CEPS Commentary*, December 25, 2009, 1.

19. No energy source is perfect or fully carbon neutral. Among the environmental concerns raised by wind energy in 2009 were the conditions under which China produces the rare earth-like dysprosium essential to manufacturing lighter magnets for wind turbines. Strategic dependence on the Chinese supply of rare earth and the manner in which Chinese industrial policy tilts the playing field in favor of Chinese-made equipment are also beginning to be more systematically analyzed and debated.

20. For an analysis of energy subsidies, see IEA, OPEC, OECD, World Bank, "Analysis of the Scope of Energy Subsidies and Suggestions for the G-20 Initiative" (Joint Report: G-20 Summit Meeting, 2010), http://www.worldenergyoutlook.org/docs/G20_Subsidy_Joint_Report.pdf.

21. Fifty-three percent of this total is for the power sector (up to the year 2030), requiring 4,800 GW in new power generation capacity—almost five times the existing capacity of the United States—80 percent of which is required in developing countries (WEO 2009, 4). More than half of the total energy demand increase is predicted to take place in developing countries. IEA dollar numbers are in 2008 dollars.

22. WEO 2009, 139.

23. WEO 2009, 139–140.

24. International Energy Agency, *The Impact of the Financial and Economic Crisis on Global Energy Investment* (Paris: IEA Publications, 2009), 24.

25. WEO 2009, 145.

26. WEO 2009, 4.

27. With a fall of 300,000 b/d in production, Mexico is paying a huge price for not having anticipated the accelerating decline in production at the supergiant Cantarell field.

28. Edward L. Morse, "Closing Keynote Address" (Russia and the Caspian States in the Global Energy Balance Conference, James Baker III Institute for Public Policy, Rice University, March 20, 2009, 7). According to Morse, reduced inputs' costs and contractors' margins could halve the break-even point for the development costs of tar sand projects from $90 per barrel in 2008 to $45 per barrel.

29. After exploding during the boom years, costs have come down significantly, though some of the cost reductions have been captured by service providers thanks to long-term contracts for drilling rings.

30. WEO 2009, 141. These deferred investments correspond to production capacities of about 2 mb/d for oil projects and 9 bcm for natural gas projects.

31. WEO 2009, 73 and 212. On average, over the 2007–2030 period, the 450 scenario would see global energy demand rise by 0.8 percent annually, gas demand rise by 0.7 percent, and coal demand drop by 0.9 percent.

32. Minister of Petroleum Ali I. Al-Naimi, "Achieving Energy Stability in Uncertain Times" (keynote address, CERAWeek, Houston, TX, February 10, 2009), http://www.saudiembassy.net/announcement/announcement02100901.aspx (accessed on March 30, 2010).

33. WEO 2009, 74 and 212. On average, in the reference scenario, demand for oil would decline by 0.2 percent per year in 2007–2010 before rebounding at 2.5 percent in 2010–2015 and slackening thereafter to average 1.5 percent over 2015–2030. In the 450 scenario, demand for oil would be 7 percent lower from 2010 to 2020 and 15 percent lower in the 2020s, with half of the savings happening in the United States (where it would decline), Europe, the Middle East, and China (where it would increase by 2.7 percent only on average).

34. Javier Blas, "Oil Demand Recovery to Be Sluggish in 2010," *Financial Times*, December 21, 2009, 11. Founded in 1966, Vitol trades 5.5 million barrels every day, which is the equivalent of 200 tankers, a level comparable to the world's supermajors. International Energy Agency, *Oil Market Report* (Paris: IEA Publications, 2010), August 2010, 4 (hereafter cited as IEA, *Oil Market Report*).

35. IEA, *Oil Market Report*, 4.

36. IEA, *Oil Market Report*, 59.

37. IEA, *Oil Market Report*, 59.

38. In its January 2009 "Oil Market Report," the IEA assumes that, for at least the early portion of the 2010s, production in the Russian Federation will decrease from a 2007 peak. Analysts at LCM Commodities have challenged this view on the basis of developments in the first three quarters of 2009 and, more importantly, of the policies that Russia is putting in place to increase oil production. They conclude that "Russian output is more likely to grow by 1–2 percent per year than to fall." Louis Capital Markets/LCM Commodities, LCM Research, "Russia Re-ducts: New Pipelines, New Energy Plans, New Growth Commitments Promise Rising Output, Exports," Special Report, August 28, 2009.

39. CNBC.com, "Oil Price to Average USD 75.40 in 2010," November 25, 2009, www.cnbc.com/id/34145910 (link expired as of September 3, 2010).

40. LCM Research, "Special Report," November 19, 2009, 9.

41. LCM Research, "The New Black (Gold): Oil Provides Haven against Dollar Weakness, Driving Physical Response to Price Breakout," *LCM Global Macro Focus*, November 2, 2009, 1–2.

42. The share of non-hydro renewable energy sources is expected to rise to 18 percent in 2030 in the IEA 450 scenario, compared to 8.6 percent in the reference scenario and to 2.5 percent in 2007.

43. Albert Bressand, "The Future of Producer-Consumer Cooperation: A Policy Perspective," in *Global Energy Governance: The New Rules of the Game*, ed. Andreas Goldthau and Jan Martin Witte (Washington, DC: Brookings Institution Press, 2010).

15

IN THE AFTERMATH OF IRAN'S LATEST REVOLUTION

Narimon Safavi

For nearly every year since 1977, Iran has been featured in a significant percentage of global newspaper headlines. Upon closer inspection, even many of the global news items that on the surface are not Iran-centered contain an important Iranian component. The years 2009 and 2010 were no exception. The 2009 Iranian election and its aftermath aside, the story of Dubai's default on its debt obligation has a huge Iranian undercurrent. Iran is also important because America's involvement in the wars in Afghanistan and Pakistan, as well as Iraq, will likely require Iranian involvement in their solutions.

The Persian Gulf countries provide a significant percentage of the liquidity necessary to make global capital markets work. Political crises in a region with Iran at its center can only affect the global markets negatively. Dubai only got past the critical stage of becoming a significant location for international business in the 1980s, after US sanctions against Iran caused many of its businesses to relocate to Dubai in order to get around international trade and investment restrictions. Otherwise, Dubai has very little oil and had always been considered a backwater in the Middle East. A conversation with an investment banker from the United Arab Emirates (UAE) in 2008 disclosed that up to 20 percent of the capital they managed was Iranian expatriate money. A group of Iranian economists recently estimated that the flow of Iranian investments to Dubai alone was approximately $260 billion in 2006–2008. Iranian investors, with very few options as to where they can invest, seem to now be going to Malaysia in droves. If the possibility of a confrontation with Iran and any other powers looms large, it will be very hard for Dubai (or other members of the UAE, for that matter) to rebuild credibility with international investors and continue to play a significant global role financially.

An effective solution to the Afghanistan and Pakistan dilemmas is unimaginable without the involvement of India and Iran. Iran has the second-largest natural gas reserves in the world, and India is one of the biggest markets for natural gas. A pipeline carrying gas through Pakistan (often called the Pipeline of Peace) will earn Pakistan billions in transit fees and will serve as a huge incentive to stabilize the relationships between the three countries (India, Pakistan, and Iran). In Afghanistan, Iran has already built a highway that connects the cities of Mashhad in Iran to Herat in Afghanistan and Dushanbe in Tajikistan, thereby connecting these three Persian-speaking countries. The city of Herat (population one million) in western Afghanistan is connected to the electrical grid of Khorasan province in eastern Iran. Iran's influence in Iraq is by now well documented and established.

Yet the prism through which we interpret all things Iranian has not changed very much in recent years. It is time for a new paradigm of evaluating Iran that moves beyond its reputation for bombastic politicians and religious zealots. Yes, Iran does have a lot of oil and gas, and is globally renowned for its rugs, caviar, pistachios, saffron, and cinema. But if we do not also take into account its newly emerged civil society, and the military's domination of its political economy, we will miss a great deal at our own peril. Often seen as a center of radical Islam, Iran is also the birthplace of the Reformist Movement of Islam (led by the recently deceased Grand Ayatollah Montazeri), which moves beyond textual literalism and posits democracy, human rights, and nonviolence as central to the societal affairs of Muslims.

A Modern Iran, at Last

In the late 1970s the philosopher Thomas Kuhn coined the phrase "paradigm shift" in his seminal book *The Structure of Scientific Revolutions*. He was referring to the phenomena of scientists detecting a need to change their underlying presumptions and worldviews in order to better explain (instead of discarding) surprising experimental results. Arguably, a similar phenomenon is under way that is changing global perceptions of Iranian society. In the aftermath of the June 12, 2009 elections and the spontaneous outbreak of widespread protests, vivid images were broadcast by global media outlets depicting a modern Iranian polity demanding its democratic rights. The cartoonish perception of Iran as a land populated by an angry, bearded, or veiled people who are steadfastly trying to develop a nuclear bomb because of their abhorrence of all that is Western started to erode. Viewers of networks such as CNN and the BBC saw a seemingly literate, articulate, often English-speaking, and smartly dressed (though minimally and even provocatively hijab observant) group of young people demonstrate a great deal of courage and political sophistication. Chants of "Death to America" and "Long live the Ayatollah" were replaced by "Where is my vote?" (which some Americans could empathize with), "Everyone . . . a Martin Luther King," and "Everyone . . . a Mahatma Gandhi." This was a savvy bunch of activists who were committed to nonviolence, making limited yet achievable demands, and never surrendering the moral high ground. And the images were there to verify that Iranians were exercising their modern subjectivity.

The physical backdrop to all of this was a country with modern cities, boulevards, and infrastructure. The world learned that Persian, after English and Mandarin, is the third most used language for blogging, even though the population of Iran is only about seventy million. After witnessing such reports, friends who have known me for decades said that they did not know these facts about Iran, and hinted that I had been hiding all of this from them. The fact was that they had been told about such realities for years, but these new images and context were somehow causing previously provided facts and a set of new perceptions to sink in. An image, or more accurately, a television broadcast, is truly worth a thousand words.

The events of the latest Revolution have even produced their own set of icons. The haunting image of life exiting the body of Neda Agha Soltan, a twenty-seven-year-old graduate philosophy student who was shot while she was recording the demonstrations, will live forever alongside the unforgettable footage of a Vietcong suspect getting shot in the head during the Vietnam War and the crash of the Hindenburg. Oxford

University has already established a scholarship for graduate students of philosophy named after Neda Agha Soltan. Neda, along with other martyrs of the Green Movement, are often mentioned by the rock star Bono at U2 concerts, as well as by other global activists. For weeks after June 12, hospitals in the United States were reporting that a number of couples were choosing to name their newborn girls Neda, even though they were not of Iranian descent.

The paradigm shift in the public perception of Iran, at least for a significant segment of the global audience, is well under way, and the images of the summer of 2009 have started to replace the images of the US Embassy Hostage Crisis of 1979 in the American psyche. The question to ask at the moment is, for a dedicated lay observer of all things Iranian, Will this be a sufficient correction in perception to provide a reasonably accurate and useful picture of Iranian society? My response is probably not.

A Century of Modern Revolutions

An important "point of rupture," as philosopher Michel Foucault would call it, in the unfolding of Iran's 2,500-plus years of history was the Constitutionalist Revolution of 1906 during the Qajar dynasty. The Qajars, an Iranian people who were weary of a corrupt dynasty of absolute monarchs and were partially aware of the concepts of Western enlightenment imported by a new Western-educated elite, rose up to demand an end to Oriental-style despotism through a system of rule of law (Mashrooteh) and checks and balances, either in the form of a republic or a constitutional monarchy. This led to the formation of the first Iranian Parliament (Majlis), which has become a sacrosanct institution in Iran as the country has evolved toward democracy. Not even the Supreme Leader of the Islamic Republic (Ayatollah Khamenei) has the power to dissolve the Majlis.

A second, and well-known, point of rupture took place in 1953 when the National Iranian Oil Company (NIOC) was nationalized by a democratically elected prime minister, Mohammed Mosadegh. This led to a coup that was engineered by the CIA and the return of a young Shah Mohammad Reza Pahlavi, who had authoritarian tendencies and had fled the country earlier in the year.

The third point of rupture for the Iranian people came in 1979 when the Pahlavi dynasty was re-toppled and, finally, the democratic aspirations of the Iranian people seemed on the verge of realization. However, crises such as the 1979 sacking of the American Embassy in Tehran by mobs and the 1980 US-backed invasion of Iran by Saddam Hussein's Iraqi/Ba'athist Army led to a radicalization of Iranian politics—and provided a perfect opportunity for extremist Islamists to declare a state of emergency and quash dissent.

The 2009 election was perceived by Iranians as an opportunity to push the cause of gradual democratic change and express their collective will by electing a Reformist president. The opening had come after it became clear that President Obama would not maintain the Bush administration's aggressive posture toward Iran, and the atmosphere of expression of dissent within Iran could thrive. The Reformists felt that they could now offer robust criticism of Ahmadinejad in the presidential debates without getting accused of being "collaborators with the enemy." Obama's Norooz (Persian New Year) address to the Iranian people, during which he quoted the Persian poet Saadi's poem about the solidarity of humanity, was a masterstroke that raised excitement in Iran about the new American president. The framing of a major election issue was set. Who was worthy of being the interlocutor to engage Obama and not squander this opportunity for a grand bargain?

Tired of violent revolutions and wars, Iranians are committed to peaceful and gradual change that is sustainable. The presidential debates were a passionate affair. People gathered in the streets after each debate, sometimes until 4:00 in the morning, conducting their own debates with the supporters of other candidates. However, results were announced on Election Day only an hour or so after the polls were closed, while people in many districts were still waiting in line to vote. Something seemed to have gone terribly wrong with the process that had elevated expectations and caused a high voter turnout of over 85 percent, which usually leads to a rejection of the status quo.

The next day, President Ahmadinejad held a rally at Tajrish Square to celebrate his reelection with about fifty thousand of his supporters. In his speech, he called the disputers of his victory petty dust and dirt. Within forty-eight hours, 3.5 million protesters (according to the helicopter photographs taken by the mayor's office) marched through the streets of

Tehran from Azadi (Freedom) Square to Enqelab (Revolution) Square demanding that their votes be counted. The stage was set for the images that would irrevocably alter the perception of Iran and redefine the concept of citizenship for Iranians themselves.

A New Iranian Citizen

A shock was delivered to Iranian politics on that Monday after the June 12 election, not just to the government (Ahmadinejad/Khamenei), but also to the opposition Reformist camp (Moussavi/Karoubi). After all, who were the three million people who poured onto the streets? According to Roger Cohen of the *New York Times*, who was in Tehran that day, "fear disappeared, and the security forces were powerless in front of the silent masses."[1] The Reformists already knew that there was a great deal of pent-up frustration with the Ahmadinejad administration in particular, and the regime in general. But a movement that could put that many people in the streets with such discipline was unimaginable. The Islamic Republic had very effectively prevented the formation of any overtly political organization that could present a systematic challenge. However, a leaderless movement of civil society appeared to have emerged and subverted seemingly innocuous organizations such as neighborhood book clubs and poetry societies into nodes of organizing protest when the opportunity arose. Through the magic of the Internet, text messaging, social networking sites, and camera phones, these organizations were able to achieve a network of common goals, slogans, and strategies, including silent protest marches and the creation of innovative barriers to the logistics of security forces. For the first time in its history, Iran's civil society, not its political parties, had achieved power that could challenge that of the state through nonviolence. All sides in Iranian politics, including the coalition that had allegedly carried out the Velvet Coup (that is, the stolen election) and the opposition, quickly realized that they had to go back to the drawing board and recalculate the balance of power. There was a new powerful player on the chessboard of Iranian politics, and neither the government nor the opposition had any idea how to control it.

Some call the current relative calm on the streets of Iran a victory for the security forces. It is more likely a pause in order to reappraise the situation and make necessary adjustments for a potential endgame. Meanwhile, the Iranian citizenry has gained a new consciousness of its role in society, has acted upon it, and is becoming more fearless while carrying on with episodic protests that are appropriating holidays and anniversaries from the government (Jerusalem Day, Student's Day, and the Memorial of Grand Ayatollah Montazeri). They have no tolerance for unrealistic utopian ideas or ideological straitjackets, and will not submit to violent paths to achieving their goals. The followers of a newly emerged Reformist interpretation of Islam only make limited demands for democratic and civil rights. Creativity in expressions of dissent—in order to find solutions to their political dilemmas—is their mantra.

In late December 2009, Borzou Daragahi of the *Los Angeles Times*, having just returned from Iran, said that many ordinary and formerly apolitical Iranian citizens had started to see themselves as part-time activists. He said that he had met a sixty-four-year-old housewife who goes about her daily chores as usual but takes a couple of hours in the afternoon to help the Reformist Movement, then goes back home and returns to her normal daily life.[2] This would have been unthinkable just two years earlier. Such citizen empowerment that aims to be sustainable and strategic, and to minimize the burnout factor and potential violent encounters, is impossible for any regime to ignore.

The Green Movement may also be presenting a new model for civil disobedience that aims to steer away from traditional organization structures with a morphology that a repressive state can attack. Amorphous networks without charismatic leadership that can be decapitated might prove more effective under such circumstances. Yet the model has its limits as well. It has been accused of being comprised mostly of a middle-class urban demographic. Although two-thirds of Iran lives in urban settings, the Green's relationships with other movements in Iran—such as its labor, women, and ethnic and religious minorities organizations—do not yet seem to be very deep.

By February 2010, when it seemed that the level of street action might be ebbing and many analysts started to call the Green Movement finished, the crisis within the Iranian regime started to raise its head in other locations. The infighting among the conservatives who sought to preserve the status quo (the Principlists), which in 2007–2008 nearly led to the impeachment of Ahmadinejad (according to some straw votes, he came within three votes) and was pushed into the background through the intervention of the Supreme Leader, again came to the fore. The Supreme Leader thought such a public fight within the ruling faction, while the Bush administration was still in power, would be unwise. In 2008 the Principlists, who can be roughly divided into three camps—a "pragmatic" wing led by the speaker of the Majlis (Ali Larijani), an "ideological" wing led by the Supreme Leader, and an Iranian Revolutionary Guard Corps (IRGC) wing led by President Ahmadinejad—were ordered to line up behind Ahmadinejad for the 2009 elections. In the fall of 2009, Iranian diplomats seemed to have reached an agreement in the five-plus-one negotiations in Geneva on Iran's nuclear technology issues. Yet upon their return to Tehran, the Iranian Foreign Ministry started to backpedal on the agreement. It is believed that the Ahmadinejad administration, while it was deprived of legitimacy in the aftermath of the elections, was being accused by a faction of the Principlists of being weak and giving away the store to the Americans. Hence, since Turkey and Brazil are easier parties for Iranian diplomats to make concessions to on the nuclear issue, an alternative strategy of engaging them on this issue was pursued.

Domestically, several monumental battles have been waged for control of various Iranian institutions such as the Tehran Metro, the monorail project, and major museums. The biggest fight is over control of the Board of Trustees of Azad University, which was elevated to debate in the legislative branch. Azad is a private university that was created after the Islamic Revolution. It now has more than thirty campuses all over Iran as well as in other countries. It has 1.2 million students enrolled, and its assets and endowments are estimated to be worth anywhere from $120 billion to $251 billion. President Ahmadinejad, through the Ministry of Education and the Revolutionary Court system, tried to wrestle control of this university away from the likes of former president Akbar Rafsanjani who serves as the chair of its board. The pro-Ahmadinejad paramilitary Basij forces showed up in front of parliament and denounced Speaker Larijani (a Principlist and recent ally of Ahmadinejad). The debate on the motion became so acrimonious that members of parliament started to use vulgar language against one another and almost broke out into scuffles. The issue remained unsettled and stuck in a political/bureaucratic quagmire as of

August 2010. Already, ambitious Principlists such as Larijani and Mo-hammad Baqer Qalibaf, the mayor of Tehran, who would like to have a chance at the presidency in 2013, are trying to distance themselves from the Ahmadinejad legacy and have begun to call him "yesterday's presi-dent." They are also calling his folksy and sometimes vulgar political rhetoric "un-presidential." It is not clear if some of these fights are still part of the Principlist versus Reformist struggle or if they represent the victorious Principlists trying to divide the postelection spoils, though the Supreme Leader is trying to be the glue that keeps the Principlists to-gether. Either way, even without street action by the Greens, Iran seems to be a backroom deal away from presidential impeachment or the in-trigue of significant purges and a potential palace coup. Overall, the new and undeniable reality of a dissatisfied Iranian citizenry and the system's inability to achieve a political solution has created a predicament that is affecting Iran's domestic and foreign policies. The government's overreli-ance on an intelligence/security paradigm seems inadequate to solving the nation's long-term problems that present themselves as a social phe-nomenon through civil society.

It's the Political Economy, Stupid

Regardless of the ideological and religious fronts that regimes maintain, the questions of power and control of the economy tend to play key roles in the evolution of a regime. Though much analysis has been done on the "Islamic" nature of the Iranian regime (IRI), very little is usually said about the nature of the economy of Iran. It is often as-sumed that Iran is much like other Middle Eastern oil producers whose unidimensional economies are about the exporting of one commodity and importing of just about everything else. The oil and energy ministries in these countries are at least as important as, if not more important than, any other ministry.

Surely Iran has some of these characteristics. After all, oil revenues ac-count for about half of the Iranian budget, and about 80 percent of the Iranian GDP is from state-controlled enterprises. Yet when one visits Iran, except in a couple of cities in the south, the petroleum industry is nearly invisible. A large segment of Iranians do not seem to be waiting to receive a handout from the coffers of a petrol-state. They are an independent and entrepreneurial lot with deep cultural beliefs in work and education, happy to run small businesses and stay away from the political baggage that government support usually brings.

In the aftermath of the Islamic Revolution, the new regime was forced to take over control of many private-sector entities. This was not so much due to ideological reasons, but was simply necessary due to absentee ownership. The old elite could not tolerate the new regime and had moved out of the country. The choice was to either shut down these enterprises and cause massive unemployment, or bring them temporarily under state control (though admittedly not very efficiently run), and reprivatize them when the situation in the country had stabilized. The range of industries affected included everything from auto manufacturing (Iran is one of the top twenty auto producers in the world and has nearly one million current and former auto workers) to textiles, petrochemicals, and a full range of service industries.

The war with Iraq (1980–1988) and the international sanctions against Iran prevented the economy from stabilizing for another decade. Wars and sanctions in particular not only destroy production capacity; they also criminalize the economy. The culture of enterprise, innovation, and the rule of law erodes, and the culture of connections, contraband, and the ability to inflict violence with impunity takes over.

During the war, the IRI realized that it could not trust the top echelon of the Iranian military whose allegiance was to the previous regime. It created the Revolutionary Guard in 1979 and the Basij (The Mobilized, later the morality police) after the war as parallel military institutions. They were the Islamic Republic's own version of the Praetorian Guard, with a dedicated and redundant army, navy, air force, and intelligence service. Iran's dependence on the West for spare parts for its military and the sanctions regime led to a complex system of smuggling and reverse engineering of previously bought Western technology. This caused Iran to grow its own native defense industry, which is almost entirely controlled by the Revolutionary Guard.

Iran has begun to produce its own updated versions of American 1970s-era technology: F-4 and F-14 fighters. It has an aerospace industry capable of launching its own satellites. When a Hezbollah rocket struck an Israeli

Navy ship in the 2006 Lebanon War, it is widely believed that the rocket launcher guidance system and the coordinates of the Israeli ship's location in the Mediterranean were provided by the Iranian Revolutionary Guard. The Israeli Defense Forces (IDF) communication system was hacked with Iranian assistance, and it seems that for much of the Lebanon War, Hezbollah was listening in on IDF communications. The West has seemingly responded with cyber warfare initiatives of its own that are targeted at Iranian nuclear facilities. The Guard is now drawing up elaborate plans for creating revenue streams from less expensive defense alternatives for developing nations. Robert Baer, a former CIA officer specializing in the Middle East, calls the Guard "the masters of asymmetrical warfare."

In short, the IRI now has its own military-industrial complex. Upon their return from the front lines in 1988, the privileged members of the Revolutionary Guard were able to negotiate commercial favors from then-President Rafsanjani. Two decades after the war, they now own ports on both Iranian coasts: the Persian Gulf and the Caspian Sea. These enterprises receive billions in transit fees from the newly independent land-locked countries of Central Asia with a voracious appetite for goods from abroad. They own numerous construction firms that are building Iran's airports and modern infrastructure. They control trading firms specializing in food items and consumer goods that drive many Iranian producers of the same products out of business. They also own investment banking firms with billions of US dollars and euros at their disposal. In one half hour in September 2009, one firm bought $7.5 billion worth of stock in the Telecommunications Company of Iran right after its privatization and IPO. In November 2009 a $2.5 billion contract to build the Baluchistan Province railroad was awarded to a contractor owned by the Revolutionary Guard. The privatization of many enterprises has finally begun along the lines of the Russian model of the 1990s, and the Guard is uniquely positioned to benefit. One could say that the Guard is on its way to creating its own versions of GE, Bechtel, AT&T, and Goldman Sachs.

In the summer of 2010, the leadership of Iran's Bazaar Merchants Association decided to go on strike against the Ahmadinejad administration's plan to increase their tax burden by 70 percent. Bazaars are a collection of central markets in various cities that have traditionally been responsible for the distribution of goods in Iranian society. They have also historically been hubs of cultural activity, as well as reputation makers, political king-makers, and the financers of political movements (such as the Islamic Revolution). Although the issue was settled a few weeks later when the government quietly backed down, many of these elite merchants are of the belief that the IRGC is out to weaken if not destroy the bazaar because of its potential political and economic rivalry. They point out that companies that are controlled by the IRGC have drawn up plans for about three hundred big-box, Walmart-type outlets, with their own distribution networks across the country that will severely damage the bazaar's future prospects.

Another economic wild card is the Ahmadinejad administration's plan for the removal (called "smartening") of subsidies for basic goods such as food and gasoline. In place of the subsidies, the government plans to pay a cash stipend to citizens who qualify on the basis of need. Some see this as part of a strategy to create a new patronage system. The policy was scheduled to begin in late 2010, but delays have occurred, and its ramifications will probably be better known by the middle of 2011.

In hindsight, the Guard leadership's overt support for Ahmadinejad in the 2005 and 2009 elections, and the break with the taboo of military intervention in politics, was an attempt by a new elite (which had historically used its position in the military to negotiate economic privilege) to try to consolidate power by getting a good grip on the nation's politics. We have come a long way from the early revolutionary days of radical clerics, political Islam, and an apolitical military. We seem to have entered an era of Reformist or Quietist clerics (secular in politics, such as the late Grand Ayatollah Montazeri, which these days seem to dominate seminary circles), in a contentious relationship with the military-businessmen of the IRGC. Almost all of the leadership of the Guard has outside financial interests, and, when it suits them, they seem to be able to get very pragmatic about their professed radicalism. A vast majority of the Grand Ayatollahs in the holy city of Qom disapprove of the current close relationship between religion and the state. In June 2010 the residences and offices of several liberal Grand Ayatollahs were attacked by thuggish-looking groups of "Seminarians" no one had seen before. The "Seminarians" called the Grand Ayatollahs traitors and collaborators with the enemy. The irony of today's Islamic Republic is that such bold attacks on high-ranking clerics had never before occurred in Iran, even in the era of anticlerical monarchy.

There is also internal resentment simmering within the Guard rank and file as a result of this privilege. According to the exit polls of the 2001 presidential election (before the politicization of the military), 70 percent of the Revolutionary Guard rank and file voted for the Reformist Mohammad Khatami. In 2010 several mid-ranking officers of the Guard defected to Western countries and spoke of deep schisms within the Guard. In July of that year, General Yadollah Javani, a senior leader of the Guard, admitted that a significant percentage of the Guard supports what he called the Fetneh, which is a derogatory term used by Iranian officials to refer to the sedition caused by the opposition (the Greens).

Toward a New Paradigm

The events of the summer of 2009 and Principlist infighting in 2010 probably mark the beginning of an endgame for the IRI as we know it. Either the coalition that is alleged to have stolen the election will conduct a successful purge and crackdown, and turn Iran into an Islamic version of Burma or North Korea (which, after the infighting, seems highly unlikely), or it will break up, and elements of the coalition will create a new coalition with the Reformist side or even the secular forces. They will have to engage in a level of profound reform of the system that would be satisfactory to the vast majority of the Iranian people. Though currently out of power, the Reformists still hold several trump cards. The talented tent of Iranian society that is integral to running enterprises seems to be behind them. Only the Reformists seem to be able to deliver a solution to the country's sense of crisis that is more politically based and does not stem from a "security" paradigm. Reformist figures such as former president Khatami are the only leaders of any significant stature and prestige who could play a reassuring role in the eyes of the international community to create a potential grand bargain that has diplomatic, human rights and economic components. There will be no significant inflow of foreign investments, which the country and its elite desperately need, without such a grand bargain. In a speech in August 2010, Ayatollah Khamenei called for a restart of the "politics of maximal inclusion."

Radical solutions seem unlikely, and a great percentage of the current Iranian elite will likely play an important role in Iran's foreseeable future.

"Reformolutionaries" (radical goals, reformist means), not revolutionaries, are the ones likely to offer actionable solutions to the Iranian people.

History tells us that the price of getting Iran wrong can be high. It is the dominant power in the Persian Gulf region, a very strategic part of the world. Along with China, Russia, and India, it is one of the primary powers that has controlled the Asian landmass—which comprises nearly two-thirds of the global population—for centuries. Iran is an intellectual leader and trendsetter for much of the region, just as it was when it made political Islam fashionable in the 1970s (and one day could with Reformist Islam). For cultural, economic, and historical reasons, Iran's sources of soft power extend as far east as Central Asia and the western borders of China, as far south as northern India and Jammu Kashmir, as far north as the Caucasus's (southern Russia), and as far west as the Atlantic coast of Morocco. Steven Kinzer, a former Istanbul bureau chief for the *New York Times* says, "When you study the history of the Middle East, you see that most of the countries in the region are made-up; they were invented by British diplomats drawing lines on maps fifty or a hundred years ago. But when you go to Iran, you realize immediately that this is the opposite of a made-up or fake country. This is a nation that has existed for twenty-five centuries on more or less the same plot of land, and whose people have a very strong sense of themselves and their nationhood."[3] In his 2010 book *Reset*, Kinzer advocates a more Iran-Turkey–anchored US policy in the Middle East.[4]

Clearly, the outside world's sanctions-and-nuclear-tech-oriented approach to Iran since the 1980s has not worked. To paraphrase award-winning scholar Trita Parsi, author of *Treacherous Alliance—The Secret Dealings of Iran, Israel and the United States*,[5] it has most likely hurt the Iranian people more than the regime. It has created incentives for the development of a nascent military-industrial complex. Normalized relations with Iran, which closely monitor human rights, will probably do more to propel the country along the one-hundred-year-old path of democratization than isolation by the great powers. Any assessment of Iranian politics has to go beyond the chess game of personalities and take into account the role of Iranian civil society and Reformist Islam, which will likely redefine the Islamic world's language of politics and liberate religion from the pitfalls of statecraft and its new political economy.

Though likely to drive a tough negotiation, the new Iranian elite is counting on a grand bargain with the West to make the assets acquired through the privatization program (Asl E 44, the forty-fourth amendment of the constitution) more valuable and to cash in on the windfall that the inflow of international investments will bring to a less isolated Iran. The traditional prism of who is more pro-West or anti-West is bound to reach its limits in this context. One could say that the fight among the Iranian elites is about who gets to negotiate the grand bargain with the West and better position him- or herself for the spoils it is bound to bring.

However, the potential Israeli-Iranian conflict is not a very useful prism through which to assess Iranian foreign policy. The Palestinian-Israeli conflict is between two small nations almost two thousand kilometers away from the Iranian border and of almost zero intrinsic strategic value to Iran. Championing the Palestinian cause brings only rhetorical value that sometimes is directed toward Arab populations in the region to help agitate against their governments. Iran has at times signaled that, given the right deal, it is willing to assume a more neutral posture on the Palestine-Israel issue. The latest attempt to strike a deal was made by Reformist President Khatami in a grand bargain offered to the Bush administration in 2003 that would resolve all outstanding issues with the United States on bilateral ties, terrorism, and sanctions. The response from the Bush administration was "We do not make deals with evil."

A significant portion of the Iranian government seems committed to increasing the private-sector share of the economy. Yet the current geopolitical situation, the country's near-perpetual state of crisis, and international sanctions help keep Iran locked in a state-centric economic mode. The Wikileaks documents that were revealed in November 2010 indicated that there may have been a serious infiltration of the Iranian nuclear programs by Israeli intelligence agencies, and that US plans to reengage Iran diplomatically were not supported unanimously within US policymaking circles. They also showed that Iran's Arab neighbors have a very hostile view of the country's government and are not likely to be significant investors in Iran's near-term economic development projects. These relationships are key to Iran's plans for projects such as the development of the South Pars natural gas reserves in the Persian Gulf that Iran shares with Qatar. The South Pars reserves are probably one of the three largest in the world.

These circumstances also prevent Iran from reforming its business culture. Its stock exchange suffers from serious transparency and governance issues that preclude it from attracting significant international capital, despite the fact that it was one of the best performing exchanges in the world in the early 2000s and 2008. The arrest of two IRGC members by Nigerian authorities for smuggling massive amounts of armaments destined for other West African countries, through a private-sector entity, indicates that the Iranian military-industrial complex intends to reach new markets, regardless of legality and international conventions.

Critical to the peaceful evolution of Iranian society will be the ability to convince the new Iranian military-business elite that their long-term interests, including the attraction of international capital, lie with the transition to a rule-of-law-based capitalism rather than a version of crony/gangster capitalism. I believe this matter to be even more important than clerical rule or the secularization of Iranian politics.

With a new paradigm of understanding Iran, the outside world can play a more constructive role in ensuring that Iran stays on a peaceful, evolutionary course. Meanwhile, the people of Iran are convinced that time is on their side.

Notes

1. Roger Cohen, "A Revolution in Crisis." Speech, Northwestern University, Evanston, IL, October 7, 2009.

2. Borzou Daragahi, An interview with Michelle Norris, *All Things Considered*, NPR, December 21, 2009.

3. Stephen Kinzer, "The Folly of Attacking Iran." Speech, Northwestern University, Evanston, IL, February 19, 2008.

4. Stephen Kinzer, *Reset* (New York: Times Books, 2010).

5. Trita Parsi, *The Treacherous Alliance: The Secret Dealings of Israel, Iran, and the United State* (New Haven, CT: Yale University Press, 2007).

16

CLIMATE CHANGE: FEASIBLE POLICY AND FUTURE CARBON MARKETS

Brian Fisher and Anna Matysek

Global greenhouse gas emissions and the world's reliance on fossil fuels are expected to grow significantly over the coming decades, particularly in developing countries. As scientific understanding of the climate change problem has improved, it has become increasingly clear that substantial emissions reductions will be required to avoid significant increases in global average temperature.

The following is a review of climate change policy rather than of the science of climate change. Although there is much uncertainty about the nature of climate change, we have taken the broad scientific consensus as presented by the Intergovernmental Panel on Climate Change (IPCC) as given and as a reasonable representation of the state of the science.

The nature of the emission reductions being discussed in the international climate negotiations go well beyond mitigation efforts at the margin because they involve major energy system transitions. To achieve this in a way that does not stifle economic growth, particularly in the developing world, is a challenge of unprecedented proportions. Technological change and economic transformation on a massive scale will be necessary. And this must be backed up with institutional frameworks and financial incentives to bring the technologies into play.

The difficulty of the task is clearly illustrated by Table 16.1, which was compiled by the Intergovernmental Panel on Climate Change.[1] Analysis of Table 16.1 shows that to limit the global mean temperature increase (compared to preindustrial levels) to between 2.0 and 2.4 degrees Celsius in the future, it is likely that global carbon dioxide emissions would need to peak between the years 2000 and 2015 and then decline steeply thereafter. There is no real political prospect that such abatement will occur in that timeframe, so the only reasonable conclusion to draw is that there will be significant global warming in the future, and that policymakers are faced with developing both mitigation responses and policies that encourage adaptation to the consequences of climate change.

In the shorter term, business will not face coordinated global climate policy; rather the operating environment in each country or region is likely to be quite different and developing countries are most unlikely to take on legally binding emissions reduction targets. As a consequence, the introduction of mitigation policies either unilaterally or plurilaterally in developed countries will lead to potential losses in export competitiveness and demands that trade measures be taken against countries that have not imposed mitigation policies. This prospect was heightened following the global financial crisis that led to a greater frequency of claims and counterclaims about the sources of global trade and current account imbalances, none of which of course have anything to do with climate change, at least at this point in time.

International Architecture

The key international agreements on climate change are the United Nations Framework Convention on Climate Change (UNFCCC) and its Kyoto Protocol. At the regional level, discussions under the auspices of agreements such as the Asia-Pacific Partnership on Clean Development and Climate (APEC) and within the European Union (EU) are also important in shaping any future agreements reached under the UNFCCC. The G-20 will also become an increasingly important forum for discussion of climate change and associated issues.

United Nations Framework Convention on Climate Change

The UNFCCC came into force on March 21, 1994, and it provides the overarching framework for intergovernmental efforts to deal with climate change. The UNFCCC has been ratified almost universally, with a membership of 194 parties along with the European Economic Community.

The objective of the Convention is the stabilization of greenhouse gas concentrations "at a level that would prevent dangerous anthropogenic interference with the climate system" (UNFCCC, Art. 2). Key principles (Art. 3) under the Convention include (1) intergenerational equity; (2) consideration of mitigation and adaptation costs for developing countries; (3) the precautionary principle, which, tempered by cost-effectiveness, should be the basis for action; (4) sustainable development, recognizing that economic development is necessary to enable mitigation; and (5) promotion of open international economic systems and repudiation of unjustifiable restrictions on international trade, including on measures taken to combat climate change either unilaterally or otherwise.

The Convention clearly distinguishes between, and establishes distinctly different commitments for, developed country parties (those included in Annex I of the Convention) and developing country parties. For the purposes of the Convention, there are many countries included in the "developing" country group that have per-person incomes well in excess of many countries included in Annex I. The first anomaly in this respect is that South Korea and Mexico (both members of the OECD) are not listed in Annex I; therefore, they were not allocated emissions reduction targets under the Kyoto Protocol. In addition, for the purposes of the Convention, countries such as Singapore are considered to be "developing."

Article 4 of the Convention establishes "common but differentiated responsibilities" for parties. Parties included in Annex I are required to "adopt national policies and take corresponding measures on the mitigation of climate change" (Art. 4.2a). Actions of Annex I parties are reviewed periodically as required by Article 4.2b. Articles 4.3, 4.4, and 4.5 commit developed country parties to providing funding, technology, and know-how to assist developing country parties in meeting their commitments under the Convention and, in particular, to adapting to climate change.

The division between the developed and the developing country parties that is enshrined in the Convention has led to legal and political blockages to the negotiations over "developing countries'" possible future commitments to reducing emissions.

At the eleventh Conference of the Parties to the Convention (COP11) in 2005, a process was initiated to consider future action on climate change beyond 2012. This discussion, known as the Dialogue on Long-Term Cooperative Action under the Convention, is an open and nonbinding process. The discussions are "without prejudice to any future negotiations, commitments, process, framework or mandate under the Convention, to exchange experiences and analyse strategic approaches for long-term cooperative action to address climate change."

The Dialogue was originally scheduled to conclude at COP13 in December 2007, but the process is continuing, and the thirteenth session of the Ad Hoc Working Group on Long-Term Cooperative Action was held at COP15 in Copenhagen in December 2009. The main objectives of this negotiation are to establish binding emission reduction targets for Annex I countries, together with concrete actions by developing countries to attempt to reduce emissions from "business as usual" levels, and to provide a means of funding emission reductions in developing countries. At COP15, the Copenhagen Accord was drafted by the United States, China, India, South Africa, and Brazil, and the COP formally took note of it. The Accord is not a legally binding document, but it acknowledges the "need" to keep warming below two degrees Celsius. In its current form, however, the Accord will lead the world to at least three degrees of warming, assuming that it leads to concrete actions.

Given the progress to date in the COP negotiations, it seems unlikely that it or any of the processes within the COP will be a catalyst for rapid agreement on a global emissions reduction regime. What seems more likely is that slow progress will be made to more closely integrate regional schemes, with emerging project-based or sectoral schemes to curb emissions growth in developing countries. Of course it is also possible that the United States and China could construct a joint deal paving the way for significant emissions reduction, but not without large wealth transfers from West to East.

Kyoto Protocol

The Kyoto Protocol came into force on February 16, 2005, and has been ratified to date by 183 countries and the European Economic

Community. Parties to the Convention that are not parties to the Protocol (such as the United States) are able to participate in meetings of the parties as observers (Art. 13).

The Protocol builds on the UNFCCC by establishing legally binding targets and timetables for the reduction of greenhouse gas emissions by countries listed in Annex B. Annex B to the Protocol is effectively those countries listed in Annex I to the Convention, minus Turkey (some countries' names changed between the agreement of the Convention and the Protocol as a consequence of the reorganization in Eastern Europe). As noted earlier, the specific listing of countries in Annex I and Annex B means that not all industrial countries have emissions reduction targets under the Protocol.

Article 3.9 specifies that consideration of emission reduction commitments for parties included in Annex I for the second and subsequent commitment periods shall be initiated at least seven years before the end of the first commitment period (2008–2012). In accordance with that provision, the first Conference of the Parties serving as the meeting of the Parties to the Kyoto Protocol (CMP1 in 2005) began the process by establishing the Ad Hoc Working Group on Further Commitments for Annex I Parties under the Kyoto Protocol (AWG). The fifteenth session of the AWG was held in Copenhagen in December 2009.

Achievements to Date

Reflecting international concern about the possible effects of climate change, the great majority of national governments are parties to the UNFCCC. The Kyoto Protocol to the Convention is the most significant outcome of the international negotiations on climate change response policy so far.

As a result of the Convention and the Kyoto Protocol, international awareness of global climate change has been greatly heightened over the years since 1994. The Convention has provided a forum for the exchange of information and ideas. A range of nonbinding actions have been promoted, and techniques for measuring and reporting emissions have been developed.

However, seventeen years after 155 countries originally signed the Convention, and after thousands of person-years of negotiating effort, the fact is that the Protocol (in its current form) will do little to curb global greenhouse gas emissions or to move toward stabilizing atmospheric concentrations of greenhouse gases. A great deal remains to be done to design an effective agreement to reduce global emissions following the establishment of the political framework at Copenhagen and the negotiations at the sixteenth Conference of the Parties held in Cancun in December 2010.

Possible Future Outcomes

The EU has historically been a leader on the issue of climate change. At the February 2007 EU Council meeting, the EU endorsed a unilateral target of a 20 percent emissions reduction on 1990 levels by 2020. In addition, at the same meeting, the EU indicated that it is willing to commit to a deeper cut by 2020 (30 percent against the 1990 level) provided that other developed countries commit to a similar target and that the economically more advanced developing countries "adequately contribute according to their responsibilities and respective capabilities."[2]

In an announcement on March 13, 2007, the United Kingdom went beyond the EU commitment when the country announced its own target of a 60 percent emissions reduction by 2050 and a 26–32 percent reduction target by 2020.[3] It is anticipated that these targets will be enacted in legislation, thus becoming legally binding.

The EU's approach is very similar to the one it adopted during the Kyoto negotiations: announce a stringent target and attempt to persuade others to follow.

In late November 2009, President Obama announced that the United States was prepared to commit to achieving a 17 percent reduction in emissions by 2020 compared with a base year of 2005. This commitment is substantially less than that desired by the EU because of the reference under the Kyoto Protocol to a 1990 base year, and because of Europe's preference for continuing to count emission reductions from a 1990 base. The US commitment is equivalent to about a 5 percent reduction compared with a 1990 base. Such a cut is less stringent than the one the Clinton administration agreed to in the Kyoto negotiations for achievement by 2012. It follows that considerable differences still remain between developed countries on what can be feasibly achieved in the short to medium term. From a practical political perspective these differences deepened with the electoral losses suffered by the Obama administration in the 2010 mid-term elections.

The stance of the G-77 developing countries, which includes China, has not changed. They continue to state, with justification, that their key priority is economic development and poverty eradication. A key driver in developing countries is an effort to increase energy efficiency in light of likely future increases in real energy prices and concerns about energy security. For example, China's announced aim to reduce the emissions intensity of GDP is largely motivated by a desire to increase the efficiency with which its economy uses energy. Of course, this action has the secondary benefit of reducing the growth in greenhouse gas emissions, but it falls far short of a policy that would lead to a reduction in emissions. Although under the Copenhagen Accord China has recognized the need to keep global warming to two degrees Celsius, the agreement is not binding and China's obligation under it is only voluntary.

The inherent difficulties in the negotiations, and the lack of institutional frameworks in the vast majority of developing countries to support sophisticated market mechanisms such as international emissions trading, leaves project-based mechanisms as the only meaningful way of engaging developing countries in the medium term under the Convention.

The success of project-based mechanisms hinges on the provision of financial assistance from developed countries, such as the assistance offered under the Clean Development Mechanism (CDM). However, significant progress must be made in furthering the scope and extent of the CDM and related schemes in forestry and land management if substantial reductions in emissions are to occur in developing countries. The maintenance of the CDM as an operational mechanism also provides a possible source of emissions credits for any new domestic emissions trading schemes that might be introduced in Annex I countries.

This suggests that any international regime adopted post-2012 should allow for the possibility of linking any UN-recognized market-based unilateral domestic emissions trading scheme to any project-based scheme that succeeds the CDM.

Conclusion

There is a growing body of evidence that suggests that if "dangerous climate change" is to be averted, substantial action must be taken to reduce global emissions. However, despite many years of negotiations under the UNFCCC and the Kyoto Protocol, the international community is a very long way from achieving a truly global framework that will make the required mitigation inroads over the next few decades. The difficulties experienced in the negotiations at COP15 in Copenhagen at the end of 2009 are strong testimony to this fact.

One of the key reasons for this lack of progress, despite all best efforts, is that individual countries have very different priorities and political imperatives. This divide is particularly stark between developed and developing countries. However, given that the climate problem cannot be solved in the absence of key developing countries such as China and India, it is crucial that the means be found to engage these increasingly large emitters in any future policy architecture.

Although international emissions trading has long been portrayed as the best possible policy approach, it will be a long time before a global scheme emerges. In addition to the difficulties associated with engaging developing countries, it is not clear that many Annex B countries have the necessary institutional frameworks to properly support a monitoring and enforcement regime that is compatible with a viable international emissions trading scheme.

Despite these difficulties, some countries have either introduced or signaled that they will introduce emissions trading schemes. Even so, the political difficulties with introducing such schemes remain significant. For example, in 2009 the Australian government failed to get the Australian parliament to agree to its proposed domestic emissions trading scheme. In 2010 the minority Australian government, with the support of independents and the Greens, announced a new process to reconsider this and related policy instruments.

Some commentators believe that governments can relax once a domestic emissions trading scheme is introduced. However, contrary to popular belief, unilateral schemes will do little on their own to solve the global climate problem. Effort needs to be made to coordinate such schemes with mitigation efforts by other major emitters. In addition, greater attention needs to be paid to technology policy.

The unprecedented scale of technology development and deployment that will be required over the coming decades suggests that a priority area is the development of agreements that focus on technology R&D and the widespread deployment of resulting innovations. At present, the scale of technology R&D is not commensurate to the task at hand. Governments should urgently address this issue to stem the historic downward trend in energy R&D expenditures. The long lead times, spillover effects, high risk, and intellectual property constraints associated with new developments all suggest that there may be an incentive for countries with similar resource bases or interests to collaborate and subsequently enjoy the benefits of any innovations.

Until at least 2020, the policy environment that international businesses are facing is one that is likely to be characterized by a large number of loosely related policy regimes across countries and regions, with a mixture of some market-based measures and (potentially quite significant) regulation designed to discourage the emission of greenhouse gases. This will add to the complexity of doing business, particularly across international borders.

Governments' primary focus to date has been on attempts to negotiate regimes that will lead to the mitigation of greenhouse gas emissions and control the rise in global average temperature to be no greater than two degrees Celsius, which is essentially a politically defined target. However, there is currently no evidence that global emissions are on a trajectory consistent with holding the average global temperature increase at two degrees Celsius or below by 2100. In fact, global emissions are continuing to grow significantly despite international negotiating efforts. It is already more likely that, subject to the science, the present global emissions pathway will result in at least three degrees Celsius of warming by the year 2100. The implication is that it will be necessary for the world to adapt to a significant level of climate change in the coming decades. This has implications for many businesses. For insurance, the implications are potentially negative as claims for climate-related damages increase. This situation presents a possible opportunity for plant and animal breeding and genetic

Table 16.1 Characteristics of Post-TAR Stabilization Scenarios

Category	Radiative forcing (W/m²)	CO₂ concentration (ppm)	CO₂-eq concentration (ppm)	Global mean temperature increase above pre-industrial at equilibrium using "best estimate" climate sensitivity (°C)	Peaking year for CO₂ emissions	Change in global CO₂ emissions in 2050 (percent of 2000 emissions)	No. of assessed scenarios
I	2.5–3.0	350–400	445–490	2.0–2.4	2000–2015	−85 to −50	6
II	3.0–3.5	400–440	490–535	2.4–2.8	2000–2020	−60 to −30	18
III	3.5–4.0	440–485	535–590	2.8–3.2	2010–2030	−30 to +5	21
IV	4.0–5.0	485–570	590–710	3.2–4.0	2020–2060	+10 to +60	118
V	5.0–6.0	570–660	710–855	4.0–4.9	2050–2080	+25 to +85	9
VI	6.0–7.5	660–790	855–1130	4.9–6.1	2060–2090	+90 to +140	5
						Total	177

Source: IPCC (2007, p. 15)

engineering as pressure mounts to breed new drought-resistant and more temperature-tolerant cultivars and animal breeds. For the pharmaceutical industry, the implications are potentially positive as new drugs and chemicals will be required to counter the spread of temperature-related diseases. While the implications are potentially negative for the insurance industry, there may be some upside for construction as it becomes more necessary to secure existing cities and other economic and environmental assets against rising sea levels. Of course, the observations regarding potential opportunities for individual industries depend on reaching an agreement to mitigate the growth in greenhouse gas emissions to the extent necessary to avoid a climate-driven collapse in world economic growth. Such an outcome would clearly be in no one's long-term best interest.

1. The understanding of the climate system response to radiative forcing as well as feedbacks is assessed in detail in the IPCC's Fourth Assessment Report. Feedbacks between the carbon cycle and climate change affect the required mitigation for a particular stabilization level of atmospheric carbon dioxide concentration. These feedbacks are expected to increase the fraction of anthropogenic emissions that remain in the atmosphere as the climate system warms. Therefore, the emission reductions to meet a particular stabilization level reported in the mitigation studies assessed here might be underestimated.

2. The best estimate of climate sensitivity is three degrees Celsius according to the IPCC's Fourth Assessment Report's Summary for Policymakers.

3. Note that global mean temperature at equilibrium is different from expected global mean temperature at the time of stabilization of global greenhouse gas (GHG) concentrations due to the inertia of the climate system. For the majority of scenarios assessed, stabilization of GHG concentrations occurs between 2100 and 2150.

4. Ranges correspond to the 15th and 85th percentile of the post-Third Assessment Report (TAR) scenario distribution. CO_2 emissions are shown so that multi-gas scenarios can be compared with CO_2-only scenarios.

Notes

1. Intergovernmental Panel on Climate Change, "Summary for Policymakers," in *Climate Change 2007: Mitigation. Contribution of Working Group III to the Fourth Assessment Report of the Intergovernmental Panel on Climate Change*, ed. B. Metz, O. R. Davidson, P. R. Bosch, R. Dave, and L. A. Meyer (Cambridge: Cambridge University Press, 2007), 15.

2. Council of the European Union, 2785th Council Meeting, Environment, 6272/07 (Presse 25), February 20, 2007, 13.

3. United Kingdom, Department for Environment Food and Rural Affairs, "New Bill and Strategy Lay Foundations for Tackling Climate Change—Miliband," March 13, 2007, http://webarchive.nationalarchives.gov.uk/20100401103043/http://www.defra.gov.uk/news/2007/070313a.htm.

PART

VII

CRISIS AND REFORM

17

WERE BANKS BUST IN 2009? AND DID THEY REALLY NEED MUCH MORE CAPITAL?

Tim Congdon

As they returned to their desks early in the New Year of 2010, bankers were asking, "When will our institutions again be regarded as well capitalized by central banks and regulators?" On December 17, 2009, the Basle Committee on Banking Supervision had announced consultative proposals on the promotion of "a more resilient banking sector,"[1] which were already becoming known as Basle III. The proposals did *not* contain precise numbers for a new regulatory minimum level of capital, but the aim is clearly for more consistency between countries in accounting standards and the regulatory calibration of risk assets. The move toward greater consistency was intended to have taken effect quite quickly, after only a few months of consultation in early 2010. To quote the press release, "The fully calibrated set of standards will be developed by the end of 2010 . . . with the aim of implementation by end-2012."[2]

The resulting negotiation were to directly involve twenty countries (that is, the G-20), including China, India, Saudi Arabia, and Argentina. These countries had utterly different agendas, but—in their attempts to attract well-paid international financial and business service industries—they were all competing with non–G-20 "city-states" (such as Singapore, Hong Kong, Dubai, and Qatar). Would a new, fully articulated bank capital regime have been agreed to by the end of 2010? The likelihood had to be low. Great uncertainty about the banking industry's regulatory framework would probably persist through 2010. This in itself was undoubtedly negative for economic activity, implying that near-zero interest rates will persist for many months yet to come.

Officialdom—with much public support from movers and shakers in the financial sector—was unanimous for most of 2009 that "banking needs more capital." (The private views of the movers and shakers were—and remain—usually very different and often unprintable.) The underlying thought was hardly complex: The more capital a bank had relative to its risk assets, the greater its ability to withstand losses and the lower the probability of another financial crisis. After the macroeconomic trauma that followed the collapse of Lehman Brothers in September 2008, no one could be surprised that in the closing weeks of 2009 the Basle Committee on Banking Supervision endorsed—among other things—a new maximum leverage ratio in the banking sector. But the exact meaning of the new leverage ratio, as well as of such other objectives as more international

---

Box 17.1

Four Points Arguing against Higher Capital-to-Asset Ratios in Banking

---

1. In the fifteen years leading up to the mid-2007 closure of the international interbank market, the world's leading economies enjoyed the so-called Great Moderation, while Basle I (and, for a time, Basle II) capital rules were in force. The Great Moderation saw more stable and benign macro outcomes than any period of comparable length in the twentieth century. The often-repeated argument since mid-2007—that the Basle I rules were too easygoing, and so risked instability—is far from proven.
2. Higher capital ratios will raise the cost of bank finance and handicap commercial banking in its competition with other forms of capital raising.
3. If implemented too quickly, the introduction of higher capital ratios will cause banks to further shrink risk assets, leading to another phase of balance-sheet retrenchment, negligible or low monetary growth, and weak economic activity.
4. Although the main novelty of the Basle Committee's latest proposals is an insistence on international harmonization, in practice this will prove to be a pipe dream. Those nations that fully enforce the new, tighter rules will find that they lose wholesale banking business to other, more liberal jurisdictions. The United Kingdom and its financial center, the City of London, are particularly vulnerable.

consistency in accounting standards, was still largely a matter of guesswork. This chapter argues that, as far as the US *commercial* banking industry is concerned (as distinct from its *investment* banks), the case for a tougher capital regime was difficult to establish from industry-wide data, even in 2008 and 2009. Opposition to higher capital ratios in the banking sectors of the United States and other countries was intense in late 2009 and 2010, and continued to be so in the beginning of 2011. Four points against a move to higher capital-to-asset ratios are developed in the sections that follow and are summarized in Box 17.1.

Claims of Systemic Global Banking Problems Overlook Two Key Facts

The financial crisis since mid-2007 has been so severe—the worst since the 1930s in most countries—that many people take it for granted that "something was wrong with the system as a whole" instead of with the management of particular organizations and events. The claim that the problem was general instead of institution specific leads to the argument that capital ratios for the whole system need to be boosted in order to make it safer. This claim overlooks two obvious counterarguments.

First, banking authorities agreed to the first set of international capital regulations (Basle I) in the late 1980s, and these regulations took effect before the end of 1992. While the post-2007 crisis has been of appalling severity, banks were subject to more or less the same capital regime in the fifteen years from 1992 to 2007, a period celebrated as the "Great Moderation" because of its benign macro outcomes. (In qualification, a somewhat different set of rules—Basle II—was adopted in 2004, although these rules were not fully and universally implemented before the onset of the crisis in mid-2007.) If the Basle capital regime was to blame for the crisis, why was it not also responsible for the Great Moderation? As macro outcomes were so good for so long, is it really beyond dispute that the capital rules were too lax and needed to be tightened up?

Second, although thousands of banks have been affected by the crisis to some extent, numerous institutions are now emerging—usually after a round of capital raising—with relatively little damage. The United States is commonly seen as the main source of the crisis. Given the apparent

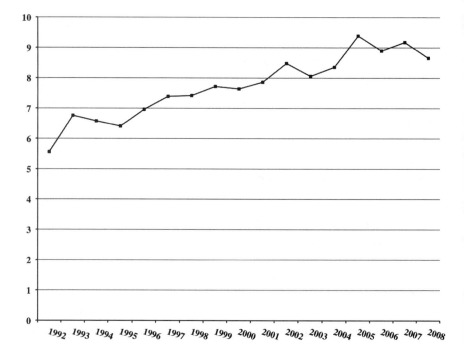

Figure 17.1 "Capital Account" as a Percent of the Ten Largest US Banks' Net Assets
Note: Total capital—not equity capital alone—was *much higher* relative to large US banks' assets in the mid-2000s than it had been fifteen years earlier, while the late 1990s and most of the 2000s are generally regarded as a period of impressive macro stability. In other words, from a macro stability viewpoint, a case can be made that nothing much was wrong with US banks' capital regime when the financial crisis broke in mid-2007.
Source: Federal Reserve Bulletin

consensus that more bank capital should now be raised, the implication is that US banks were operating with a low level of capital, relative to current risks and past standards, by the mid-2000s. Particularly disreputable practices are alleged to have been the tranching of mortgage-backed securities and the willingness of banks to hold these securities. As has been said many times in retrospect, large decreases in house prices could wipe out the value of the more risky mortgage-backed securities and hence part of the banks' capital. But what is the evidence? Figure 17.1 shows the ratio of capital—both equity and bond capital—to the ten largest US *commercial* banks' assets. (Note that Figure 17.1 relates to commercial banks under

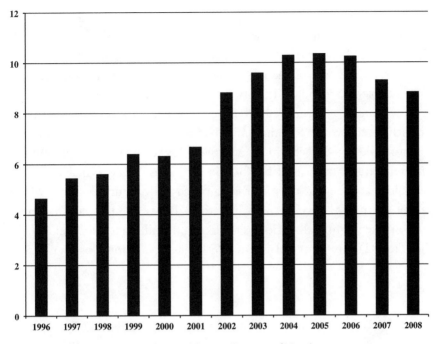

Figure 17.2 Mortgage-Backed Securities as a Percent of Net Assets
Note: Mortgage-backed securities originated in the 1980s, not in the 2000s, and have therefore been an important asset for US banks for a long time. The chart shows that the big jump in banks' holdings took place in 2002, a few quarters *before* the housing boom started.
Source: Federal Reserve Bulletin

Fed supervision, not to the entire banking industry.) The message is striking: Capital has been much higher relative to assets over the last decade than it was in the early 1990s. In 2009, banks' capital-to-asset ratio rose markedly, and available data for 2010 indicated that this trend continued. As of January 2011, US banks are much better capitalized than they were before the Basle I rules came into effect.

Figure 17.2 confirms that big US banks had a strong appetite for mortgage-backed securities during the boom in the housing market and structured finance from 2003 to 2006. During these years mortgage-backed securities were roughly 10 percent of their assets, about double the ratio in the late 1990s. However, Figure 17.2 also shows that the big surge in banks' holdings occurred *before* 2003 (that is, before the housing bubble).

The surge is probably best explained by banks' attempts to increase their earning assets when loan demand was weak, not by poor credit appraisal. In any case, US *commercial* banks' holdings of mortgage-backed securities were predominantly of the least-risky tranches, with their initial ratings being triple-A or similar. (Investment banks are another story.)

Since July 2009 the Federal Reserve has in fact been publishing a monthly series on US commercial banks' "net unrealized gains/losses on available-for-sale securities." Mortgage-backed securities represent the greater part of their available-for-sale securities, while available-for-sale securities account for most of the so-called toxic securities about which many journalists have been so hysterical. Between July and December 2009 these net unrealized losses fell from $55.1 billion to just over $10 billion. (See Figure 17.3.) Relative to US banks' total capital of over $1,000

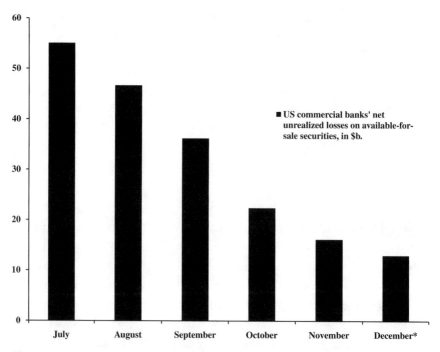

Figure 17.3 How Bad Is the Problem of So-Called Toxic Securities in the US Banking System?
Note: The remaining loss of just over $10 billion is a tiny fraction of banks' capital.
*December relates to December 16, not the monthly average.
Source: Federal Reserve

billion, and indeed relative to the system's operating profits *in one year*, the $10 billion loss was a fleabite. As many bankers and observers remarked in late 2007 and 2008, the supposed problem of toxic securities in *commercial* banking was and remains much exaggerated. (In the spring of 2010 the value of the toxic securities reported on the Federal Reserve website became positive. In other words, the banking system was making capital gains on its available-for-sale securities. In late July 2010 the positive number exceeded $10 billion. At the time of writing in January 2011, the latest figure was from December 22 and stood at $1.6 billion, which is of course a trifling for the system as a whole.)

The overall conclusion is that, as far as the United States is concerned, many executives in the *commercial* banking sector have had excusable difficulty understanding why international regulators were able to persuade themselves that extra capital was needed. The *investment* banks did indeed have a serious problem in 2008, because most of them (including the most risky tranches of asset-backed securities) had been manufacturing inordinate quantities of "structured products" during the boom and still held large amounts of inventory when the crisis broke. They did suffer losses running into many tens of billions of dollars. In this sense the post-2007 crisis was specific to this particular type of institution and, in fact, largely to the well-known names (Lehman Brothers, Bear Stearns, Citigroup, and Merrill Lynch, plus some specialist mortgage lenders in the commercial banking sector).

The majority of US commercial banks were and still are in a different position. They also have had their difficulties, which is hardly surprising given that peak-to-trough falls in house prices and commercial real estate were, respectively, 30 percent and more than 40 percent. But these difficulties should be kept in perspective and were *not* appreciably worse than in other postwar recessions. Since most banks survived the postwar recessions, why should extra precautions be taken with capital now? There is a regular monthly series that provides a crude guide to US banks' level and change in capital. This is the Federal Reserve's "Assets and Liabilities of Commercial Banks in the United States" published on its website. In November 2009 the figure was $1,327.6 billion, compared with $1,173.1 billion a year earlier; in November 2010—after hundreds of billions of write-offs—it was $1,362.6 billion. The media alleged at various points in the crisis that the US banking system was "bust" or "insolvent." Even columnists such as Martin Wolf of the *Financial Times*—taking his cue from Nouriel Roubini of Roubini Global Economics—have indulged in this sort of scare-mongering. Of course, no banking system can withstand slides in asset values of, say, 40 to 70 percent. But, despite severe asset price oscillations from 2007 to 2010, the US *commercial* banking system plainly was not bust at any stage in the Great Recession. In fact, the preliminary data suggested that American banks have over 15 percent more capital in January 2011 than they did two years earlier, while their risk assets have fallen. The May 2010 issue of the *Federal Reserve Bulletin* contained its regular annual article on US commercial banks' "Profit and Balance Sheet Developments." The item for "capital account" was 10.5 percent of net consolidated assets in 2009, compared with 9.9 percent in 2008, with an average in the nine years leading up to 2008 of less than 9.5 percent. The article confirmed that, despite an unusually high incidence of losses on residential mortgage assets, the US commercial banking system was fully solvent throughout 2008 and 2009.

In any case, asset value slumps of over 40 percent are due to incompetent central banking and monetary policy. In the three years leading up to late 2007, the Federal Reserve allowed broad money (on the M3 measure) to grow at an annual rate well into the double digits, setting the scene for the housing and real estate bubbles. (See Figure 17.4.) No individual bank was responsible for the monetary excesses of that period or can be blamed for the subsequent collapses in asset prices. It would be wrong for bankers and their regulators to set capital ratios to anticipate such violent asset price movements. To summarize, US commercial banks appear to have significantly more capital now than at the end of 2008. Assuming that American house prices stabilize or continue rising, the US banking system is far from being bust. If regulators attempt to impose further large increases in capital requirements, the banking industry and its customers would be right to resist. Contrary to the impression given by the media, a good case can be made that the crisis in the United States—the country that is supposed to have been the main culprit for the disaster—has been institution specific rather than general and systemic.

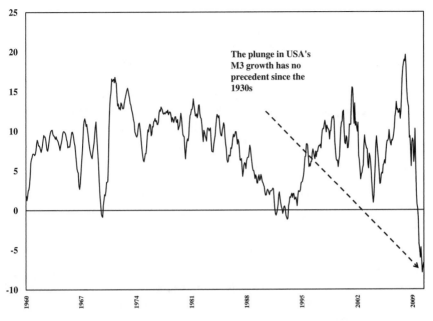

Figure 17.4 The True Cause of Asset Price Volatility in the Latest American
Business Cycle: Incompetent Monetary Policy
Note: The chart shows the annualized growth rate of the US M3 (in percent). The
last value is for June 2010, but even in December 2009 the value would have been
negative, at −5 percent.
Source: Data from March 2006 on is courtesy of Shadowstats.com. Earlier data
courtesy of the US Federal Reserve.

Advocates of Higher Capital Ratios Do Not Sufficiently
Recognize for the Pitfalls of Implementing Them

The ratio of bank loans (primarily banks' risk assets) to national
income depends partly on cost. The higher the cost of bank loans (that is,
the spread over cost of funds, which is usually approximated by interbank
rate), the lower the equilibrium ratio of bank loans to national income.
The cost of bank loans has to be sufficient to deliver a positive return on
banks' capital. If other influences on profit outcomes (including expectations of loan losses) are held constant, and if the rate of return on bank
capital is taken as given, then the cost of bank loans is a positive function
of banks' capital-to-asset ratios. It follows that the higher banks' capital-
to-asset ratios are—as determined by regulators and central bankers (usually

Box 17.2

Algebraic Argument on Banks' Profits and Loan Margins

Let a bank's assets be split between cash, C, with c representing the ratio of cash to assets, and earning assets or loans, L. Then total assets $A = C + L$ or $A = c.A + L$. So $L = (1 - c) \cdot A$. Profits (P) are equal to the loan margin or profit "spread" on assets, s, multiplied by the earning assets, L, or

$$P = s.L = s \cdot (1 - c) \cdot A,$$

while the rate of return on capital (K) is P/K, which is

$$P/K = s \cdot (1 - c) \cdot A/K.$$

So

$$s = P/K \cdot (1/[1 - c]) \cdot K/A.$$

It is clear that, if the loan margin is given, the rate of return on capital is inversely related to the cash/assets ratio (or indeed in practice the cash/deposits ratio) and the capital/assets ratio.

after consultation with the banks themselves)—the lower is the equilibrium level of banks' risk assets relative to national income. The foregoing argument (which can be summarized in algebra—see Box 17.2) has an obvious message. If regulators increase capital-to-asset ratios, they must expect banks to shrink risk assets. Nevertheless, throughout 2009 regulators and politicians were simultaneously demanding that commercial banks raise capital-to-asset ratios and expand lending (that is, increase risk assets)! Like Alice in Wonderland before breakfast, commercial bankers were being asked to pursue the impossible.[3]

In a message in the German newspaper *Bild Am Sonntag* on December 27, 2009, Jean-Claude Trichet, president of the European Central Bank, decided to remind banks of their duty. In his words, "The economy's continued gradual recovery in 2010 is dependent on the efforts of all of us. Banks must perform their central role in the supply of credit to the economy."[4] Trichet must have been fully informed of the latest Basle Committee proposals. How many times has it been repeated that the banks cannot be expected to "supply credit" if they are being also required to raise the ratio of their capital to their risk assets, since "bank credit" and risk assets come to the same thing? Trichet's final sentence was that "Confidence is the key word for 2010." Well, well. Does anyone remember the great military strategist who told his generals that the answer to their logistical dilemma was simple, to move their forces "by land, by sea, and by air?" To reiterate the main point being emphasized here, the more capital that banks are required to hold relative to their risk assets, the higher is the cost of bank loans to their nonbank customers, and the lower is the equilibrium ratio of bank loans (to the private sector) to national income. The idea that a lower ratio of bank loans to national income implies a lower capital stock (and hence lower living standards) can be debated, but the view is certainly arguable, and is indeed a commonplace in the literature on financial development.

Implementation of Higher Capital Requirements Should Be Phased In over Time

In a weekly International Monetary Research e-mail from September 14, 2009, I pointed out that there was "a paradox of excessive regulation":

> Governments in the leading advanced countries are agreed that banks must have higher ratios of capital to assets to make them safer and so to prevent a recurrence of the crisis of 2008/9. But there is a paradox—the paradox of excessive bank regulation— here. Capital-to-asset ratios can be increased in two ways, by boosting capital or shrinking assets. If banks shrink their assets, their deposit liabilities will also decline. But deposits can be used to make payments and are money. In other words, the current drive to make banks less leveraged and safer is having the perverse consequence of destroying money balances. This destruction of money damages company liquidity, hits asset prices and reduces spending. Bizarre though it may sound, the current regulatory pressure to curb the risks in bank balance sheets strengthens deflationary forces in the world economy. That *increases* the risks of a double-dip recession in 2010.

Not only is the logic of this argument unassailable, but also its empirical validity was amply confirmed by financial trends in the closing months of 2009 and 2010. Under pressure from regulators, governments, and the media, banks have continued to cut back on risk assets in order, at least supposedly, to strengthen their balance sheets. Meanwhile money growth almost everywhere in the advanced world (except Australia) was negligible and recovery disappointing.

The December 17, 2009, statement from the Basle Committee said that the implementation of the new rules would be phased in so as not to jeopardize recovery. But suppose the effective increase in the capital-to-asset ratio were to be 20 percent. (If it were to be less than this, why had there been so much kerfuffle?) If the increase were to take effect by the end of 2012, as the committee's proposals stated, either the banks would have to raise yet more capital or to reduce risk assets by significant amounts of roughly 5–15 percent a year. If risk assets had to be reduced at this pace, the growth of broad money would undoubtedly continue to be weak.

Perhaps the banks did have a capital problem in late 2009. If so then—because of the feedback from the potential contraction of money to asset prices and loan losses—any increase in capital ratios ought to have been allowed to take effect very gradually, say over five to ten years. Imposing an early deadline (the end of 2012 was a very early deadline in this context) would exacerbate the debt-deflationary processes that are now under way in, for example, several eurozone member states. The larger principle to be applied in this context is straight forward: the earlier the deadline for the completion of the move to the higher capital-to-asset ratios, the worse is the macroeconomic outlook over the short term. Why was there such a rush in late 2009 to implement the process of balance sheet rehabilitation? In practice, most banks' balance sheet rehabilitation would come—and ought to come—from a recovery in asset prices and retentions from profit, not from new capital raising.

Shanghai Could Become the Financial Capital of the World by 2030

If there was a new emphasis in the December 17, 2009, Basle Committee proposals, it was on the need for the harmonization of rules and regulations across the main jurisdictions. In some countries central banks and regulators are so close to commercial banking systems that many commentators say that regulatory officialdom has been "captured";

in others—notably the United Kingdom in 2008—the central bank and regulatory authorities have been virtually at war in the recent past. Different degrees of application of a given regulatory framework can matter as much to outcomes as differences in the regulatory framework itself.

A common saying is that international regulation should aim at a "level playing field." But participants in the current and recent sounds of Basle discussions are kidding themselves if they think that a totally flat playing field across all jurisdictions will ever be achieved. The United Kingdom was traditionally a very hospitable location for banks, with the Bank of England acting as a benign and (mostly) efficient regulator. This has changed, possibly for good. There is little doubt that ambitious new Asian centers would like to attract as much international financial business as possible. (High concentrations of such business boosts land values, and the elites in these societies usually own much of the land.) Quite apart from the city-states (Singapore, Hong Kong, Dubai, Qatar, Bahrain), the big player in the background is China—more specifically Shanghai. China is by far the world's largest creditor nation, and its national output, measured at purchasing power parity, was about $8.5 trillion in 2009 compared with the United States' $14 trillion. (See Table 17.1.) No one can predict exactly what will happen to different countries' output by 2020 or 2030, but there has to be a possibility that—if the trend growth differential of the 2000s (that is, about 6 percent a year, with 8 to 9 percent growth in China compared to 2.5 percent

Table 17.1 The World's Leading Nations in 2008, Measured in Terms of Purchasing Power Parity GDP

Country	2008 purchasing power parity GDP, billions of "international $"	2008 purchasing power parity GDP, as a percent of world total
United States	14,204	20.4
China	7,903	11.3
Japan	4,355	6.2
India	3,388	4.9
Germany	2,925	4.2
Russia	2,288	3.3
United Kingdom	2,176	3.1

Source: World Bank

Table 17.2 The Chinese and American "Savings Pools" in 2006 and 2008

Country	GDP in 2008 in terms of purchasing power parity, billions of "international $"	Gross fixed capital formation as a percent of GDP, national data	Allowance for current account deficit/surplus on external payments, percent of GDP	Size of national "savings pool," roughly, billions of "international $"
United States	14,204	20 (in 2006)	−4	2,300
China	7,903	43 (in 2008)	6	3,900

Source: World Bank data and International Monetary Research Ltd. calculations

in the United States) persists—China's GDP will catch up with US GDP by 2020.

Because the Chinese save a much higher proportion of their incomes than Americans, the Chinese "savings pool" was already more than 50 percent larger than the United States' in 2008 (See Table 17.2.) At present, China's government—which remains a government of Communist Party members—is resisting international pressure to revalue its currency and ease its exchange restrictions. However, attitudes and thinking can change very quickly. If the Chinese yuan were to be declared fully convertible and the Chinese authorities decided that they wanted their country to take a lead in international financial business (that is, with the appropriate central bank support, legal framework, etc.), it is difficult to see what the traditional G-7 countries could do to stop Shanghai from becoming the financial capital of the world in the 2020s or 2030s. Whether China would then pay much attention to the deliberations of the Basle Committee is moot. Meanwhile the non G-20 city-states are well aware of the dynamics of the current geopolitical situation, and it has to be asked whether over the next few years they will pay much attention to the Basle Committee's conclusions either. (They may pay lip service to them in public and chuckle privately about stealing business from the West. Hong Kong's financial business boomed in 2010.)

The message here is simple: Jurisdictions that go along with the spirit as well as the letter of Basle III (when it emerges) will find themselves marginal and irrelevant players in the subsequent round of negotiations (that is, Basle IV, if the Bank for International Settlements still exists and matters) after the next crisis. They will be marginal and irrelevant because overregulation will cause the relocation of financial business from them to other centers. So they will no longer host much of the business to which the rules are supposed to relate. This warning applies with particular force to the United Kingdom, where a significant part of the nation's output (over 4 percent) was being generated by international financial services in the mid-2000s. It is hardly surprising that Goldman Sachs has announced a review of its operations in the United Kingdom as a response to the special tax on bankers' bonuses. HSBC has also signalled that it could move its global headquarters from London because of the adverse regulatory environment.

Central Banks and Governments Should Focus on Increasing Money Supply, Not Just Capital Requirements

The world's central banks, financial regulators, governments, and media are at present in the grip of a very bad idea. The idea is that, because banks are better able to cope with losses on their assets the higher their capital buffers are (that is, the higher their capital-to-asset ratios are), society benefits from ever-increasing amounts of banks' capital and ever-rising levels of banks' capital-to-asset ratios. There are at least two oversights in this line of argument:

1. Suppose that the comparison is between two stable nations (in so-called steady states, to use economists' jargon) with different capital-to-asset ratios in the banking system. Because the cost of bank loans rises with banks' capital-to-asset ratios, and because the equilibrium levels of risk-taking and the capital stock depend partly on the cost of bank finance, the equilibrium levels of risk intermediation and the capital stock are *lower* in the nation with a highly capitalized banking system than in a nation where the banks are light on capital.

2. Suppose that instead the comparison of the passage from one steady state to another, with banks' capital-to-asset ratios being increased. If capital is unchanged, a fall in banks' assets is necessary, leading—in all probability—to a decrease in the quantity of money. Banks' assets could remain unchanged if the shift to the higher level of bank capitalization

occurred through bank capital raising. But that involves depositors converting their claims on the banks into equities and bonds. Equities and bonds cannot be used to make payments and are not money. So again the quantity of money falls and reductions in the quantity of money are deflationary.

It would be much better if central banks took active and aggressive steps to boost their quantity of money. This would help asset prices, and rises in asset prices could then convert loan loss write-offs into loan loss write-backs. This would be a simple, painless, and wholly welcome form of bank recapitalization. One might criticize this idea on the basis that deliberate money creation is inflationary. However, in current circumstances, it would be antidisinflationary. Contrary to the opinion of Alan Greenspan, Martin Feldstein, Allan Meltzer, and other American monetary conservatives in mid-2009, the big threat to the recovery in 2010 was not a return of inflation but a continuation and intensification of deflation.

The year 2010 saw many interesting debates on the December 2009 set of the Basle Committee's proposals. On July 26, 2010, the Basle Committee for Banking Supervision issued a press release in which its chairman, Nout Wellink, acknowledged the importance of the phase-in period for the new capital rules. In his words, "Many banks have already made substantial strides in strengthening their capital and liquidity base. The phase-in arrangements will enable the banking sector to meet the new standards through reasonable earnings retention and capital raising."[5] According to newspaper reports, the implication was that the phase-in period for the new Basle III capital rules would be extended to January 1, 2018 or even run into 2019. The Basle Committee had shelved the December 2012 deadline. The case for gradual implementation of new bank capital arrangements had been accepted, implicitly raising doubts about the wisdom of the sudden and arbitrary bank recapitalization exercises in late 2008. Rules regarding how to handle "systemically important" institutions in times of crisis were described as works in progress, to be finished later in 2010 or 2011. During the negotiations, Germany, France, Canada, and Australia tended to resist has file pressure to undermine the banking industry from UK and US representatives. The world's banking systems and their customers had shown that they could fight the central bankers, regulators, politicians, and journalists who had done so much harm both to their industry and to the world during the Great Recession.

Notes

1. Bank for International Settlements, "Strengthening the Resilience of the Banking Sector" (consultative document, Basel, Switzerland, December 2009), 1.

2. Bank for International Settlements, "Consultative Proposals to Strengthen the Resilience of the Banking Sector Announced by the Basel Committee" (press release, Basel, Switzerland, December 17, 2009), http://www.bis.org/press/p091217.htm.

3. Lewis Carroll, quoting Alice in Wonderland on one of her many predicaments: "Why sometimes I believed as many as six impossible things before breakfast!"

4. Jean-Claude Trichet, "Special Commentary," *Bild am Sonntag,* December 27, 2009.

5. Nout Wellink, "The Group of Governors and Heads of Supervision Reach Broad Agreement on Basel Committee Capital and Liquidity Reform Package" (press release, Basel, Switzerland, July 26, 2010), http://www.bis.org/press/p100726.htm.

18

THE TOBIN TAX: CREATING A GLOBAL FISCAL SYSTEM TO FUND GLOBAL PUBLIC GOODS

Andrew Sheng

The Tobin Tax: Sand in the Wheels of Speculation

In the early 1970s, when the US dollar abandoned convertibility against gold and ushered in the era of flexible exchange rates, Yale economist and later Nobel Laureate James Tobin suggested a tax on currency trading to "put sand in the wheels of currency speculation." As he put it, "The tax on foreign exchange transactions was devised to cushion exchange rate fluctuations. The idea is very simple: at each exchange of a currency into another a small tax would be levied—let's say 0.1 percent of the volume of the transaction. This dissuades speculators as many investors invest their money in foreign exchange on a very short-term basis. If this money is suddenly withdrawn, countries have to drastically increase interest rates for their currency to still be attractive."[1]

Since the idea required a drastic change in global tax regimes and went against the idea of free markets, particularly the drive toward frictionless financial markets, the proposed tax was never adopted or considered seriously in official circles. Most economists, international banks, and governments do not like the idea of the Tobin tax proposal because they feel that it would be difficult to implement and may even add instability to foreign exchange markets.

The Recent Financial Crises Have Renewed Interest in the Tax

When currency speculation became controversial again during the 1997–1999 Asian financial crisis, the idea of a Tobin tax was revived as part of the antiglobalization movement. Again, the idea was deemed by the official Group of Eight (G-8) circles as not worth considering. The idea went against the grain of the free market ideology, which advocates liberalizing financial markets and encourages the free flow of capital. After all, booming financial markets in the early 2000s seemed to confirm that the ideology worked well in creating limitless prosperity. We now know, however, that the result of this ideology was massive leverage that eventually created the financial bubbles and crisis.

Despite these setbacks, the antiglobalization movement did not wholly abandon the idea of the tax, and it retained minority support in Europe and the United Kingdom. The 2007–2009 global financial crisis also brought renewed attention to the Tobin tax idea. In November 2010, the European Commission announced that it supported a financial transactions tax (FTT) at the global level, but a financial activity tax within Europe. Apparently, Germany and Austria support the FTT, but others may not agree. The FTT would be pushed to assist development aid and climate change within the G-20 forum. Among emerging markets, Brazil, Venezuela, and Argentina have also displayed support for some form of a Tobin tax.

Support for the Tax Is Found in an Unlikely Location

Strangely enough, the idea of the Tobin tax seems to have resonance in the United Kingdom. First among its supporters are charities that are interested in raising revenue to fund aid for development. Intelligence Capital Ltd., a City of London firm, found that a turnover tax on sterling was feasible and could be unilaterally implemented by UK authorities.

In August 2009, Lord Adair Turner, chairman of the UK Financial Services Authority, supported the idea of new global taxes on financial transactions in an effort to constrain the size of financial institutions that have grown too big for society. The financial services companies in the City of London came out strongly against this idea.

Critics of the tax contend that currency speculation is useful for liquid markets, price discovery, and risk management. Hence, a Tobin tax would constrain currency speculation and hurt global market liquidity.

Unfortunately, the global financial crisis has shattered conventional wisdom about global governance. Bank of England Governor Mervyn King's dictum that we have global banking in life but national banking in death characterizes the fact that large, complex financial institutions are larger than sovereign nations, ineffectively regulated in compartments at national levels, and not bound by any global laws. Their demise means that national governments have to pay for the global banks' mistakes, but ultimately the whole world pays in the form of higher inflation, near zero interest rates, increased taxation, and lost jobs.

The Westphalian System's Relevance to Finance Wanes

The Westphalian system of national sovereignty and voluntary cooperation is cracking at the seams in this highly interconnected and interdependent world. The G-20 has improved the legitimacy of global governance, but the "What to Do" is confused by turf battles over "Who Bears the Loss" and "Who Will Have the Control". It is useful to remember that the present fiscal trend of accelerating expenditure and decreasing tax revenues in order to restore excess consumption, which in turn is funded by excess leverage despite limited global resources, is just a race to another crisis.

The world is caught in a collective action trap. The gaming nature of nation-state and private-sector behavior is such that there is a tendency to race to the bottom. No country is able to tighten monetary policy alone for fear of inviting hot money that negates the policy. Additionally, no country is able to tighten financial regulation for fear of business migrating to other financial centers. Furthermore, no country is able to raise taxation for fear of massive tax arbitrage.

The Triffin Dilemma Goes Global

In hindsight, global imbalances were caused by the violation of the Triffin Dilemma writ large. The Triffin Dilemma states that the reserve currency central bank faces the dilemma of running monetary policy that is inconsistent with domestic needs. When the reserve currency country has excess consumption, its central bank should be running tighter monetary policy, but in a world of free capital flows, the efficacy of monetary policy is weakened. The trouble is that when all four reserve currency central banks (Federal Reserve Bank, European Central Bank, Bank of England, and Bank of Japan) are faced with rising fiscal deficits and hidden leverage that was pumped into the system by massive financial engineering, the systemically important countries collectively generate a global credit bubble that can only be financed by lower and lower interest rates.

The reality is that we now have a global economy without a corresponding global monetary policy, global financial regulation, or global fiscal system.

In the same way, a disjointed regulatory environment has led to excess consumption that ultimately feeds into global warming, which can only be controlled by hard budget constraints in the form of current taxation, not future taxation. We are reminded of the effects of global climate change by recent typhoons, floods, earthquakes, and droughts, as well as the estimate that biodiversity loss could cause as much as US$2–5 trillion annually, while the total cost of the current financial crisis is less than $4 trillion.

Advocates of global governance reform suggest that the current problems can be solved through a global currency or a global financial regulator. They forget that the precondition for global government action is a global fiscal system. The European currency system has demonstrated unequivocally that a single currency cannot function without some form of fiscal compensation for those who suffer regionally from the consequences of monetary policy that may not suit local conditions. We cannot agree on a global fiscal system because all taxation is currently local.

The Turnover Tax Has Many Merits

A turnover tax has many merits. First, it is a user-pay tax that is less regressive than other forms of taxation. It is akin to a gambling tax on socially negative activities. Second, a turnover tax can be countercyclical, being increased or decreased depending on the level of speculative fever in the markets. When the risk of a bubble collapse rises, the tax rate can be increased to fund safety nets in the event of a crisis. It complements capital adequacy tools. Third, a turnover tax can finance global public goods that currently have no other forms of financing. Fourth, a turnover tax will reduce financial institutions' profits and hence their capacity to pay excessive bonuses that promote too much risk-taking at the expense of society. Fifth, the turnover tax collection system will generate data on financial transactions that will help regulators monitor excessive speculation, market manipulation, and insider trading, all of which currently prevent effective global financial market supervision.

Of course, the financial sector would object to any form of new tax. But those who prosper through public subsidy in the form of deposit guarantee and enjoy higher profits at public risk deserve to pay some tax. Those who argue for frictionless finance have created a windmill spinning at supersonic speed that has fractured the global financial structure. A minimal turnover tax will impede infinite financial derivative layering that creates complexity, opacity, and potential for systemic risks.

Just how much can governments raise from a turnover tax? Based on the Bank of International Settlement's Triennial Survey data in 2007, the global annual value of foreign exchange turnover was roughly US$800 trillion. Adding another US$101 trillion of stock market trading based on the World Federation of Exchanges statistics would give total annual financial trading, excluding bonds and other over-the-counter transactions, of roughly US$900 trillion. Using a turnover tax of 0.005 percent would yield US$45 billion, roughly equivalent to the US$50 billion of annual aid pledged to Africa.

Global public goods are currently funded by equity (based on the Bretton Woods system that allocates weighted voting quotas to participating institutions) or by direct national grants. These mechanisms are not sustainable. We need a global tax to fund global public goods. But for a turnover tax to work, it is vital that all of the G-20 countries agree to impose a single, uniform rate of, say, 0.005 percent to avoid a race to the bottom from the onset. This would put into place the module of fiscal standardization and tax mechanism that improves conditions for future coordination in monetary policy and financial regulation. The tax can be collected at the national level based on buyer-pay. The tax collected could be credited to a global fund, with a formula that would allow national governments to use part of the proceeds to resolve domestic crisis problems.

A global turnover tax can fund noncontroversial global public goods, including international initiatives that promote education, before moving on to confront more controversial matters, such as funding to tackle climate change. Global problems are global tragedies of the commons. We cannot build a global fiscal system to tackle global problems overnight, but we must begin the debate.

Notes

1. James Tobin, "A Proposal for International Monetary Reform." *The Eastern Economic Journal,* Vol. 4 (1978): 153–159.

19

FISCAL IMBALANCES, ECONOMIC GROWTH, AND TAX POLICY: PLUCKING MORE FEATHERS FROM THE GOLDEN GOOSE

Jack Mintz

Burgeoning public deficits and debt will require significant fiscal correction in many countries in the coming years. Although some argue that higher rates of inflation will be tolerated to monetize debt burdens, this scenario would require a reversal of monetary policy that has successfully targeted inflation since the 1990s. A more likely course is fiscal discipline either in the form of expenditure cuts or tax increases. For some countries—especially Japan and the United States—with relatively low tax burdens and large unfunded liabilities, tax increases will be the more likely course of action.

These scenarios will be laid out in more detail below in terms of their implications for tax levels and the structure of taxes. Given the necessity for capital investment and the rising cost of capital, governments will likely rely more on consumption-based, rather than income-based, taxes as they decide which feathers they will pluck from the golden goose.

The Great Global Recession and Public Debt

Without a doubt, one of the long-term effects of the current global recession has been the sharp increase in government deficits throughout the world—in some countries more so than in others. According to the International Monetary Fund, global public deficits are expected to have reached 6.0 percent of GDP in 2010 and to fall to less than 3.3 percent by 2015. However, experiences differ sharply by country, with imbalances particularly large in the biggest countries: the United States (11.1 percent of GDP in 2010), Japan (9.6 percent), and the eurozone (8.3 percent).

As for other countries, impaired fiscal imbalances will have sharply diverged in 2010. The United Kingdom's public deficit is expected to have reached 10.2 percent of GDP in 2010. Spain's deficit is projected to have been 9.3 percent of GDP, while India's is projected to have been 9.6 percent. Much smaller deficits are expected to have occurred in China (2.9 percent), Canada (4.9 percent), and Brazil (1.7 percent). A surplus was expected in Saudi Arabia (1.9 percent).

But these 2010 deficits are not projected to be temporary. IMF forecasts of worldwide gross public debt as a share of GDP are expected to stabilize at around 79 percent by 2015, about 20 percent more than pre-recession levels. However, yawning differences in countries' experiences are forecast. The advanced G-20 debt burden is expected to rise to 110 percent of GDP by 2015, about 37 points higher than pre-recession years. However, emerging markets are expected to experience a decline in debt burdens after 2011, keeping well below 40 percent of GDP by 2015.

Growing debts in advanced countries will also put pressure on government imbalances as interest charges to service debt will almost double from 1.9 percent of GDP in 2007 to 3.2 percent of GDP in 2015. Debt burdens are especially worrisome in the world's largest economy, the United States. Forecasts are for large, unsustainable deficits in the 2010s that are not expected to dip below 6 percent, assuming a continuation of the Bush tax cuts and patches to the annual advance minimum tax to avoid greater coverage. US all-government gross debt is forecast to nearly double from 62 percent of GDP in 2007 to 111 percent in 2015. Given its poor saving rate, much of the rising debt will need to be provided for by foreign markets in Asia and the Middle East that have better balance sheets.

Public fiscal imbalances arising from the great recession are game changers for advanced economies. By 2015 governments with large debt burdens will be severely constrained in their ability to manage the economy as they seek exit strategies from the fiscal problems they face.

Some Problems Do Not Go Away: Pre-Recession Long-Term Pressures

Other major economic trends were already affecting fiscal policy before the great recession. Slower growth in the labor force—due to increased numbers of retirees as a result of population aging and low fertility in advanced economies—has begun to lead to much lower saving rates as retirees consume their wealth. With tighter labor and capital markets, productivity is impaired as wage and capital costs rise.

Demographics are also intensifying public imbalances. Age-related expenditures on pensions and health care are significant unfunded liabilities that will lead to increased public expenditures over time. For the United States, public health care and social security spending—currently 11.6 percent of GDP—is expected to rise by 5.8 percent of GDP until 2030 and an additional 3.2 percent of GDP by 2060. European health care, long-term care, and social security spending are expected to rise by 5.3 percent by 2050. While some age-related expenditures will decrease with respect to child-related programs such as education, child tax deductions, or credits due to past lower fertility rates, tax-to-GDP ratios are expected to decline as elderly populations pay less tax during retirement years compared to working years.

The other significant trend impacting fiscal policy has been the shift of resources to Asia and Latin America, where the economic growth rate has been at least double that of advanced economies. If anything, the great recession accelerated this shift. China, India, Brazil, and other large economies have emerged with stronger economies and much better balance sheets than North America and Europe.

As world economic growth is restored, demand for commodities will accelerate as manufacturing and service sectors grow faster in emerging economies. The differences between Asian and Western economic growth will be especially pronounced in energy markets. Advanced countries will cap their demand for fossil fuels to curb greenhouse gas emissions. They will seek greater energy efficiency and alternative energy supplies, including nuclear, biomass, and wind resources. In the meantime, Asian demand for fossil fuels will accelerate, thus increasing prices for oil and coal.

It's All About Capital

The combination of demographics, Asian growth, infrastructure needs, reorientation of energy systems, and public imbalances poses a significant challenge for economies to find sufficient resources to finance capital spending. New technologies can only be adopted if businesses invest in machinery, structures, and engineering. Investments to augment physical and human capital will require money and training. Unfunded liabilities are more easily paid off if economies improve their productivity rates.

However, the incentive to invest in capital will most likely diminish in the coming years as capital costs rise, savings become less abundant, and risk is better priced in financial markets. Public debt imbalances will create greater demand for capital, squeezing out private investment.

Implications for Fiscal and Tax Policies

The large deficits and debt many countries face will require major corrective actions to improve fiscal sustainability. Deficits can be financed or reduced in three ways: bonds can be issued to the public or central banks, expenditures can be cut, or taxes can be increased.

Issuing bonds to the public is not a solution for those countries with large deficits that are expected to prevail over a long period. In order to stabilize debt burdens, it would be necessary to reduce deficits to a level whereby debt financing would grow no faster than the economy. Otherwise, a debt spiral will develop that will require future corrective actions.

Selling public debt to central banks would lead to growth in the monetary supply and higher inflation. Unless monetary policy no longer targets inflation, central banks would eventually need to sell bonds back into the market to raise interest rates and slow down the economy. Given recent statements by most central bank authorities, including the Federal Reserve, the European Central Bank, and the Bank of England, it is unlikely that the monetary policy that has successfully reduced inflation since the 1990s would be easily given up.

This leaves fiscal policy as the only means to correct fiscal imbalances either in the form of expenditure cuts or tax increases. Politically, spending cuts will be more difficult to achieve in many countries given the growth of age-related spending. The Obama health care plan is a case in point. It adds little to the federal deficit on the presumption that Medicare payments will be cut back in order to fund the expansion of benefits to the uninsured. Ultimately, Congress could reverse any current commitments to reduce health care spending that add to the deficit. The recent relaxation of limits to Medicare spending from earlier legislation passed does not augur well that Congress will be able to maintain the fiscal discipline needed to control health care spending.

For many countries, tax adjustments will be the more likely course of action, especially in low-tax jurisdictions such as the United States and Japan, where the revenue-to-GDP ratio is close to 30 percent. The more difficult issue is determining which tax to increase in order to fund the deficits.

A Case in Point: The United States

Several countries have been raising taxes on the rich and tightening up corporate tax loopholes. The United States is the best example. The United States is looking to let the Bush tax cuts expire for those with incomes above $250,000. The country has already introduced a new surtax on high-income Americans to help pay for health care reform legislation. Although these tax increases will help the United States deal with the deficit, they compromise economic growth.

The United States already has an uncompetitive corporate tax regime, with one of the highest tax burdens on capital investment in the world, so there is not a lot of room available for increased taxation of industry (see Figure 19.1) without affecting competitiveness. The most significant changes could arise with respect to energy taxes, but little new revenue will be raised. For example, a windfall profits tax on oil and gas companies will be easily soaked up by large subsidies paid to alternative energy and new carbon-reducing technologies. Corporate tax increases will not be sufficient to fund large deficits, so more revenue would need to be raised by taxing people. Marginal tax rates on high-income Americans will soon reach 50 percent, and this figure will be even higher once payroll taxes are included. However, there is a limit on the extent to which income taxes

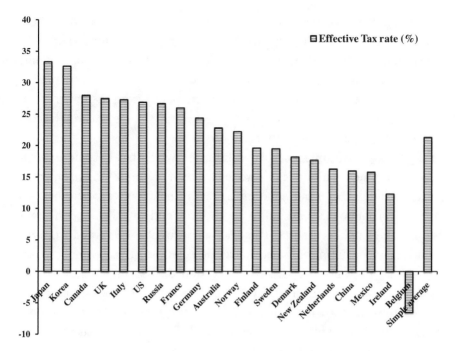

Figure 19.1 Effective Tax Rate on Capital Investment for Twenty Countries (2009)
Note: The effective tax rate on capital is calculated as the annualized value of corporate income taxes, sales tax on capital purchases, and other capital-based taxes as a share of the pretax rate of return earned by new investment projects. The US rate includes the impact of bonus depreciation—without it, the effective tax rate on capital would be 35.7 percent.
Source: School of Public Policy, University of Calgary

can help fund the deficit, leaving only one option for the United States to correct its fiscal imbalances: rely on a general source of revenue from the broad population. This could be a broad tax increase that would be borne by a majority of the population.

Consumption-Based Taxation Is the More Likely Candidate to Fund Deficits

For advanced economies that are subject to Asian competition, greater reliance on income and payroll taxes will be harmful in time, especially given capital and labor shortages with an aging population. If anything, advanced economies will need to rely less on taxes that affect mobile factors if they are going to generate greater productivity to help pay the bills down the road. More progressive income taxes discourage savings and investment as well as human capital acquisition. Income and payroll taxes have more of an effect on the working population, thereby increasing the burden of taxes on the younger generation that is bearing the cost of providing age-related public services.

This leaves consumption-related taxation, which has become increasingly important as a source of revenue for many countries. Consumption taxes include general sales and excise taxes (including carbon levies), as well as corporate taxes related to expenditure and payments for the consumption of public services. Personal taxes can also be turned from income into "consumption-based" levies by exempting the "normal" return on savings from taxation or letting people deduct savings from earnings and taxing withdrawals from accounts that are used for consumption.

The most popular form of general sales tax in the world is the value-added tax (VAT), which did not even exist before 1950. Now there are few countries without a VAT, although the United States is among the few. A 10 percent VAT in the United States would roughly raise revenues equal to 5 percent of GDP, which would significantly address its fiscal problem. The VAT would also reduce the need to raise corporate and personal income tax rates, which would be harmful to capital markets.

Excise taxes, typically applied to alcohol, tobacco, fuel, and automobile purchases in many countries, are another candidate for higher taxation. Carbon taxes as adopted in Norway, Sweden, and recently British Columbia, Canada, can be a source of revenue to help pay for public services, including green subsidy programs. Some countries are considering auctioning allowances under carbon cap-and-trade systems to raise revenue as well. The 2009 Markey-Weitzman cap-and-trade bill in the United States would give 85 percent of allowances to industries, especially to the politically sensitive coal industry. However, as this bill looks moribund, new legislation seems to focus on new spending and tax cuts to fund carbon-reducing strategies.

Some countries have adopted a different approach to taxing consumption by applying a tax on businesses' net revenues, with no deductions for payroll and interest expenses. Italy's Imposta Regionale sulle Attività

Produttive (known as IRAP) and Hungary's regional tax are examples of this form of tax, which is similar to an accounts-based VAT without border adjustments (exports are taxed and imported costs are deducted). A Californian tax reform commission in 2009 recommended the adoption of this tax in lieu of retail sales and corporate income taxes, although it looks as though this proposal will not be adopted.

Another way to engage in consumption-based taxation is to assess levies for the use of public-provided services. This would include development of highway tolls, water pricing, education tuition fees, and co-payments or user fees for health and long-term care costs. These "nontax" government revenues have increased among OECD countries in recent years, accounting for a larger share of revenues raised by governments.

Little Room to Maneuver

The fiscal imbalances governments face, including unfunded liabilities related to age-related program expenditures, have imperiled balance sheets, especially in advanced economies. Countries with large public deficits and growing debt, including Japan, the United Kingdom, and the United States, are painting themselves into a corner whereby tax increases will be a necessity in order to stabilize debt burdens. While governments will look to raise taxes in the most politically acceptable way, which often means imposing higher levies on corporations and the rich, there is little room to maneuver. Broad tax increases affecting the whole population will be necessary, and these will likely be related to consumption rather than savings and investment. Economies need capital to fund retiree consumption, to adopt new technologies to compete with growing emerging markets, and to fund public infrastructure projects, including new energy systems. The future of tax policy is to raise taxes in many countries, but to gear them toward consumption-related levies.

20

DODD-FRANK FINANCIAL REFORMS HAVE A BROAD SCOPE, AND WILL LIKELY HAVE A MODEST IMPACT

Michael T. Lewis

In 2010 the 111th Congress passed, and President Obama signed, two historic pieces of legislation. One, of course, was health care reform. The other, which is the focus of this chapter, was financial regulatory reform. Known as the Dodd-Frank Act after its principal authors, Senator Christopher Dodd (D-CT) and Representative Barney Frank (D-MA), the law will affect most financial entities and weigh on transactions ranging from complicated derivative schemes to the purchase of a gift card at the mall. Clocking in at over 2,300 pages—ten times the length of the earlier Glass-Steagall Act—Dodd-Frank granted new or expanded powers to ten regulatory agencies, established a new independent consumer protection panel, and mandated the creation of what could be more than five hundred new rules governing the operation of financial firms. Its impact will depend greatly on how these rules are crafted and implemented. The law's true benefits—and true costs—will not be fully apparent for a very long time.

That said, we can confirm that Dodd-Frank provides improvements and avoids some major pitfalls, but it also creates some brand new problems. Perhaps more significant, however, is what the law fails to address: government-sponsored enterprises (GSEs) that were critical causes of the housing and financial crises and that remain a grave concern for taxpayers, if not the integrity of the financial system.

Dodd-Frank will exert a marginal drain on financial profits and boost the cost of capital modestly, not to mention increasing employment for securities lawyers. Firms will adapt quickly, as they usually do, to mini-mize the impact of new restrictions. Consumer protection provisions will likely increase the costs of financial services for most consumers, echoing Congress's ill-conceived efforts in 2009 to curtail "excessive" credit card penalties. As often happens, the poor who need the options the most will end up worse off.

The new regulatory regime will almost certainly not be tested anytime soon. Though the administration is anxious "never [to] let a good crisis go to waste," the fact is that the financial crisis has already passed. Before legislators even put pen to paper, the industry had already undertaken its own sweeping corrections. It is safe to say that major institutions (and regulators) will not repeat the missteps of the past decade. As a case in point, mortgage and other lending standards have become tighter and more rigorous. Financial firms have also made great strides in reducing excessive leverage.

It is virtually certain that the next financial crisis will look very little like the 2008–2009 debacle. And serious systematic problems are not likely to occur for some time (following the example of the savings and loan crisis of the late 1980s and early 1990s, after which the financial system stayed in good order for a decade).

With or without Dodd-Frank, there are not likely to be any further bailouts (additional FDIC takeovers of smaller banks are another matter, but for the most part they do not fall under the new legislation). Politi-cians will be quick to claim credit, but there will be no practical way to determine whether any is deserved.

Dodd-Frank's Missing Pieces

Far more important than anything that Dodd-Frank does are the things that—for good or ill—it does not do. The most obvious deficiency is its silence on GSEs. Although Senator Dodd and Representative Frank found space to empower regulators to crack down on retail payday loans and to order companies to report purchases of "conflict gold" from Africa, they somehow neglected to say anything about some of the chief cul-prits behind the housing bubble and subsequent financial collapse. Fannie Mae and Freddie Mac facilitated—if not encouraged—all the mortgage-underwriting excesses of the 2000s. GSEs have already become the most expensive part of financial rescue efforts, and taxpayers remain potentially liable for hundreds of billions of dollars in additional losses. Yet policymakers want GSEs to support more questionable mortgage lending. Einstein was a physicist, not a political scientist, but his definition of insanity—doing the same thing over and over again and expecting a different result—seems on point here.

On the plus side, the final version of Dodd-Frank omitted most of the more onerous provisions of earlier drafts, as well as demands for even more sweeping restrictions from the left and right wings. (See Table 20.1.) Shares of major financial firms rallied as the bill neared completion, reflecting the fact that they can live with—and still profit under—this new regime.

Most critically, the Federal Reserve remains fully independent; it is even a bit more powerful than it used to be. The Fed's role in the bailouts had sparked opposition within Congress. Members from across the political spectrum were calling for complete audits of the Fed's past actions and closer monitoring of its policy decisions. Fed insiders also worried that their regulatory powers and prerogatives would be infringed upon or given to other agencies. Instead, there are no restrictions and no greater scrutiny of monetary policy, any audits will be limited and conditional, and the Fed's core regulatory powers remain intact, with even a few new areas of responsibility added. In FMI's view, some greater transparency in Fed lending would have been a welcome improvement. Nonetheless, anyone who has listened to the tortured, confused, and flat-out ignorant questions posed by all-too-many Congressmen to Fed officials testifying before them knows that political oversight should only go so far. The Fed's political independence is a necessary, though clearly not sufficient, ingredient for sound monetary policy.

Key Dodd-Frank Provisions

The biggest flash point in the debate over the Dodd-Frank law was bailouts, with Democrats claiming that the law would put an end to them while Republicans argued that it continued the "too-big-to-fail" mindset, guaranteeing more bailouts. Who is right? Both are, to some extent. Since any too-big-to-fail firms would remain nearly as big under

Table 20.1 Key Provisions of Dodd-Frank Financial Regulations

Fannie Mae / Freddie Mac	***No Action****
Too-Big-to-Fail Bailouts	Regulators get broad powers to "unwind" failing financial firms; court approval necessary if a firm resists
	All costs to be paid by fees on financial firms with assets >$50B
	Large complex institutions to provide and update "funeral" plans
	Recoupments on executive compensation in failed firms
Federal Reserve	Fed mostly escapes new congressional oversight, gains some expanded regulatory powers
Banks and Financial Firms	Volcker Rule bars banks from proprietary trading and from sponsoring or investing in private equity or hedge funds
	Multiple exemptions greatly limit effect of regulations in practice
	Raises FDIC coverage to $250K, up from $100K
	Increases capital requirements on banks
	Originators of mortgage-backed securities (MBS) must retain 5 percent ownership
	SEC registration for hedge funds over $150M
	Allows investors to sue rating agencies
Rating Agencies	Prevent MBS sellers from "shopping around" for rating agencies
Derivatives	Most over-the-counter derivatives to be traded on public exchanges / clearinghouses
	Banks barred from trading derivatives for their own benefit
Corporate Governance	Proxy access to allow outside shareholders greater ability to nominate board of directors
	Say on Pay: mandatory but nonbinding shareholder votes on executive compensation
Consumer Protection Financial Bureau	Independent agency funded through Fed (that is, no chance of congressional repeal) will have power to oversee services ranging from mortgages to gift cards; auto loans are exempt
Affirmative Action	Office of Minority and Women Inclusion within every agency will apply "fair employment tests" to regulated firms

The Dodd-Frank financial reform law spans 2,300 pages, but its full scope and impact will not be known until the new and expanded regulatory agencies issue more than 500 new rules.

Source: Free Market Inc.

Dodd-Frank, there is still a risk of bailouts. Technically, these would not be taxpayer funded, because any such action would trigger a new levy on all other large financial firms to cover the costs (though those firms—or rather, their shareholders—are taxpayers, as are their customers who would ultimately pay higher prices).

The law gives regulators broad powers to "unwind" the positions of large entities that are deemed to be threats to financial stability before it is too late. For example, if the Feds had been armed with Dodd-Frank, they would have had specific power to seize Lehman Brothers before its collapse and to force a more orderly liquidation. Now—after the fact—the government has the power to recoup top executives' compensation.

To facilitate such a move, large firms are required to provide and update "funeral" plans that would lay out how best to shut them down should the need arise. It is unclear how comprehensive these plans will be. Compiling instructions that are detailed enough to be truly useful would be expensive for the firms and would require substantial disclosure of proprietary information. Regardless, any such unwinding process is apt to be very complicated as counterparties seek to protect their own interests.

Another key battle was fought over the Volcker Rule. Named for the former Fed chairman's crusade, the rule bars banks from proprietary trading and from directly sponsoring or investing in private equity or hedge funds. Initially, banks worried that this would hurt their profits, but the final version is riddled with exemptions that will allow most to continue with some minor reshuffling.

Some parts of Dodd-Frank are benign, even favorable. It requires originators of mortgage-backed securities to retain 5 percent ownership in the hope that having "skin in the game" will ensure greater underlying quality. Extending FDIC protection to accounts of up to $250,000 corrects for erosion by inflation of the previous $100,000 cap. Provisions to prevent "shopping around" for rating agencies can prevent abuses. Increasing the ability to sue those agencies will add accountability and multiply costly nuisance suits. Trading many derivatives on exchanges will increase transparency. Corporate governance provisions create the impression that shareholders have more of a say on executive pay and other matters, but the provisions will have minimal practical effect. Collectively, these provisions will create modestly higher costs for financial firms that will ultimately translate into a higher cost of capital.

Consumer Protection Juggernaut

The most problematic element of Dodd-Frank has absolutely no connection to the financial crisis. Not wanting to "let a crisis go to waste," Congressional Democrats used the financial reform bill to create the Consumer Financial Protection Bureau. Knowing that odds for controlling Congress in 2011 were dwindling, Democrats made the agency independent and all but invincible. Because the agency is funded through the Fed, a new Congress will not be able to reduce or eliminate its budget. Nor can Congress directly overrule its regulations. President Obama can veto any GOP attempt to abolish the agency. Except for auto loans, the agency may regulate "abuses" in most financial products. However, as Congress should have learned from the credit card penalty fiasco, firms demand a reasonable rate of return. If forced to cut some fees, they will raise others.

Finally, Dodd-Frank creates affirmative action offices in every regulatory agency. Discrimination was already illegal, but financial firms can expect a lot more paperwork, as well as implicit pressure to meet hiring quotas.

Impact of the Midterm Elections

By many standards, the November 2010 elections were historic; among other things, the Republican Party not only recaptured the US House of Representatives, they won their biggest majority in more than half a century. The new Congress will likely have a far-reaching impact on taxes and fiscal policy in general. The new health care law will surely come under major attack. The financial reforms, however, will likely stand more or less unchanged.

Democrats still control the Senate, and their liberal block is large enough to filibuster a bipartisan bid to change the law. Regardless, Republicans do not have enough votes in either chamber to override an Obama veto. Through their House majority, Republicans control the power of the purse, but that holds little sway over the financial regulations. As mentioned above, Democrats insulated the new consumer protection agency from Congressional interference by giving it dedicated funding through the Fed. The other financial regulations are difficult to target through appropriations. Any substantive legislative revision will not be possible until after the 2012 elections, and then only if we get a new president elected.

21

THE FUTURE OF CORPORATE COMPLIANCE

Carole Basri

The future of compliance lies in the shadow of the global financial crisis of 2008. Predictably, demands for greater regulation immediately followed the crisis. However, we do not need more regulations that will create more administration and more extensive compliance programs. We need better targeted regulations that are consistently enforced, that foster corporate integrity, and that streamline the compliance process. Reductions in the number of compliance officers or the funding of compliance programs will be counterproductive, yet this is precisely what is happening today.

What we need now is a compliance cocktail that combines the requirements of Sarbanes-Oxley (SOX) reporting, codes of conduct, attestation, and hotlines with a holistic view of compliance and ethics. The seven steps of the Federal Sentencing Guidelines, which deal with the sentencing of corporate entities, should be disseminated and utilized along with a comprehensive risk-assessment protocol. This "compliance" cocktail is the powerful concoction that can alleviate the financial and ethical excesses of the 2008 financial crisis and prevent their recurrence. It will require a more global outlook for compliance programs of the future.

Reductions in Compliance and Ethics Departments

Reductions in compliance and ethics department head counts at financial institutions have commenced as part of the reductions in workforce resulting from the global financial crisis. It is difficult to think of a worse time to make such reductions. Yet major banks, insurance companies, and other financial institutions are implementing across-the-board cutbacks affecting these critical functions. According to the *Wall Street Journal*, "In addition to the [Citigroup] investment bank, the layoffs will be felt in Citigroup's wealth-management division, compliance and legal departments throughout the company."[1] As the article indicates, Citigroup's layoffs will be felt in, among other divisions, the compliance and legal departments. Yet Citigroup received $50 billion in bailout funds and a guarantee of over $300 billion on troubled assets from the US government.[2] At this time it is critical for compliance, ethics, and internal control functions to be expanded, not reduced. However, many financial institutions are reportedly cutting back on compliance efforts in order to reduce their number of employees and their expenses.

Compliance under SOX

SOX, which was passed in July 2002, mandates under Section 406 that the SEC requires corporations to adopt a code of ethics for senior financial officers and that such a code of ethics be a basic component of an effective compliance program. The final rules for disclosure required under Sections 406 and 407 state that "companies must comply with the code of ethics disclosure requirements promulgated under Section 406 of the Sarbanes-Oxley Act in their annual reports for fiscal years ending on or after July 15, 2003. They also must comply with the requirements regarding disclosure of amendments to, and waivers from, their ethics codes on or after the date on which they file their first annual report in which the code of ethics disclosure is required."[3]

Sections 302 and 906 of SOX require that CEOs and CFOs of public corporations covered by the SEC must certify in the company's annual and quarterly report that they have reviewed the reports and that the reports are not misleading; they are responsible for establishing and maintaining internal controls; and they have evaluated the effectiveness of the company controls within the ninety days preceding the report. Thus, under SOX, an effective corporate compliance program should have CEOs and CFOs attest that internal controls are adequate. However, this does not require effective auditing and monitoring of all risks that a best-practice gaps analysis may disclose. Further, Section 301(4) requires that the audit committee establish procedures for "the confidential, anonymous submission by employees of [the corporation] regarding questionable accounting or auditing matters." Thus, under SOX, anonymous hotline reporting is required. This reporting is part of setting up an open-door reporting policy for an effective compliance program.

SOX was critical in pressuring public corporations to adopt compliance programs. However, the emphasis under SOX is on attestation by the CEO and CFO, codes of conduct, and establishing hotlines. If a holistic compliance and ethics program under the Federal Sentencing Guidelines is to be "effective," it would require a different approach; it would not emphasize attributes that every company must have, such as a code of conduct or a hotline. A holistic program would require the compliance officer as well as the officers and directors of the corporation to think about what makes a compliance program effective. They would not be checking off a list of three or four component parts.

An effective compliance program under the Federal Sentencing Guidelines requires not only a code of conduct but policies and procedures as well as internal controls to foster the compliance program. Also, there needs to be a central authority, such as a compliance officer, who is responsible for the compliance program. There must be board oversight of the program as well as leadership from the CEO and top management to encourage participation in the compliance program.

This is only the beginning. Thorough background checks must be carried out to ensure that the people responsible for compliance and ethics have the highest ethical standards. Further, it is important that these standards, procedures, and internal controls be communicated to all employees, officers, and directors through appropriate mandatory training programs that are tailored to each person's individual needs (including relevant contractors, subcontractors, and agents). Tailoring of the compliance program should be related to the risks encountered in performing each function within the corporation. Tailoring of the compliance training should also be based on the specific industry involved.

Additionally, it is critical to regularly audit and monitor the compliance program in such areas as antitrust and competition, employment and labor, intellectual property, securities, conflicts of interest, environmental concerns, and other issues. It is also critical to set up an open reporting system—including hotlines—and to report and publicize detected criminal conduct and violations of the compliance program. Furthermore, it is essential to promote and consistently enforce, through appropriate incentives and discipline, the compliance program. This means having clear guidelines that are uniformly enforced for promoting the compliance program. These could consist of rewards for positive job evaluations related to ethics and compliance, as well as consistent discipline, including job termination for failure to uphold the code of conduct and important policies applying thereto.

Finally, the compliance program must be continually updated and modified to reflect current laws and regulations, as well as current risks. None of this is possible without creating ethics awareness for the directors, officers, and employees, as well as supporting the entire compliance program with a risk assessment to determine best practices and gaps within the corporation. As such, it was anticipated that SOX would have prevented the excesses of WorldCom, Enron, Adelphia, and Tyco that came to public awareness in 2001 and 2002.

Causes of the Global Financial Crisis Prior to Enactment of SOX

Before examining why SOX failed, it is important to understand certain financial improprieties that occurred prior to the enactment of SOX. These include:

- Developing Country Debt Crisis (1983)
- US Savings and Loan Crisis (1980s)
- Resolution Trust Company, which created REITS (Real Estate Investment Trusts) (late 1980s)
- The 1988 Basel Capital Accord (1988)
- The beginning of derivatives (early 1990s)
- Proliferation of derivatives and Special Purpose Entities (SPEs) (1990s)
- Asian Financial Crisis (1997–1998)
- Collapse of Long-Term Capital Management (LTCM) (1998)

- The repeal of Glass-Steagall (1999) and the adoption of Gramm-Leach-Bliley Financial Modernization Act (GLBA) (1998)
- The failure of dot-coms (2000)

Causes of the Global Financial Crisis after SOX and Prior to September 18, 2008

It is also important to understand the events and economic climate after the July 31, 2002, passage of SOX and prior to September 18, 2008. These events include:

- The increasing complexity of derivative products, including CDSs (Credit Default Swaps) and CDOs (Collateralized Debt Obligations)[4]
- The ascendancy of rating agencies
- Alt-A subprime lending
- Basel II (2005–2006)
- The subprime housing crisis in the United States, including the rise of "NINJA" (no income, no jobs, no assets) financing
- The rise of hedge funds
- The oil crisis (2008)
- The collapse of Bear Stearns, Fannie Mae, Freddie Mac, and Lehman Brothers (2008)

Understanding the causes of the global financial crisis will go hand in hand with regulatory reform and increasing targeted global compliance and ethics programs.[5]

Why SOX Failed

SOX was supposed to remedy the financial improprieties and excesses that existed prior to July 31, 2002. The debacles of WorldCom, Enron, Adelphia, and Tyco were only the last in a long series of financial abuses. Further, after SOX, despite the subprime mortgage crisis in the United States, rating services failed to calculate the risk of credit default swaps (CDSs), collateralized debt obligations (CDOs), and other financial abuses. Until September 18, 2008, there was no general sense that SOX had not alleviated the possibility of a global financial meltdown, or at least a US financial meltdown. No one seemed to question SOX's ability to create greater transparency and integrity in the US financial market. However, SOX ultimately failed to deliver the kind of protection its framers anticipated.

SOX failed because it was too rigid and detailed (for example, by requiring attestations from the CEO and CFO of a corporation and all of its subsidiaries), while not going far enough in creating a holistic compliance and ethics regiment for corporations. SOX should have made a difference in tapping down financial irregularities and corruption since it required more robust auditing, increased accountability of financial officers and CEOs, anonymous hotlines, and codes of conduct for senior corporate officers. Further, SOX should have prevented the current financial debacle for, at least, US banks and financial institutions. It did not.

This is because SOX did not provide a holistic program based on an ethical culture. To accomplish this, culture changes are needed at all levels of the corporation, from the board of directors and the CEO to the officers and employees. There needs to be, as Malcolm Gladwell writes in his seminal book *The Tipping Point: How Little Things Can Make a Big Difference*, a tipping point[6]—in this case, a concerted compliance program to create a tipping point within the corporation that fosters integrity and ethics among all employees, officers, and directors.

Creating a Culture of Ethics Using the Compliance Program

It is critical to create a culture of ethics using the compliance program. First, the corporation needs to create ethics awareness within the company. Then, the corporation needs to apply the seven steps of the US Sentencing Guidelines for business organizations, as revised in November 2004, on a mandatory, as opposed to a voluntary, basis.

The seven steps need to be performed with a foundation of an underlying best practice/gaps analysis, also known as a risk assessment. This best practice/gaps analysis should be performed by trained, independent outside compliance and ethics experts. Where bailout monies are provided, this analysis should be undertaken in cooperation with the US Department of Justice or the SEC. At each financial institution receiving government bailout funds, a monitor should be appointed by the Department of Justice in cooperation with the US Attorney General's office to create monitorships, similar to those in deferred prosecutions, to oversee the allocation of funds. In each case, the monitor should set up a compliance program to oversee the bailout and conduct a risk assessment to determine that all identifiable risks to the corporation have been ascertained.

Additionally, where federal bailout money is used, executive compensation and bonuses must be transparent and should be monitored through a more rigorous executive compensation compliance program than heretofore. Accountability for taxpayer money is essential to the integrity of the bailout regime. According to the *Wall Street Journal*, President Obama said that it was "shameful" that Wall Street workers received more than $18 billion in bonuses in 2008 while their firms were receiving taxpayer help.[7]

Five principles have been enunciated by the US Treasury Department regarding compensation: compensation plans should properly measure and reward performance; compensation should be structured to account for the time horizon of risk; compensation practices should be aligned with sound risk management; golden parachutes and supplemental retirement packages should be reexamined to determine whether they align the interests of executives and shareholders; and promote transparency and accountability in the process of setting compensation.

The Government's Role in Creating a Culture of Ethics

The government has a crucial role in creating a culture of ethics within corporations, particularly now in the era of the Troubled Asset Relief Program (TARP) and the Term Asset-Backed Securities Loan Facility (TALF). The US government, at the federal, state, and local levels, needs to provide vigilant enforcement of all applicable laws and regulations. As set forth in Malcolm Gladwell's *Tipping Point*,[8] in the "broken window" scenario, minor infractions of the law can signal that much larger violations are in fact occurring. Therefore, by fixing the "broken windows" and charging violators who break the windows, law enforcement signals that those who violate the law through minor infractions (such as breaking windows or drinking alcohol in public) will not be tolerated by the police and will lead to arraignment and conviction for so-called petty crimes.

The reverse is true. Failure to fix windows or to provide adequate street lights, as well as failure to sanction violators for "petty" crimes, leads criminals to believe that major crimes such as drug peddling, prostitution, carjacking, and murder will be tolerated in a particular locale.

Similarly, a recent article in the University of Chicago's *Journal of Law and Economics* titled "Weathering Corruption" found that when a natural disaster occurred that triggered windfalls of federal disaster relief, for each $100 per capita of Federal Emergency Management Agency (FEMA) disaster relief given, the average state's corruption increased by nearly 102 percent.[9] This suggests that when states "attract more disaster relief," it "makes them more corrupt." Natural disasters create a "bad" locale where lack of control by the federal government through FEMA and the lack of normal policing permit "petty" criminal acts to occur without an adequate response. This lack of police response sends a signal to those willing and able to embezzle disaster relief funds that there will be little or no criminal sanctions.

In the same way, decreasing head counts in government enforcement functions (in justice, the SEC, and the police force at state and local levels), as well as in corporate compliance departments, sends the wrong message to the "bad" people in corporations, particularly in the troubling times of the global financial crisis. Indeed, in any organization, 5 percent of people are "good" or intuitively moral, 5 percent of people are "bad" or intuitively amoral, and the rest (approximately 90 percent) are followers.[10] The "bad" people could perceive the bailout as an opportunity for absconding with more money.

If we can tap down the activities of the "bad" people and reward and reinforce the activities of the "good" people, the net effect will shift the 90 percent of followers in a positive direction. This can be done in several ways, including the following:

- Creating "train the trainer" programs to establish acceptable norms in small groups of fifteen to eighteen people
- Performing a best-practice gaps analysis/risk assessment for corporate risks

- Implementing reasonable auditing and more monitoring programs, including an anonymous hotline reporting system (which, according to the 2004 Report to the Nation on Occupational Fraud and Abuse by the US-based National Association of Fraud Examiners, can initially reduce the amount of corruption by 50 percent)
- Designing and utilizing an appropriate and systematic incentive for all members of the corporation, and extensive corporate governance training for the board of directors
- Rigorously following the seven steps of the US Sentencing Guidelines

Further, the program should not be overly complex; it should be simple and easy for everyone in the corporation to understand, including those overseeing the compliance program, such as directors, officers, and monitors. Simplicity of design leads to elegant, understandable, and workable compliance programs. This is the goal of an "effective" compliance program that creates a culture of ethics.

The Public's Role in Creating a Culture of Ethics

The public has an important role in creating a culture of ethics, not only in corporations and government, but in civil society in general. This means creating ethics awareness programs in all levels of society. It will involve creating ethics and compliance curriculums—including advanced degrees—at law schools, business schools, and other professional schools; creating required ethics public awareness programs at grade schools, high schools, colleges, and universities; creating a public awareness program for the general public on the importance of ethics and compliance in corporations, as well as in any organization using the seven steps of the US Sentencing Guidelines; and requiring that a risk assessment be performed in any corporation or organization prior to adopting the seven steps. Further, it is important to make the public aware of what the seven steps of the Federal Sentencing Guidelines are. Citizens should know how to perform a rudimentary risk assessment in order to take personal and civic responsibility for the corporations and organizations to which they belong.

Additionally, it is important to urge government representatives to create International Standard Organization (ISO) standards for compliance programs and for conducting internal investigations in corporations. It is also important to promote better cooperation between federal, state, and local law enforcement and regulators in the United States, as well as in other countries and with international organizations. US Generally Accepted Accounting Principles (GAAP) standards should be updated to reflect the more holistic European GAAP standards to prevent, for example, the financial abuses of off-balance sheet, special purpose entities (SPEs). Moreover, the SEC, or its equivalent in other countries, should require independent certified triple bottom-line audits of corporations for financial, environmental, and corporate social responsibility issues, and the filing of these audits.

Finally, the public should be aware that there is a connection between criminal activity, counterfeiting goods, money laundering, and terrorism. These elements frequently work together to promote their agendas. For example, the 1993 World Trade Center bombing was financed by counterfeit Hard Rock Café souvenirs.

Checklist for Creating a Future of Transparency and Integrity in the Corporate World and Civil Society

Listed below are the eighteen steps to creating a future of transparency and integrity in the corporate world and civil society:

1. Update SOX to be holistic.
2. Make the US GAAP more holistic (as in Europe) and create global rather than US-centric compliance programs.
3. Require a third-party certification of a compliance program (similar to the annual report certified by a public accounting firm).
4. Require an independently certified triple bottom-line audit of corporations for financial, environmental, and corporate social responsibility issues. This audit should be filed with the SEC in the United States or its equivalent in other countries.
5. Audits and certifications of the compliance program, the environmental program, and corporate social responsibility should be made transparent and available to investors and the public on the Internet.
6. Hire more personnel to the SEC—or its equivalent in other countries—to monitor suspicious activity reports (SARs), annual reports on

compliance programs, environmental programs, corporate social responsibility reports, and financial reports.

7. Promote better cooperation between federal, state, and local law enforcement and regulators in the United States, including state attorney general's offices, the Justice Department, the SEC, and police departments. This should also be done in other countries and with international organizations such as the International Monetary Fund (IMF), World Bank (WB), United Nations Global Compact, Interpol, OECD, etc.

8. Hire more personnel to the US Justice Department—or its equivalent in other countries—to prosecute criminal actions by directors, officers, and employees of corporations, and to supervise deferred prosecutions where an effective compliance program must be overseen.

9. Hold more CFOs, general counsel, outside counsel, and public accounting firms accountable for activities of corporations that constitute criminal liability due to failure of these professionals to uphold legal as well as ethical standards.

10. Create awareness that there is a connection between criminal activities, counterfeiting goods, money laundering, and terrorism. These elements frequently work together to promote their agendas.

11. Provide rigorous background checks for those involved in auditing and monitoring in the corporation. Background checks should be carried out for the legal department and the compliance office, as well as for all officers and directors, in order to promote people of integrity to positions of importance.

12. Update corporate compliance programs to be holistic ethics programs that undertake best-practice gaps analyses and risk assessments on a yearly basis.

13. Create an anticorruption academy under the auspices of Interpol and the United Nations that fosters compliance and ethics programs at major corporations and financial institutions.

14. Create ISO standards for compliance programs and for investigations.

15. Create ethics and compliance curriculums—including advanced degrees—at law schools, business schools, and other professional schools.

16. Create required ethics public awareness programs at grade schools, high schools, colleges, and universities.

17. Create a public awareness program for the general public on the importance of ethics and compliance in corporations, as well as in any organization using the seven steps of the US Sentencing Guidelines. A risk assessment should be required in any corporation or organization prior to adopting the seven steps.

18. Make the public aware of what the seven steps of the Federal Sentencing Guidelines are and how to perform a rudimentary risk assessment. Each citizen should be able to take personal and civic responsibility for the corporations and organizations to which they belong.

Notes

1. David Enrich and Robin Sidel, "Citi to Cut More Jobs, Raise Rates on Its Plastic," *Wall Street Journal*, November 14, 2008.

2. "Your Citibank," *Wall Street Journal*, February 28, 2009.

3. Release Nos. 33-8177; 34-47235; File No. S7-40-02 as of January 24, 2003; Effective Date: thirty days after publication in the Federal Register.

4. See Richard E. Grove et al., *ABCs of Swaps and Other Derivatives 2009* (New York: Practising Law Institute, 2009).

5. Committee of Capital Markets Regulation, *The Global Financial Crisis: A Plan for Regulatory Reform*, May 26, 2009, http://www.capmktsreg.org/pdfs/TGFC-CCMR_Executive_Summary_(5-26-09).pdf.

6. Malcolm Gladwell, *The Tipping Point: How Little Things Can Make a Big Difference* (New York: Little, Brown and Company, 2000).

7. Damian Paletta, Jonathan Weisman, and Deborah Solomon, "U.S. Eyes Two-Part Bailout for Banks," *Wall Street Journal*, January 30, 2009.

8. Gladwell, *The Tipping Point*.

9. Peter T. Leeson and Russell S. Sobel, "Weathering Corruption," *Journal of Law and Economics* 51, no. 4 (November 2008): 667–681.

10. Joseph Koletar lecture, "Lateral Investigations" University of Pennsylvania School of Law, Philadelphia, PA, November 15, 2004).

PART

VIII

NEUROECONOMICS

22

THE HUMAN SIDE OF INVESTMENT
DECISION-MAKING

Thierry Malleret

What Was the Investment World's Mindset before the Recent Crash?

On four occasions while I was working at the World Economic Forum in 2006, I gathered a group of economists, prominent investment bankers, and insurers to brainstorm about the impending risks that could derail the "Goldilocks scenario" that then prevailed. The disconnect between the concerns and warnings of the economists—among them Roubini Global Economics' Nouriel Roubini and David Rosenberg, then with Merrill Lynch—and the indestructible optimism of the investment bankers and insurers was startling. This series of meetings subsequently led to a session at Davos in January 2007 aptly titled "Housing Deflation: What's the Hissing Sound?" Among other panelists, economist Robert Shiller and then president of the central bank of Germany Axel Weber warned about the impending real estate crisis and its possible cascading effects on other asset classes. A lively discussion ensued with the few people in the room who had bothered to attend the session. Several of them argued convincingly that it "would all end up in tears." The exuberant Davos consensus of 2007 paid little heed.

Apart from the fact that Davos has been an effective contrarian indicator—every single crisis has been missed by the Davos consensus since the 1990s—the lesson that arises from this brief recollection is dead simple: The conventional wisdom that today claims that "nobody saw it [the crisis] coming" is mistaken, or rather incomplete. It misses the second half of the sentence: "Nobody saw it coming because nobody wanted to see it coming!" Why is it so? Because the theory of rational choice, which suggests that when confronted with uncertain outcomes we make the best possible decision based on all the relevant information, is wrong. Besides the fact that most of the information we deal with is of an asymmetric nature, we find it very difficult as human beings to make rational decisions based on the objective assessment of several possible alternatives. In fact, our decisions are subjective and profoundly influenced by our emotions, beliefs, and feelings. As such, we often disregard the available information, or we misinterpret it.

Neuroeconomics Will Be the Big Winner in 2011

At the risk of being provocative, I would predict that, while "traditional" economics was one of the major casualties of the crisis, the big winner of 2011 will be neuroeconomics, and more generally the idea that markets are efficient and good at self-correcting. Indeed, many of the long-held ideas at the core of economics (most notably the theory of efficient markets) have been shattered. Conversely, the phenomenal progress made in neuroscience over the past few years is changing the way we see ourselves and how we make decisions. We now understand why, faced with the ever-growing complexity of our world, we are all victims of what Herbert Simon called in 1957 "bounded rationality" (research for which, twenty-one years later, he was named Nobel Laureate in Economics). The truth is that our human brains, shaped by evolution, have specialized in fast decision-making under threat, not in the ability to process the complex interactions that govern any decision in today's world. Indeed, in the literature on psychology and cognition, there is ample evidence that as human beings we are unable to process more than seven (plus or minus two) "chunks" of information over brief periods. We also find it exceedingly difficult to manipulate more than four variables in relation to one another at the same time. Yet is there an investment decision in existence that does *not* require considering at least seven pieces of information and four interrelated variables? There almost certainly is not! In the same vein, our language, whose syntax is sequential (words follow one another in a predetermined way), forces us to describe complex, nonlinear systems in inappropriate linear terms.[1] Also, we tend to construct artificial "mental" boxes that often make us confuse random fluctuations with causal patterns. All of this leads to important distortions in the way we strive to interpret and assess complex issues. One of the most important issues in the investment world is the one associated with the search for the "catalyst." Investors often try to identify a catalyst that might trigger a reversal or a major trend in the markets, such as a surge in bond yields, a flight to safety, an increase in commodity prices, or a particular market collapsing. In complex, nonlinear adaptive systems such as the markets or the economy, this is never true: An event always has more than one cause, all of which are intertwined in a web of complex interrelationships. The obsession with the search for one cause is particularly evident in discussions about the origin of the current financial and economic crisis. There have been thousands of articles and interviews ascribing the responsibility of the crisis to one particular group: bankers, traders, the US Congress, regulators, rating agencies, the gullible consumer, and so on. As much as we would like to identify the culprit—it would make the mitigation of a future similar risk much easier— there simply is not just one guilty party. The causes are multiple and involve interdependent relationships of many different players and factors.

Thus, paradoxically, in a world of increasing complexity and magnitude, we strive to make sense of the overabundant information and complex interactions by oversimplifying. By what process do we do this? Principally by letting our brains rely on "shortcuts," which are also called heuristics or cognitive biases (or illusions). There are seventy-eight of them, but four are the prime suspects when it comes to the mistakes that investors tend to make.

Overconfidence: characterized by the belief that one is always right, or at least more often than other people. The propensity to be overconfident is particularly strong among individuals who think of themselves as above average and who receive performance-related incentives and compensation packages disproportionately larger than those of others. Financial market participants qualify on both counts. A great majority tend to believe that they are "better than average," and that, as a consequence, they will outperform the market (or conversely, they will not be submitted to the risk of underperforming).

Availability: characterized by the interpretation of a story or an event through the lens of a superficially similar account. One effect of this heuristic—particularly prevalent in the financial markets—is to view the future only in terms of the immediate past: the like-the-past fallacy. I would posit that a good half of the dozen or so research pieces that I read on a daily basis contain somewhere among the various investment recommendations: "If history is any guide. . . ."

Anchoring: characterized by the tendency to cling mentally to any number one hears in a particular context, even when it is factually far off the mark. Many investors still retain valuation models learned years ago in a totally different context, or they use historic ratios, volatilities, reversions to the mean, and correlations that have become meaningless because the world has changed. The much-expected Nikkei's reversion to the mean, for example, is the market equivalent of *Waiting for Godot*—it may never come, but many investors still desperately anchor on the 37,000 peak.

Confirmatory evidence: characterized by the fact that we tend to form opinions by falling back on intuition or hunches and then look for confirmatory evidence to reinforce these. When someone confirms our views, they are in turn reinforced in the reward system of our brain. We then seek further evidence to validate our views, shutting off contradictory information. The case of Greece during the first half of 2010 is particularly illustrative of this bias. For several consecutive months, the overwhelming consensus in the market and among opinion-makers was that Greece was likely to fail, taking the eurozone with it. Any piece of news was portrayed as a watershed event that was about to precipitate the nation's collapse. Demonstrations, for example, were often described in "apocalyptic terms"—depicted as if they were about to rock the country's social contract, when in relative terms they were poorly attended. Doomsayers, however, were only too happy to disregard evidence that would contradict their view.

Cognitive illusions operate at the level of the individual, but their effects on investment decisions are amplified by additional problems related to group behavior. A particularly powerful one is the herd instinct, or the desire to conform to the accepted norm or wisdom. New research shows that one of the key drivers guiding investors' decisions is the fear of losing one's job, which is the so-called career risk. In such conditions, a fund manager may well be tempted "to fail conventionally rather than to succeed unconventionally," as Keynes used to say. This has been suggested as one of the possible reasons for the powerful market rally experienced since March 2009. Evidence suggests that most institutional investors were initially highly skeptical of the rebound, but then many decided to buy into the market, not wanting to miss an upturn—thus creating a positive feedback loop.

Why Neuroeconomics Disproves the Theory of Rationality

Since the 1970s, with the pioneering work of Daniel Kahneman and Amos Tversky, we have understood how heuristics distort our ability to make rational decisions. Kahneman and Tversky investigated the apparent anomalies in human behavior that lead to asymmetries in the choices we make. In particular, they investigated how the framing of an identical issue can lead to either risk-averse or risk-seeking behavior. In a nutshell, this is the greatest insight of behavioral economics: all the decisions we make can be greatly influenced by small changes in the context. However, neuroeconomics has put to rest the notion entrenched in classical economic and financial theory that we systematically apply rational calculations to all the investment decisions we make. Now that we can observe neural activity in the brain through imaging as well as other techniques, we know that each time we make an investment decision (or a decision of any kind), emotions, feelings, habits, and instincts interfere with our attempt to make a rational choice.

We tend to oppose emotion and reason as if they were two different compartments of our brain, but new research shows that the cognitive or rational processes, which address logical questions and affective processes that relate to emotional responses, are in fact an artificial construction. As Olivier Oullier states, "Our brain does not seem to generate emotions and rationality in an independent fashion. Rather, it might be dealing with a complementary pair, a kind of 'emo-rationality.'"[2]

Why Neuroeconomics Only Has Limited
Relevance to Investors

What light does this shed on our capacity as investors? Simply, that we are much more fallible than we like to imagine and much less in control than we think. For example, research conducted in 2007 by John Coates (a former Wall Street trader who is now a neurophysiologist at Cambridge University in the United Kingdom) has shown that hormones play a critical role in how traders perform. By analyzing hormonal levels on the trading floor of a London bank, he revealed that testosterone, a hormone that plays a critical role in sexuality but also in impulsive and risky behaviors, and cortisol, a hormone whose level increases under stress, have to remain within a certain concentration range for traders to perform well on the market. Beyond certain concentration levels, testosterone can lead to senseless decisions that are much too risky. Yet not many traders of our acquaintance would choose to ascribe their investment prowess to testosterone levels rather than to their intellect and a unique capability to make fast decisions in a most complex environment!

If neuroeconomics provides such incontrovertible evidence relating to the making of flawed decisions, why are so many investors still "neuroskeptics"? Why is it that so very few investment companies have neuroeconomists or cognitive psychologists on their board, their trading floor, or their investment committee? Probably because neuroeconomics does not help to make better decisions; it only helps to avoid bad ones, which is much less noticeable. It pays more to sell a collateralized debt obligation to a client than to warn him or her about the hidden risks, many of which would be apparent if one ever paid attention to a bias as obvious as overconfidence. But the fundamental reason for which we still do not pay enough attention to the lessons of neuroeconomics may be simpler yet. On repeated occasions, I have asked renowned neuroeconomists why so very few investors pay for their services. Their response is often the same: Investors perceive themselves to be highly intelligent, and they do not like to be told that some of their decisions may be beyond their control. The illusion of control is indeed a powerful driver of our lives. As nobody enters married life thinking that he or she might get divorced, nobody enters the investment world thinking he or she might fail. Doing the opposite would require humility, which is a quality not found in abundance within the world of investment. Potentially a victim of this hubris, my prediction for 2011 may in the end be nothing more than wishful thinking.

If it is, how disconcerting! When Richard Thaler and Cass Sunstein published *Nudge–Improving Decisions About Health, Wealth, and Happiness* with Yale University Press in 2008, they showed that what's come out of behavioral economics—and by extension neuroeconomics—can lead to improved decisions in terms of better health or sounder investments. Soon, some of their ideas on how to nudge made their way into policy-making. Today, for example, many governments try to harness some of their insights for specific policy purposes. The governments of the United States, the United Kingdom, and France, just to name three, have a policy unit devoted to "nudging."[3] So far, these efforts are mainly devoted to the areas of health (with a particular focus on obesity) and pensions. How long will it take before the investment world takes notice of the benefits of "nudging"?

Notes

1. All of these limitations are explained in Sean Cleary, "Cognitive Constraints and Behavioral Biases," chap. 4 in *Learning from Catastrophes: Strategies for Reaction and Response*, vol. 1, ed. Howard Kunreuther and Michael Useem (Upper Saddle River, NJ: Wharton School Publishing, 2009).

2. Olivier Oullier, "The Useful Brain: How Neuroeconomics Might Change Our Views on Rationality and a Couple of Other Things," chap. 10 in *The Irrational Economist: Making Decisions in a Dangerous World*, vol. 1, ed. Erwann O. Michel-Kerjan and Paul Slovic (Philadelphia: PublicAffairs, 2010).

3. These policy units are led by Dr. David Halpern in the United Kingdom and by Dr. Olivier Oullier in France; while Cass Sunstein has become the "regulatory czar" in the Obama administration.

THE DIMINISHING RETURNS OF
THE INFORMATION AGE

Mark Roeder

At the dawn of the Internet age in the mid-1990s, many pundits predicted that the Internet would empower billions of people to become smarter, or at least better informed, simply by making so much information easily accessible. But information is not knowledge. People do not automatically become smarter by being immersed in a sea of data any more than security guards in an art gallery become art experts through a process of osmosis. Information must be chewed on, tested, and digested before it can become knowledge. Indeed, too much information can be a bad thing. This is because the only way most of us can cope with vast oceans of data is to skim the surface and glean the fragments of information that seem most relevant. Many of us are able to scan vast amounts of information by jumping from hyperlink to hyperlink with astonishing dexterity. This behavior is facilitated by a dazzling array of new gadgets, such as Apple's iPad, which provide simple and instantaneous access to the Net.

How Skimming Is Hurting Our Ability to Think

Although it may appear that skimming is simply the Internet version of "speed reading," this would be to underestimate its influence on the way we process information. Nicholas Carr, writing in the *Atlantic*, says:

> What the Net seems to be doing is chipping away my capacity for concentration and contemplation. My mind now expects to take in information the way the Net distributes it: in a swiftly moving stream of particles. Once I was a scuba diver in the sea of words. Now I zip along the surface like a guy on a Jet Ski. I'm not the only one. When I mention my troubles with reading to friends and acquaintances—literary types, most of them—many say they're having similar experiences. The more they use the Web, the more they have to fight to stay focused on long pieces of writing. Some of the bloggers I follow have also begun mentioning the phenomenon.[1]

Carr highlights one of the great paradoxes of the modern media, particularly the Internet, which is that despite offering so much depth of information, it encourages our thinking to be shallower. Reading, unlike speaking, is not an instinctive skill for human beings that is coded in our genes. It has to be learned and practiced. Over time, the way we read conditions the way we think, which in turn rewires our brain through the process of neuroplasticity. For centuries our reading habits have encouraged us not only to broaden our knowledge but to reflect on the human condition and the world we live in through works of literature and philosophy. Such deep reading is indistinguishable from deep thinking. Nowadays, however, technology is conditioning us to read in the "shallows" and never dwell on one subject for too long. Playwright Richard Foreman believes this process is transforming us into "pancake people"— spread wide and thin as we connect with the vast network of information accessed by the mere touch of a button. Indeed, the very businesses that run the Internet do not like us staying on one site for too long or surfing at too leisurely a pace. This is because they derive their advertising revenue from the number of sites visited, and the faster we move from one site to another, the better.

People not only move between Internet sites, they also skip from media to media—from e-mails, phone calls, blogs, Facebook, text messages, Twitter, television, and radio. Our evolution into media omnivores is also affecting the way we think. A recent study led by Clifford Nass, a professor at Stanford University, investigated whether cognitive abilities might be affected by the range of media that people regularly use. The results of the study were surprising, suggesting that heavy "multitaskers"—people who often switch between many tasks—are actually slower at identifying changes to content than light multitaskers. The heavy multitaskers also had more trouble filtering out irrelevant information, greater difficulty concentrating on particular activities, and, perhaps most surprisingly, more difficulty moving between tasks in an effective way. Until now it was generally assumed that heavy multitaskers would be more adept at responding quickly and accurately to content changes, but the reverse seems to be the case. The researchers concluded that "human cognition is ill-suited both for attending to multiple input streams . . . and for simultaneously performing multiple tasks."[2]

The Idols of the Information Age Failed to Detect the Big Story

There are certain professions that breed multitaskers and "super-skimmers"—people whose job it is to scan and process information at lightning speed. Financial traders are such people. They are immersed in a sea of Blackberries and Bloomberg screens gushing out torrents of financial data, which they rapidly sift through in order to optimize their trades. It is not a job for the slow or dim-witted. Traders are usually acutely bright young men. Yet, they were among the first to be drowned by the tsunami of the global financial crisis. Why? Because they could not detect the tectonic shifts occurring on the ocean floor that would generate the destructive wave. They were skimmers trying to cope with too much information. They are the personification of the diminishing returns of the Information Age.

In the 1960s an interesting experiment was conducted that demonstrated the folly of having too much information. Two groups of people were shown a fuzzy and indistinct outline of a fire hydrant. The resolution was gradually increased for one group through a series of ten steps. For the other group, the resolution was increased over just five steps. Then the process was stopped at a point where each group was looking at an identical picture and was asked what they could see. It turned out that the members of the group who saw fewer intermediate steps saw the picture earlier than the group that was presented with more steps. The extra informa-tion encouraged them to speculate more about what the image was, thus clouding their judgment. The first group saw the fire hydrant more di-rectly for what it was, unhindered by too many layers of information.[3]

The Internet, too, has a multilayer structure. In fact, it has so many lay-ers that one can easily get lost. Paul Kedrosky, a senior fellow at the Kauff-man Foundation, said that the Internet was supposed to be "the great democratizer of information. It was supposed to empower individual in-vestors, make murky financial markets more transparent, and create a new generation of citizen investors. . . . It was supposed to shrink the world and turn it into a village, where everything happened in the public square and corruption and greed would have no place to hide. As the 1990s man-tra goes, 'Information wants to be free.'" However, this new "freedom of information" created a giant jigsaw puzzle comprising countless pieces of information that were constantly and frenetically changing. All the relevant information was there, but there was no way to look at it in a way that made sense. The Internet also greatly accelerated people's ability to make transactions, thus generating more momentum in the markets. This, in turn, fueled the bubble. "We are in the midst of the first financial crisis of the mature Internet age," said Kedrosky, "a crisis caused in large part by the tightly coupled technologies that now undergird the financial system and our society as a whole."[4] For example, one reason for the global financial crisis was, perversely, the sheer abundance of financial in-formation available online, which created a "smog" of data. This made it difficult for even the most sophisticated financial analyst to grasp the whole picture and comprehend the scale of the emerging problem.

Selective Consumption of Information Leads to Insulated and Polarized Societies

The Internet not only causes our thinking to become shallower, it also causes it to be narrower. This is because, unlike traditional media such as a newspaper or television show, we can choose to see only the in-formation we want to see. So, when we go online, we act as our own edi-tor and gatekeeper for the news, and we tend to screen out opposing viewpoints. In fact, we often look for information and perspectives that confirm our existing mindsets and prejudices. Nicholas Negroponte of MIT calls this self-censored media product "The Daily Me."[5] It represents another step toward a world in which people increasingly isolate themselves in a bubble of self-sustaining beliefs and immerse themselves in like-minded communities. Although we may like the idea of a debating chamber, in reality we prefer an echo chamber. In one classic study, Republicans and Democrats were offered various research reports from a neutral source. Both groups were most eager to receive coherent arguments that corroborated their preexisting mindsets. Bill Bishop, author of *The Big Sort: Why the Clustering of Like-Minded America Is Tearing Us Apart*, says that as the United States grows more politically segregated, "the benefit that ought to come with having a variety of opinions is lost to the righteousness that is the special entitlement of homogeneous groups."[6] A twelve-nation study found that Americans, particularly highly educated ones, are the least likely to discuss politics with people of different views.

People's tendency to confirm their existing beliefs causes them to form like-minded communities on the Internet in locations such as social networking sites and virtual worlds. Communities such as Facebook, MySpace, Second Life, and the Twitterscape, help connect millions of people in environments that are conducive for building relationships. They also offer the potential for new types of democratic processes, such as direct voting online, and the scope for alternate views to be put forward outside of the mainstream. The downside to Web communities is that they can cause people to become more cut off from the rest of society. In their paper "Electronic Communities: Global Village or Cyber Balkans," professors Marshal Van Alstyne and Erik Brynjolfsson said that "individuals empowered to screen out material that does not conform to their existing preferences may form virtual cliques, insulate themselves from opposing points of view, and reinforce their biases. . . . This voluntary Balkanisation and the loss of shared experiences and values may be harmful to the structure of democratic societies."[7] They warned that we should have no illusions that the Internet will create a greater sense of community. The danger is that when people suppress or are oblivious to information that contradicts their existing mindset, they are far more likely to believe they are heading in the right direction and ignore warning signs. This phenomenon may help to explain the increasingly polarized political environment in the United States.

The Rise of the Online Oligarchy

Perhaps one of the more disappointing, and counterintuitive, aspects of the Internet is that it is not the free and open marketplace of ideas that we would like to believe. Many of the world's most popular Internet news sites are owned by major news organizations such as CNN, the *New York Times*, News Limited, and the BBC, which tend to mirror the editorial slant of their own television and newspaper outlets. During the first quarter of 2009, websites owned by newspaper groups in the United States attracted 73.3 million unique visitors on average (over 30 percent of all Internet users). According to Nielsen Online Research, this was a record number that represented a significant increase over the same period in 2008. The vast majority of popular news sites continue to be owned by the richest media companies. Based on an analysis of data from Advertising Age and Nielsen Online, of the twenty-five most-visited news websites in 2008, twenty-two were owned by the one hundred richest media companies.[8] In effect, we are seeing the emergence of an online oligarchy that is dominated by the old guard. Some media companies have invested huge resources into their online sites. This enables them to generate lucrative revenue because advertisers are able to more accurately track audiences and their response rates to online advertising. People gravitate to the big, established online news sites because they are distrustful of a medium that, as *The Daily Show* host Jon Stewart points out, "combines the credibility of anonymous hearsay with the excitement of typing."

Meanwhile, the traditional media, particularly television news, has undergone a profound transformation in recent years. This has much to do with the way news is presented. Whereas the media used to provided us with relatively unvarnished reports of what was happening, it increasingly tends to magnify and sensationalize news stories. This trend is particularly prevalent on television, where news stories are often magnified out of all proportion to their intrinsic newsworthiness and are then repeated relentlessly through the twenty-four-hour news cycle.

The cumulative effect of these changes is to create a perceptual environment in which the world around us seems to be moving faster. Events seem to happen more instantaneously and evolve more rapidly. They also seem to be more important and consequential, as if every news story is a big story. This makes us feel as if we should know about them, so we "plug into" this fast-moving machine to get our daily "fix" of the news, which for many people can be quite addictive. We become conditioned to see the world as a series of rapidly escalating events that generate a powerful, self-perpetuating momentum. We voyeuristically and vicariously ride the wave of these events as they ebb and flow.

The Internet Has Begun to Affect Our Perceptions of Reality

Gradually, this conditioning seeps into the way we experience our own "real" lives. We become more accustomed to a momentum-driven world in which we are content to go with the flow and to observe rather than participate or challenge. This is particularly so for the big issues of our time that develop enormous momentum, or "Big Mo," as it is sometimes called. We are less inclined to resist such powerful momentum and may even see such resistance as futile. It is so much easier to surrender to the flow.

This conditioning may not be just a matter of perception. Recent studies of the human brain using imaging technology (fMRI) indicate that the persistent use of communications technology activates reward pathways that have been linked to addiction. The brain appears to rewire its neural pathways through a process called neuroplasticity. Hence, there may be a biological basis to some people's addictive tendencies for the fast-moving news cycle. This is reflected in the amount of television we consume, which now averages around four hours a day in developed countries (over five hours in the United States) and accounts for the major share of people's leisure time.

The momentum-driven nature of the news also means that news stories tend to take on a life of their own and become "stuck in the groove." This is because when a newsworthy event happens, the media develops a story line around it that is magnified and reinforced by the globally integrated nature of the media. Eventually this story line develops its own powerful momentum, so that even when facts arise that contradict it, they are resisted or ignored and are ultimately overwhelmed by the media juggernaut that is already moving in a certain direction. This is why so many news stories, particularly big ones, seem to have a predetermined air about them. Rarely are we surprised by a sudden turn of events.

One of the most destructive ideas promulgated by the media in recent years was that debt did not matter because people could get richer through rising house prices. Economist Paul Krugman wrote,

> Until very recently Americans believed they were getting richer, because they received statements saying that their houses and stock portfolios were appreciating in value faster than their debts were increasing. And if the belief of many Americans that they could count on capital gains forever sounds naïve, it's worth remembering just how many influential voices—notably in right-leaning publications like the *Wall Street Journal*, *Forbes*, and *National Review*—promoted that belief, and ridiculed those who worried about low savings and high levels of debt."[9]

Once a story line becomes established in the public's mind, even if it is false, it becomes difficult to dislodge. Long after it became clear just how serious the global financial crisis was, people were still rushing to buy homes they could not afford and ramping up their credit card debt. It was as if they did not want to hear the bad news. This is one of the great paradoxes of the modern media: It actually conditions people to be less able to absorb real news. It is equivalent to someone who is always babbling and hyping everything up: When he or she actually has something consequential to say, you do not hear it. Social commentator and columnist Frank Rich observed, "One of the most persistent cultural tics of the early twenty-first century is Americans' reluctance to absorb, let alone prepare for, bad news. We are plugged into more information sources than anyone could have imagined even fifteen years ago. The cruel ambush of 9/11 supposedly 'changed everything,' slapping us back to reality. Yet we are constantly shocked, shocked by the foreseeable."[10]

The decline of news quality has not gone unnoticed by the public. A poll conducted by the Washington-based Pew Research Center suggests that more than half of Americans believe that US news organizations are politically biased, inaccurate, and do not care about the people they report on.[11] Meanwhile, media diversity is in decline everywhere, particular with regard to news coverage. Although there are now over 1,600 network and cable channels in the United States, up from just a handful twenty-five years ago, most of these amplify news feeds from a small number of major media companies.[12] Thousands of local independent newspapers have closed down across the country, further reducing the diversity of viewpoints. The number of channels in the United Kingdom has increased from eleven in 1990 to over 530 today, but the number of newsrooms has actually decreased. In a case of more is less, most major media companies in the Western world have simultaneously reduced their independent news-gathering resources while expanding their distribution networks.

The Challenge for Media Companies

This trend will continue because large media companies are finding it difficult to charge for their news-gathering activities when consumers can get their news for free on the Internet. This recently prompted some companies, such as News Limited, to begin charging for their online news content through the introduction of "pay walls," which prevent nonsubscribers from accessing content. Companies hope that these services will prove popular with users of tablet computers such as Apple's iPad, which has already sold millions of units and is specially designed to optimize the reader experience on the Web.

Whether these attempts to boost revenue will succeed remains to be seen. The trouble is, having been conditioned to receive their news for free, many consumers may balk at paying a fee. As Les Hinton, the CEO of Dow Jones, explained, the challenge for online newspapers is "getting the horse back into the stable."[13] Also, as mentioned earlier, many online consumers prefer to be able to "skim" through various sites, and so would be reluctant to get locked into a small number of expensive subscriber sites.

One possible solution would be for media companies to offer "skimmer packages" for media "omnivores" and "diver" packagers for those who want to delve more deeply into specialist media—or a combination of both. Another solution would be to make news sites "semipermeable" so that only the headlines and top layer information is available for free (for "skimmers"), while the rest is available on subscription (for "divers")–thus overcoming the problem with "solid pay walls," which tend to alienate many users.

The advent of such flexible packages could lay the groundwork for a much-needed model to "monetize" parts of the Internet, while also facilitating consumers' need to "skim and roam" the Net relatively unencumbered. These innovations will require a high degree of cooperation between competing media and technology companies. They will also require the development of a common payment system for consumers to simplify the subscription process. Such a system is already being developed by a start-up company called Journalism Online, but there is much work to be done and the outcome remains uncertain.

One thing is certain, though: The coming battle between pay and free-to-view models of online journalism will transform the business model of a medium that is over four hundred years old. In the meantime, until these commercial and quality issues are sorted out, the cumulative effect of the trends outlined in this chapter will be to create a "diminishing law of returns of the Information Age" for both consumers and media companies. Indeed, this is the great paradox of our world today. Never before have we had access to so much information, yet so little understanding of how to manage it.

Notes

1. Nicholas Carr, "Is Google Making Us Stupid?" *Atlantic Monthly*, July/August 2008, http://www.theatlantic.com/magazine/archive/2008/07/is-google-making-us -stupid/6868/. See also Gary Small and Gigi Vorgan, *iBrain: Surviving the Technological Alteration of the Modern Mind* (New York: Harper Collins, 2008). See also Sharon Begley, *Train Your Mind: Change Your Brain* (New York: Ballantine Books, 2007).

2. Eyal Ophir, Clifford Nass, and Anthony D. Wagner, "Cognitive Control in Media Multitaskers." *Proceedings of the National Academy of Sciences,* August 24, 2009. See also Mark Henderson, "Media Multi-taskers Are in Danger of Brain Overload," *Times of London*, August 25, 2009.

3. Nassim N. Taleb, *The Black Swan* (New York: Random House, 2007).

4. Paul Kedrosky, "The First Disaster of the Internet Age," *Newsweek*, October 27, 2008, http://www.newsweek.com/2008/10/17/the-first-disaster-of-the-internet -age.html.

5. Quoted in Nicholas D. Kristof, "The Daily Me," *New York Times*, March 19, 2009.

6. Ibid.

7. Marshal Van Alstyne and Erik Brynjolfsson, "Electronic Communities: Global Village or Cyber Balkans," Sloan School of Management Working Papers, MIT Sloan School, March 1997.

8. Nate Anderson, "Online Oligarchy: Old Guard Dominates 'Net News Coverage," *Ars Technica*, March 17, 2008, http://arstechnica.com/old/content/2008/03/online-oligarchy-old-guard-dominates-net-news-coverage.ars (accessed on November 19, 2010); PBS, "Democracy on Deadline: Who Owns the Media?" http://www.pbs.org/independentlens/democracyondeadline/mediaownership.html (accessed on August 4, 2010).

9. Paul Krugman, "Decade at Bernie's," *New York Times*, February 16, 2009, A23.

10. Frank Rich, "What We Don't Know Will Hurt Us," *New York Times*, February 22, 2009, WK10.

11. Pew Research Center for the People and the Press, "Views of Press Values and Performance: 1985–2007," August 9, 2007.

12. Project for Excellence in Journalism, "The State of the News Media 2007: An Annual Report on American Journalism," http://www.stateofthemedia.org/2007/index.asp.

13. Quoted in Takashi Kitazume, "Shift to Charging for Online News Inevitable, Dow Jones Chief Says," *Japan Times*, June 14, 2010.

GLOSSARY

A/H1N1 VIRUS: An influenza virus that originated from animal influenza viruses and is unrelated to the human seasonal H1N1 viruses that have been in circulation among people since 1977.

ACCREDITATION: The act of providing official authorization or approval.

AFRICAN UNION: A group of African countries formed in 2002 that aims to protect the security of the continent. The African Union also seeks to increase development, combat poverty and corruption, and end Africa's many conflicts.

ALT-A LOANS: Loans that are given to someone with a generally clean credit record, but who suffers some deficiency such as incomplete documentation, an unsteady income, an inability to make regular payments, and so on.

ANC ALLIANCE: The alliance between the African National Congress (ANC), the South African Communist Party (SACP), and the Congress of South African Trade Unions (COSATU). The SACP and COSATU have not contested any elections, but they field candidates through the ANC, hold senior positions in the ANC, and influence party policy and dialogue. Also known as the Tripartite Alliance.

ANNUS HORRIBILIS: A horrible or disastrous year.

ARBITRAGE: The nearly simultaneous purchase and sale of securities or foreign exchange in different markets in order to profit from price discrepancies.

ASSET BUBBLE: Price movement that is unexplainable based on fundamentals.

ATTESTATION: To affirm to be true or genuine; often accomplished by a witness's signature.

AYATOLLAH: High-ranking title given to Usuli Twelver Shī'ah clerics. The title is bestowed upon experts in Islamic studies, ethics, and philosophy.

BA'ATHIST: Adherent to the Ba'ath party, which is a secular political party that espouses Arab nationalism in opposition to Western imperialism. Its most famous leader was Saddam Hussein in Iraq.

BALANCE OF PAYMENTS: The quantity of a country's own currency that is flowing out minus the amount flowing in.

BASIJ FORCES: Group of pro-government vigilantes in Iran that are part of the Revolutionary Guard.

BASLE (BASEL) ACCORDS: Set of banking supervision accords that are issued by the Basel Committee on Banking Supervision, which maintains its secretariat at the Bank of International Settlements. Two sets of accords have been issued, and the third is in development.

BOUNDED RATIONALITY: School of thought that posits that an individual's ability to make rational choices is limited by the cognitive limitations of the individual's knowledge and cognitive capacity. Bounded rationality is a central theme in behavioral economics. It is concerned with the ways in which the actual decision-making process influences decisions.

BRETTON WOODS: An agreement signed in 1944 by representatives of forty-four countries that outlined rules and regulations for an international monetary system. It established a fixed exchange rate linked to the US dollar, with other countries pegging their currency to the dollar. It created the International Monetary Fund (IMF), as well as the precursor for the modern World Bank.

BULLION: Bar or ingot form of gold, silver, platinum, or palladium; occasionally used by central banks for the settlement of international debt.

BUSINESS CYCLE DATING COMMITTEE: Committee on the National Bureau of Economic Research that maintains a chronology of the US business cycle. The chronology identifies the dates of peaks and troughs that frame economic recession or expansion.

CAPACITY UTILIZATION: This metric measures the extent to which the nation's capital is being used in the production of goods. The utilization rate rises and falls with business cycles. As production increases, capacity utilization rises, and vice versa.

CAPITAL ACCOUNT: The component of a country's balance of payments that records the nation's outflow and inflow of financial securities.

CAPITAL CONTROLS: When government restricts capital flows into or out of a country.

CAPITAL FLOW: When investment money from one country goes to another country.

CAPITAL GOODS: Durable goods that are used to produce other goods for consumption.

CAPITAL REQUIREMENTS: Standardized requirements that determine how much liquidity is required to be held for a certain level of assets for banks and other depository institutions. It is monitored and enforced by various regulatory agencies.

CAPO: A high-level official in a criminal organization.

CARBON TAX: Environmental tax that is levied on the basis of the carbon content of products that utilize energy resources.

CARRY TRADE: An investment strategy in which an investor sells a certain currency with a relatively low interest rate and uses the funds to purchase a different currency yielding a higher interest rate.

CARTELIZATION: The process of bringing a market for goods or services under the control of a cartel.

CASCADING EFFECTS: Direct, indirect, complex, or cumulative effects that manifest themselves throughout an organization or system.

CLEAN DEVELOPMENT MECHANISM: An arrangement that allows a country with an emission-reduction or emission-limitation commitment under the Kyoto Protocol (Annex B Party) to implement an emission-reduction project in developing countries. It provides a standardized emissions offset instrument (certified emission reductions).

COGNITIVE BIAS: Human tendency to acquire and process information by filtering it through one's own likes, dislikes, and experiences.

COLLECTIVE ACTION PROBLEM: When the uncoordinated actions of a given actor in a group may not result in the best outcome he or she can achieve.

COMMON MARKET: A customs union with provisions to liberalize the movement of regional production factors, including people and capital.

COMPARATIVE ADVANTAGE: Economic concept maintaining that a country should focus its resources on the export of goods and services it can produce most efficiently.

CONVERTIBILITY: An agreement between different currencies or currency systems that sets a ratio for exchanges between their units. It can be a formal agreement or left to the free market.

CORE INFLATION RATE: The consumer price index minus food and energy prices. The Federal Reserve examines this metric closely in determining the Fed funds rate.

CORPORATE COMPLIANCE: The observance of statutory and company regulations on lawful and responsible conduct by the company, its employees, its management, and supervisory bodies.

COST OF CAPITAL: The required return that is necessary to make a capital budgeting project worth pursuing.

CREDIT CRUNCH: A period of time when credit is costly and/or difficult to obtain.

CROWDING-OUT EFFECT: The reduction in private consumption or investment that occurs because of an increase in government expenditures.

CURRENCY PEG: A publicly announced fixed exchange rate that is often made against a major currency or basket of currencies and maintained by monetary authorities.

CURRENCY SPECULATION: The process of buying, selling, and/or holding currencies in order to make a profit from favorable exchange rate fluctuations.

CURRENT ACCOUNT: A country's trade deficit plus interest payments on what the country borrows from foreigners to finance the trade deficit.

CUSTOMS UNION: A free trade area that also establishes a common tariff and other trade policies with nonmember countries.

DAVOS: Annual meeting held by the World Economic Forum that gathers politicians, business leaders, economists, and other luminaries to discuss key issues facing the global economy.

DEBT DEFLATION: Economic theory originally articulated by Irving Fisher that holds that recessions and depressions are due to the overall level of debt shrinking.

DEBT SPIRAL: The phenomenon of a country's debt load growing rapidly, which leads to even more debt in the form of increased interest payments. The increased interest payments lead to bigger deficits, which in turn lead to an increased national debt load.

DECOUPLING: When the performance of one economy is not affected by the performance of another economy.

DEFLATION: A general decrease in price level that often occurs during periods of stagnant or declining economic growth.

DELEVERAGING: The reduction of financial instruments or borrowed capital previously used to increase the potential return of an investment. It is the opposite of leverage.

DEVALUATION: The significant reduction of a given currency in relation to other currencies and/or gold. It is performed by a central bank in countries with fixed exchange rates.

DUTCH DISEASE: The negative externalities that arise when there are large increases in a country's income. The situation is often associated with the discovery of natural resource deposits.

ECHO CHAMBER: A forum or setting where all the participants agree with one another's views.

EMISSIONS STANDARDS: Rules and requirements that limit the amount of pollutants that can be released into the environment by various entities.

EN BLOC: As a whole.

EUROZONE: A group of European countries that uses the euro as a common currency.

EXCESS RESERVES: The amount of reserves that are held by a bank or financial institution above the reserve requirement.

EXCHANGE-TRADED FUND: A financial security that tracks an index, a commodity, or a basket of assets much like an index fund does; however, it trades on an exchange and experiences price changes throughout the trading day.

EXCISE TAX: Taxes paid on purchases of goods or activities. They are often incorporated into the price of the product or activity.

EXPATRIATE: A person who withdraws oneself from one's country, either temporarily or permanently, in allegiance and/or residence.

FED FUNDS RATE: The short-term interest rate at which US depository institutions lend to each other overnight within the Federal Reserve System.

FEEDBACK LOOP: A channel or pathway that is formed by an "effect" returning to its "cause"; it generates either more or less of the same effect.

FIAT MONEY: Money that has value solely through governmental decree, not through any intrinsic value or ability to be redeemed for specie or commodity.

FLOATING EXCHANGE RATE: When the value of a currency is allowed to fluctuate according to market forces and is not fixed by government entities.

FOREIGN DIRECT INVESTMENT: Investment of foreign assets into domestic structures, equipment, and organization. Excludes foreign investment in domestic stock markets.

FOREIGN EXCHANGE RESERVES: Liquid assets held by a central bank or government entity that are used to intervene in the foreign exchange market.

FRAGILE STATES: States that fail to provide basic services to poor people because they are unwilling or unable to do so.

FREE TRADE AREA: A group of countries within which tariffs and non-tariff trade barriers between members are generally abolished. The group lacks a common trade policy toward nonmembers.

FRONTIER MARKET: Emerging market countries with high volatility, low liquidity, and higher risk/return ratios that are not as prominent as major emerging market countries such as China and Brazil.

GAAP (GENERALLY ACCEPTED ACCOUNTING PRINCIPLES): The common set of accounting principles, standards, and procedures that companies use to compile their financial statements. They are a combination of formal standards and traditional practices.

GDP DEFLATOR: A price index that is used to adjust a country's output for changes in prices of goods and services included in the GDP.

GLASNOST: Soviet policy that allowed open discussion of political and social issues and increased dissemination of news stories.

GLOBAL COMPETITIVENESS REPORT: Report by the World Economic Forum that is derived from the Global Competitiveness Index (GCI), which is based on twelve pillars of competitiveness. It provides a comprehensive picture of the competitiveness landscape in countries around the world at all stages of development.

GOLD STANDARD: The commitment by participating countries to fix the prices of their domestic currencies in terms of a specified amount of gold. It originated in England in 1717 and first broke down during World War I. Eventually replaced by the Bretton Woods System.

GOLDILOCKS SCENARIO: A period of robust economic growth with low inflation.

GOVERNMENT-SPONSORED ENTERPRISES: Privately held corporations with public purposes that were created by the US Congress to reduce the cost of capital for certain borrowing sectors of the economy.

GREAT MODERATION: The period of time beginning in the mid-1980s that is associated with rapidly rising growth along with low and stable prices. These features are highly correlated to an increase in the probability of episodes of financial instability.

GREEN MOVEMENT: Iranian movement led by supporters of Mir Hossein Mousavi that demanded the removal of Mahmoud Ahmadinejad from office following the 2009 presidential election.

GREENHOUSE GAS EMISSIONS: Gases from fuel combustion, industrial processes, agriculture, land use change, and waste that includes carbon dioxide, methane, and nitrous oxide.

HEURISTICS: Problem-solving methodology that uses trial and error as well as rules of thumb to solve a problem faster, cheaper, and more practically than by using an optimization technique.

HEZBOLLAH: A Shi'a Islamist political and paramilitary organization that is regarded as a resistance movement in the Middle East. It is a political operation based in Lebanon that provides social services to the people of that country.

HIGHLY INDEBTED POOR COUNTRIES: A group of forty-one developing countries that are generally characterized by low per capita income levels and/or high debt-to-GDP ratios.

HIJAB: A custom in some Islamic societies in which women dress modestly outside the home.

HUBRIS: Exaggerated pride or self-confidence.

INDUSTRIAL PRODUCTION: Total output of a country's manufacturing base, utilities, and mines.

INTERNATIONAL STANDARD ORGANIZATION (ISO): A nongovernmental federation of national standards bodies from about 150 different countries. Established in 1947.

INTERREGNUM: The time between two successive reigns or regimes in which a governmental party is out of power.

KRUGERRAND: A gold coin that is minted by the South African Mint Company.

LAW OF DIMINISHING RETURNS: Economic theory that states that the marginal gains in output fall over time as one factor of production is increased while the other factors are held constant.

LEAD TIME: The amount of time between the placement and delivery of an order.

LEVERAGE: The use of credit to enhance an investor's speculative capacity and profitability.

LEWIS TURNING POINT: The point when developing countries' industrial wages begin to rise quickly as a result of surplus labor from the countryside becoming scarce.

LIFE CYCLE THEORY: Economic theory originally articulated by Franco Modigliani that posits humans choose their current consumption optimally based on future income flows and current spending requirements.

MEIJI JAPAN: The forty-four-year period from 1868 to 1912 when Emperor Meiji ruled Japan. Japan began to modernize and rose to global economic prominence during this period.

MERCANTILISM: The system of political economy that seeks to enrich a certain country by restraining imports and encouraging exports.

MOBILE FACTORS: Factors of production that are abstract and intangible. These factors are not tied to land and can be located anywhere in the world.

MONETARY BASE: The currency in circulation and reserves that commercial banks hold in their accounts with the central bank. It expresses the relations of the central bank with the other sectors of the economy.

MONETARY UNION: Two or more countries that share a common currency.

MONETIZING DEBT: A two-step process in which the government issues debt to finance its spending and the central bank purchases the debt from the public.

MORTGAGE-BACKED SECURITY (MBS): A type of asset-backed security that is secured by a mortgage or collection of mortgages that originate from a regulated or authorized financial institution.

MULTILATERAL DEBT REDUCTION INITIATIVE: A G-8 agreement from 2006 that relieved the debt burden of certain Highly Indebted Poor Countries through debt write-offs. Other countries would be eligible for debt write-offs contingent upon the meeting of certain conditions.

NETWORK THEORY: The systematizing and generalizing of the relations between the currents, voltages, and impedances associated with the elements of an electrical network; applicable to social interactions between humans as well.

NEURAL PATHWAYS: Neural tracts that connect separate parts of the nervous system.

NEUROECONOMICS: Discipline that combines neuroscience, economics, and psychology to study how humans make decisions. It examines the role of the brain when humans evaluate choices, interact with other humans, and evaluate risks and rewards.

NEUROPLASTICITY: The brain's ability to reorganize itself through the formation of new neural connections in response to new situations and environmental changes throughout life.

OUTPUT GAP: The difference between actual and potential output as a percent of GDP.

OVERNIGHT RATE: The interest rate on money market funds that are lent and borrowed overnight.

PALACE COUP: An overthrow of or challenge to a sovereign or other leader by members of the ruling family or group.

PATRONAGE SYSTEM: The postelection practice in which loyal supporters of a winning candidate and/or party are rewarded with appointive public offices.

PERESTROIKA: Policies instituted by Mikhail Gorbachev in the 1980s that brought about governmental and economic reforms.

PERSONAL CONSUMPTION EXPENDITURE: Goods and services that are purchased by a person.

POLITBURO: A Communist party's principal policymaking and executive committee.

PONZI SCHEME: An investment fraud that involves the payment of purported returns to existing investors from funds contributed by new investors.

PREMIUM: The amount by which an investment vehicle sells above its par value.

PRIMA FACIE: At first appearance.

PRIMARY PRODUCTS: Raw materials and resources that are used in the productive process.

PRIVATE CAPITAL INVESTMENT: Investment of money to purchase capital or fixed assets.

PRIVATIZATION: The sale or return of a publicly owned enterprise to private parties.

PRODUCTION SHARING AGREEMENT: An arrangement between a government and a resource production company (or group of companies) that specifies what percentage of production the government is allowed to keep for its own use.

PROPORTIONAL REPRESENTATION: A voting system that aims to secure a close match between the percentage of votes that groups of candidates obtain in elections and the percentage of seats they receive.

PROPRIETARY TRADING: When a bank, brokerage, or other financial institution trades on its own account rather than on behalf of a customer. Often done for speculative purposes.

PUBLIC SECTOR BORROWING REQUIREMENT: A term used in the United Kingdom to describe a government's budget deficit in a given fiscal year.

QUANTITATIVE EASING: When a central bank creates a supply of new money to put into a banking system that is in serious difficulty.

RAISON D'ÊTRE: French phrase that means "reason for being."

RAW MATERIALS: Unfinished goods that a manufacturer consumes in the process of producing finished goods.

REGIONAL ECONOMIC COMMUNITY: A group of countries in a shared geographical location that have in principle agreed to some form of economic cooperation, and as such pursue policies to eradicate barriers to trade and/or economic integration.

REGULATORY CAPTURE: Economic theory by Richard Posner that posits that regulatory agencies over time become dominated by the industries they are supposed to regulate.

REMITTANCES: Workers' remittances comprised primarily of wages and salaries earned by nonresident and migrant workers that are sent back to recipients from their country of origin.

RESERVE REQUIREMENTS: The amount of funds that a depository institution must hold in reserve against specified deposit liabilities.

ROBBER BARON: A nineteenth-century American capitalist who amassed great wealth through exploitation and questionable business tactics.

SAFE HAVEN CURRENCY: A currency that represents a refuge investment when political shocks hit financial markets. It also bears a negative risk premium, and its value increases with risk and/or market participants' risk aversion.

SEXENIO: The six-year term limit on Mexican presidencies.

SINGLE-MEMBER DISTRICT: An electoral system in which each district votes on one person to represent it in a legislative body.

SOVEREIGN DEBT: A debt instrument that is guaranteed by a government entity.

SOVIET BLOC: The communist nations that were closely allied with the Soviet Union. The nations' foreign policies depended on those of the former Soviet Union.

SPECIAL PURPOSE ENTITY (SPE): A business interest that is formed solely to accomplish a specific task. A business may utilize an SPE for accounting purposes, but these transactions must adhere to certain regulations.

SPECIALIZATION: The condition in which resources are primarily devoted to specific tasks.

STEADY STATE: An economy of relatively stable size that is the long-term outcome of an economy according to the Solow growth model, which models long-run economic growth using the neoclassical structure.

STOP-GO POLICIES: A sequence of alternations in official policy between trying to expand and contract effective demand, which was put in place in the United Kingdom in the 1950s and 1960s.

SUBSISTENCE AGRICULTURE: Farming in which the bulk of a farmer's output is devoted to the feeding of himself and his family, with little excess available to be sold to third parties.

TECHNOCRAT: A bureaucrat who is intensively trained in engineering, economics, or a form of technology.

TOTAL FACTOR PRODUCTIVITY: The portion of output that is not explained by the amount of input used in production.

TRAGEDY OF THE COMMONS: A metaphor that illustrates that it is hard to coordinate and pay for public goods. Individuals have no incentive to limit consumption of a public good, and thus the public good is overwhelmed with demand.

TRANCHE: A division or portion of something.

TRANSSHIPMENT: The movement of cargo between ships or between two different modes of transport.

TRIANGULATION: When a politician defines his or her ideology as being part of the political center, not the left or the right. Triangulation generally involves a politician adopting an opponent's policy position(s).

UNFUNDED LIABILITY: The amount by which a program's assets are exceeded by a program's liability at a given time.

UNWINDING: The closing out of a complicated investment position.

URBANIZATION: The rapid and massive growth of, and migration to, large cities.

VALUE-ADDED TAX (VAT): An indirect tax that is imposed on goods and services at each stage of production, from raw material to final product. A VAT is levied on the value of additions at different stages of production.

VELOCITY: The average number of times a measure of money turns over within a specified period of time.

WAREHOUSING: An attempt to maintain the price of a company's shares or to gain a significant stake in a company without revealing the true identity of the purchaser.

WINDFALL PROFITS TAX: A tax on a company or industry's profits in the wake of a sudden, dramatic spike in profitability.

WORLD ECONOMIC FORUM: An independent, international organization that aims for a world-class corporate governance system. It believes that economic progress without social development is not sustainable and that social development without economic progress is not feasible. The organization hosts the annual Davos meeting.

X-INEFFICIENCY SYNDROME: When an organization does not achieve the best results in the most efficient way in relation to the number of employees, machines, and so on, it has.

YIELD CURVE: A line that plots the interest rates, at a set point in time, of bonds having equal credit quality but differing maturity dates. It is used to predict changes in economic output and growth.

CONTRIBUTORS

LYRIC HUGHES HALE

Lyric Hughes Hale is a writer and contributor to a range of publications, including the *Financial Times, Los Angeles Times, USA Today, Current History,* and *Institutional Investor.* "China Takes Off," published in *Foreign Affairs* in 2003 and written jointly with her husband David Hale, is one of the most oft-cited surveys of China's economic ascendency. Ms. Hale studied Japanese at Northwestern University and graduated from the University of Chicago with a degree in Near Eastern Languages and Civilizations. She has lived and studied in Europe, Asia, and the Middle East. She first went to China in 1979, and has been a frequent visitor since. As a life-long Asianist, her scholarly interests include Chinese monetary policy during the 1930s, Iranian affairs, and the role of the media in developing countries, especially China. Ms. Hale is a member of the Council on Foreign Relations in New York, the Australian-American Leadership Dialogue, and is a long-time director of the Japan America Society of Chicago. She founded Women in International Trade (WIT), and was the first female president in the sixty-year history of the International Trade Club of Chicago. She serves on the advisory board of Pasfarda, which encourages and supports cultural exchanges between the United States and Iran.

DAVID HALE
David Hale Global Economics

David Hale is a Chicago-based global economist whose clients include asset-management companies in North America, Europe, Asia, and Africa. He is the founding chairman of David Hale Global Economics. Mr. Hale serves as the Global Economic Advisor to the Commonwealth Bank of Australia. He formerly worked as chief economist for Kemper Financial Services from 1977 to 1995 and Zurich Financial Services, which he joined as chief economist when it purchased Kemper in 1995. He advised the group's fund management and insurance operations on the economic outlook and a wide range of public policy issues until 2002, when he founded David Hale Global Economics. Mr. Hale holds a BS degree in International Economic Affairs from the Georgetown University School of Foreign Service and an MS degree in Economics from the London School of Economics. In September 1990, the New York chapter of the National Association of Business Economists conferred upon Mr. Hale the William F. Butler Award.

JOSHUA MENDELSOHN
Mendelsohn Global Economics

Joshua Mendelsohn is a Toronto-based independent economic advisor. His areas of focus include international economics, the US and Canadian economies, monetary policy, and financial markets. Before taking on his current role, Mr. Mendelsohn was the Senior Vice President and Chief Economist for the Canadian Imperial Bank of Commerce (CIBC) for nearly ten years and was a senior member of the bank's economics group for over twenty years. Prior to joining CIBC, Mr. Mendelsohn was an economist with the C. D. Howe Research Institute. Mr. Mendelsohn has provided advice to senior federal and provincial government officials, as well as the private sector, and has testified before parliamentary committees on both domestic and international issues. Between 1997 and 2002 Mr. Mendelsohn also chaired the Economic Policy Committee of the Canadian Chamber of Commerce. Mr. Mendelsohn has authored articles on domestic and international economic developments and issues and has been interviewed and quoted in such publications as the *Wall Street Journal*, *Business Week*, *The Economist* magazine, and *Time* magazine.

TIMOTHY HEYMAN
Heyman y Asociados

Timothy Heyman is President of Heyman y Asociados, one of Mexico's leading independent institutional asset managers. Prior to founding Heyman y Asociados, he was President of ING Baring Grupo Financiero (México), S. A. de C. V., and Baring, S. A. de C. V., Casa de Bolsa, the first foreign brokerage in Mexico. He was named Emerging Markets Allstar by Globalfinance, and for three successive years he was awarded first place for Mexican research by Institutional Investor. He is currently a member of the Listing and Index Committees of the Mexican Stock Exchange, and he is a board member of several financial and industrial companies in Mexico. A finance professor since 1982 at the Instituto Tecnológico Autónomo de México, Timothy is the author of eight best-selling books on Mexican investments, the latest being *Inversión en la Globalización* and *Mexico for the Global Investor*. Among his community activities, he has been President of the Board of the ABC Hospital, Mexico's leading private health care institution, and is currently board member of the ABC Foundation and Co-Chairman of the Imagina campaign for its new Cancer Center: he is also Treasurer of the Mexican Literary Foundation, and member of the Board of Trustees of the Mexican Council for Foreign Relations. He has a BA from Oxford and an MS in Management from MIT.

PEDRO PABLO KUCZYNSKI
The Rohatyn Group

Mr. Kuczynski began his career at the World Bank in 1961. In the private sector he was Chairman of First Boston International from 1982 to 1992, and he ran three private equity funds specializing in Latin America from 1992 to 2001. In the 1970s he ran an international mining company and was a partner of investment bank Kuhn Loeb International. He was Prime Minister of Perú from 2005 to 2006 after having served as Finance Minister since 2001. He was previously Minister of Energy and Mines and Deputy Director of the Central Reserve Bank. Since 2007 he has been a Senior Advisor and Partner of the Rohatyn Group, a firm specializing in emerging market investments. He is also Chairman of AMG, a company in special metals related to solar energy, and of Agualimpia, an organization in Perú that helps poor towns and villages set up their water systems.

ANATOLE KALETSKY
GaveKal Research

Anatole Kaletsky is Chief Economist and founding partner of GaveKal Research, Hong Kong. His book *Capitalism 4.0: The Birth of a New Economy in the Aftermath of Crisis* was published in June 2010. Anatole is best known as an economic commentator for the *Times of London* and, prior to that, on the *Financial Times*. In 1999, after twenty years as one of the world's leading economic journalists, Mr. Kaletsky joined Charles Gave and Louis-Vincent Gave to launch GaveKal. Mr. Kaletsky has been an adviser to multinational companies and financial institutions in Europe, America, and Asia, as well as a sought-after public speaker. His insights on macroeconomic and financial trends, central bank dynamics, and political developments are respected by investors worldwide. He still writes a weekly column for the *Times of London*. He is married and has three children. He speaks French, English, and Russian, and lives in London.

LOUIS-VINCENT GAVE
GaveKal and MW GaveKal Asia Limited

After receiving his bachelor's degree from Duke University and studying Mandarin at Nanjing University, Louis-Vincent Gave joined the French Army where he served as a second lieutenant in a mountain infantry battalion. After a couple of years, he left the army and joined Paribas Capital Markets where he worked as a financial analyst first in Paris, then in Hong Kong. Mr. Gave left Paribas in 1999 to launch GaveKal Research with Charles Gave and Anatole Kaletsky in London. In 2002, he left the London office and returned to Hong Kong. Mr. Gave contributes frequently to GaveKal research and was the primary author of *Our Brave New World* and *The End Is Not Nigh*. He is the CEO of GaveKal and Marshall Wace GaveKal.

ROBERT MADSEN
MIT's Center for International Studies

Robert Madsen is Senior Advisor and Economist at Asia Alternatives, a fund of funds specializing in alternative investments. He is a member of the Executive Council at Unison Capital, one of Japan's premier private equity groups. He is also a Senior Fellow at MIT's Center for International Studies, where he works on East Asian and global politics and economics. For over a decade he has written the Economist Intelligence Unit's (EIU) Japan Country Reports and contributed occasionally to that company's analysis of China and broader East Asia. Dr. Madsen consults regularly for a range of corporations and government agencies. Before joining MIT, he was a Fellow at Stanford University's Asia-Pacific Research Center, an Asia Strategist at Soros Private Funds Management, and an adviser to the Robert M. Bass Group on its investments in Japanese real estate. Dr. Madsen earned a master's degree and a doctorate from Oxford University. Dr. Madsen also holds a JD from Stanford Law School and is a member of the California State Bar.

RICHARD B. KATZ
The Oriental Economist Report

Richard Katz is Editor of *The Oriental Economist Report*, a monthly newsletter on Japan, as well as the semiweekly TOE Alert e-mail service on Japan. He is also a special correspondent at *Shukan Toyo Keizai*, a leading Japanese business weekly. Mr. Katz is the author of two books on Japan: *Japan: The System That Soured—The Rise and Fall of the Japanese Economic Miracle* (1998) and *Japanese Phoenix: The Long Road to Economic Revival* (2002). He regularly writes articles and op-eds for major magazines and newspapers, has testified before congressional committees, and did a stint as Adjunct Professor of Economics at the New York University Stern School of Business. Mr. Katz received his MA in Economics from New York University in 1996.

KEITH JEFFERIS
Econsult Botswana (Pty) Ltd.

Keith Jefferis is a macroeconomist and financial sector specialist. He is Managing Director of Econsult Botswana (Pty) Ltd. Previous appointments include Senior Lecturer in Economics (University of Botswana, 1989–1996); Deputy Director, Research Department, Bank of Botswana (1996–1998); Senior Research Fellow, Botswana Institute for Development Policy Analysis (1996–1997); Deputy Governor, Bank of Botswana (1999–2005), on appointment by then president of Botswana, H. E. Festus Mogae. He has a PhD from the Open University (United Kingdom), an MS in Economics from the University of London, and a BS in Economics with Statistics from Bristol University. He is originally from the United Kingdom and started his professional career as a Fellow of the Overseas Development Institute (ODI) working as an economist in Swaziland. He has lived in Botswana since 1989.

IRAJ ABEDIAN
Pan-African Capital Holdings (Pty) Ltd.

Iraj Abedian is the founder and Chief Executive of Pan-African Capital Holdings (Pty) Ltd., established in 2005. He was Professor of Economics at the University of Cape Town in the 1990s. From September to December 1999, Dr. Abedian was based at the IMF in Washington, DC, working on issues related to fiscal vulnerability assessment. In January 2000 he joined the Standard Bank Group at their head office in Johannesburg as Group Chief Economist, and was a member of the Standard Bank Group executive committee. He received his PhD in Economics from Simon Fraser University in Canada. He has written numerous articles and co-authored several books, including: *Economic Growth in South Africa* (1992); *Transformation in Action: Budgeting for Health Service Delivery* (1998); *Economics of Tobacco Control: Towards an Optimal Policy Mix* (1998); *Economic Globalization and Fiscal Policy* (1998).

SAUL ESLAKE
Grattan Institute

Saul Eslake joined the Grattan Institute, a nonaligned policy "think tank" affiliated with the University of Melbourne, in August 2009, as Director of its Productivity Growth program. He is also a part-time adviser to PricewaterhouseCoopers Australia and Principal of Corinna Economic Advisory. He was previously Chief Economist at the Australia & New Zealand Banking Group, one of Australia's four major commercial banks. He was a member of the Foreign Affairs and Trade Policy Advisory Councils under the government of former prime minister John Howard, and is a member of the National Housing Supply Council and the Australian Statistics Advisory Council under the government of Prime Minister Julia Gillard. He is also a nonexecutive director of Hydro Tasmania and of the Australian Business Arts Foundation.

JOHN GREENWOOD
Invesco

John Greenwood is Chief Economist of Invesco, an international asset-management company. A graduate of Edinburgh University, he did economic research at Tokyo University and was a visiting research fellow at the Bank of Japan (1970–1974). In 1974 he became Chief Economist with GT Management, based initially in Hong Kong and later in San Francisco. As Editor of *Asian Monetary Monitor* in 1983, he proposed a currency board scheme for stabilizing the Hong Kong dollar that is still in operation today. He was an economic adviser to the Hong Kong government (1992–1993) and has been a member of the Committee on Currency Board Operations of the Hong Kong Monetary Authority since 1998. He is also a member of the Shadow Monetary Policy Committee in England.

ALBERT BRESSAND
Columbia University

Albert Bressand is the Aristotle Onassis Professor of Practice in International and Public Affairs at Columbia's School of International and Public Affairs (SIPA) and Executive Director of Columbia University's Center for Energy, Marine Transportation and Public Policy (CEMTPP). Dr. Bressand formerly headed the Global Business Environment department in Royal Dutch Shell's global headquarters in London from 2003 to 2006. From 2006 to 2009, Dr. Bressand was Special Adviser to Andris Piebalgs, the EU Energy Commissioner in Brussels. Previously, he was Managing Director and cofounder of Prométhée, a Paris-based think tank specializing in the emerging global networked economy. Dr. Bressand also served as Economic Adviser to the Minister of Foreign Affairs of France and held key positions with the French Institute for International Relations and the World Bank. He has published in *Foreign Affairs, International Affairs, Futuribles, Politique Internationale, Revue d'Economie Financiére, Le Monde*, and more. His most recent book is titled *The Shell Global Scenarios to 2025.*

NARIMON SAFAVI
Pasfarda Art & Cultural Exchange

Narimon Safavi is a Chicago-based entrepreneur who is also a frequent contributor to NPR Chicago's Worldview program as an Iran analyst. Born in Tehran to an Azari-Iranian family, Mr. Safavi studied chemistry and philosophy at Illinois State University, and currently serves on the boards of the Washington DC-based National Iranian-American Council (the largest grassroots advocacy organization of Iranian-Americans) and the Pasfarda Arts & Cultural Exchange, whose mission is to build cultural bridges and foster dialogue between the United States and Iran. Previously, he was a partner in ethical diamond mining projects in Africa and served on the boards or councils of the Latino Cultural Center of Chicago, Harris School of Public Policy Studies at the University of Chicago, and Chicago Public Media. Mr. Safavi regularly appears on Persian-, Spanish-, and English-language programs on NPR, PBS, BBC, Telecinco, and other media outlets. He speaks on a wide range of topics beyond Iranian affairs, including private-sector social responsibility, cultural commentary, and art criticism, especially film. He is fluent in Persian and English, and proficient in Turkish and Spanish.

BRIAN FISHER
BAEconomics

Brian Fisher is one of Australia's most respected advisers on climate change, emissions trading, and the economic impact of current and future climate and energy policies. He is a well-known commentator on Australian agricultural, minerals, and energy commodities. He previously held the position of Executive Director of the Australian Bureau of Agricultural and Resource Economics (ABARE). He took a senior position in the Federal Department of Primary Industries and Energy before returning to ABARE as Executive Director in 1995. Dr. Fisher was previously Professor of Agricultural Economics at the University of Sydney and became Dean of the Faculty of Agriculture at the university in 1987. He was appointed Adjunct Professor of Sustainable Resources Development in 2003. Concurrent with his position at ABARE, in 1993 Dr. Fisher was appointed one of the experts completing the socioeconomic assessment of climate change for the United Nations' Intergovernmental Panel on Climate Change (IPCC) Second Assessment Report. He served as economic adviser to Australia's negotiating team at the third Conference of the Parties in Kyoto. He also fulfilled this role at the fourth, fifth, and sixth Conferences of the Parties of the United Nations Framework Convention on Climate Change (UNFCCC) and was engaged as one of the experts completing the IPCC's Third and Fourth Assessment Reports. Dr. Fisher has published more than 260 papers and monographs.

ANNA MATYSEK
BA Economics

Anna Matysek specializes in resource and environmental economics and has more than a decade's experience working in the areas of scenario design, CGE modeling, policy advice, and climate change mitigation and adaptation. Ms. Matysek has provided consulting expertise in a range of areas, including business strategy, trade and development economics, competition policy, and infrastructure development. She has also worked as a consultant on major international mergers and acquisitions transactions. As a lead author for the East and South Asia region on the World Bank–sponsored Intergovernmental Assessment of Agricultural Science and Technology for Development, she worked with a diverse team to develop economic, trade, and environmental scenarios. Ms. Matysek was a lead author in the areas of long-term and industry mitigation on the UN Intergovernmental Panel on Climate Change (IPCC) Fourth Assessment Report. This paper was completed while she was at BA Economics. She has recently become General Manager, Strategy and IOG–Business Development at Rio Tinto.

TIMOTHY CONGDON
International Monetary Research Ltd.

Tim Congdon is one of the world's leading monetary analysts. After starting his career as a journalist for the *Times of London*, he became an economist in London in 1976. He founded the economic research consultancy Lombard Street Research in 1989 after correctly warning that the excessive money growth during the Lawson chancellorship would lead to double-digit inflation. Between 1992 and 1997 he was a member of the Treasury Panel that advised the British government in a successful period for economic policymaking. His book titled *Keynes, the Keynesians and Monetarism* was published in September 2007. International Monetary Research Ltd. is his latest venture.

ANDREW SHENG
University of Malaya

Andrew Sheng is the author of *From Asian to Global Financial Crisis* (2009) and former Chairman of the Hong Kong Securities and Futures Commission. Dr. Sheng is the third holder of the prestigious Tun Ismail Ali Chair at the Faculty of Economics and Administration at the University of Malaya, and is also an Adjunct Professor at the Graduate School of Economics and Management, Tsinghua University, Beijing. From October 1998 to September 2005, Dr. Sheng was the Chairman of the Hong Kong Securities and Futures Commission. He has published widely on monetary and financial issues. In 1998, he co-chaired the Working Party on Transparency and Accountability, one of the three Working Parties formed under the Group of Twenty-two Finance Ministers and Central Bank Governors. He was the Deputy Chief Executive of the Hong Kong Monetary Authority from 1993 to 1998, responsible for the Reserves Management and External Affairs Departments. He was the Chairman of the Technical Committee of IOSCO (International Organization of Securities Commissions) and the international securities regulation standard-setter from October 2003 to September 2005. Since October 2003, he has been the Convenor of the International Council of Advisers to the China Banking Regulatory Commission. He is a member of the Malaysian National Economic Advisory Council and in June 2010, he was honored as Panglima Mangku Negara (by His Majesty the King of Malaysia), which carries the title "Tan Sri."

JACK M. MINTZ
University of Calgary

Jack M. Mintz was appointed the Palmer Chair in Public Policy at the University of Calgary in January 2008. He serves as an Associate Editor of *International Tax and Public Finance* and *Canadian Tax Journal*, and is a research fellow of CESifo in Munich, Germany, and the Centre for Business Taxation Institute at Oxford University. He is a regular contributor to *Canadian Business* and the *National Post*. He was appointed by the Federal Minister of Finance to the Economic Advisory Council to advise on economic planning. Dr. Mintz held the position of Professor of Business Economics at the Rotman School of Business from 1989 to 2007. Prior positions include President and CEO of the C. D. Howe Institute from 1999 to 2006; Clifford Clark Visiting Economist at the Department of Finance in Ottawa; Chair of the federal government's Technical Committee on Business Taxation in 1996 and 1997; and Associate Dean (Academic) of the Faculty of Management at the University of Toronto from 1993 to 1995. He recently chaired the Alberta Financial and Investment Policy Advisory Commission reporting to the Alberta Minister of Finance. In 2002, Dr. Mintz's book *Most Favored Nation: A Framework for Smart Economic Policy* won the Purvis Prize for best book in economic policy.

MICHAEL T. LEWIS
Free Market Inc.

Michael T. Lewis founded Free Market Inc. (FMI) in 1982. He earned a BS degree from MIT and an MA degree from University of California, Los Angeles (UCLA) in Economics. Before founding Free Market Inc. (FMI), Mr. Lewis was an economist at Data Resources, Inc., and Atlantic Richfield Co. He was Chief Economist from 1978 to 1982 at Stein Roe & Farnham.

CAROLE BASRI
Balint, Brown & Basri

Carole Basri is Senior Vice President of Balint, Brown & Basri, which provides temporary legal staff in New York City. She is also an Adjunct Professor at the University of Pennsylvania Law School, President of the Corporate Lawyering Association, and President of the Corporate Lawyering Group LLC. She has written four legal treatises: *Corporate Compliance Practice Guide*, *eDiscovery for Corporate Counsel*, *Corporate Legal Departments*, and *International Corporate Practice*.

THIERRY MALLERET
IJ Partners

Thierry Malleret is Senior Partner, Head of Research and Networks at IJ Partners. Prior to that, he was managing partner of Rainbow Insight, an advisory boutique that provided tailor-made intelligence to global chief executives and ultra-high-net-worth individuals. Until March 2007, Dr. Mallevet headed the Global Risk Network at the World Economic Forum, a network that brings together top-end opinion and policymakers, CEOs, and academics to look at how global issues affect business and society in the short, medium, and long term. He has organized Davos and spoken at global, industry, and regional events for several consecutive years. Prior to that, he worked in investment banking (as a Chief Economist and Strategist of a major Russian investment bank), think tanks, and academia (both in New York and Oxford), and in government (with a three-year spell in the Prime Minister's office in Paris). Dr. Mallevet has written several business and academic books, and has also published four novels. He was educated at the Sorbonne and Ecole des Hautes Etudes en Sciences Sociales in Paris and St. Antony's College at Oxford. He holds a PhD in Economics.

MARK ROEDER

Mark Roeder is an author and corporate communications executive with extensive international experience. He was Global Head of Advertising for UBS Bank, Head of Corporate Brands for Zurich Financial Services, and Head of Corporate Communications for Westpac Financial Services. He also founded his own marketing company. His upcoming book, *The Big Mo* (to be published in 2011), focuses on the increasing influence of large-scale momentum on our world.

INDEX